Quality Management:
the Theory and Practice of Implementing Change

Patrick Dawson and
Gill Palmer

To Désirée
To Dene, Len and Elsie

Longman Australia Pty Ltd
Longman House
Kings Gardens
95 Coventry Street
Melbourne 3205 Australia

Offices in Sydney, Brisbane, Adelaide, Perth, and associated companies throughout the world.

Copyright © Longman Australia Pty Ltd 1995
First published 1995

All rights reserved. Except under the conditions described in the Copyright Act 1968 of Australia and subsequent amendments, no part of this publication may be reproduced, stored in a retrieval system or transmitted in any form or by any means, electronic, mechanical, photocopying, recording or otherwise, without the prior permission of the copyright owner.

Cover design by Rob Cowpe
Designed by Rob Cowpe
indexed by Russell Brooks
Set in 11/13 Adobe Garamond
Produced by Longman Australia Pty Ltd
through Longman Malaysia, TCP

The publisher's policy is to use paper manufactured from sustainable forests

National Library of Australia
Cataloguing-in-Publication data:
Dawson, Patrick, 1958–
    Quality management.
    Bibliography.
    Includes index.
    ISBN 0 582 90884 1.
    1. Total quality management—Australia. 2. Organisational change—Australia. I. Palmer, Gill. II. Title.
658.5620994

Contents

List of Figures	ix
Contributors	x
Acknowledgments	xi

Part I: TQM in Context   1

1 Introduction

Introduction	3
TQM research programme	5
Analysing change data: a processual approach	6
Analysing managerial theory: a multiple perspectives approach	7
Objectives and structure of the book	7

2 Understanding Quality Management

Introduction	12
Quality management: context and definition	14
The emergence of quality management in Australia	19
Popular exponents of quality management	22
Common features of a quality management programme	29
Conclusion: quality management	35

3 TQM and its Place in Management Theory

Introduction	38
Part one: TQM and the history of management thought	*39*
Contextualising the development of managerial ideas	41
Part two: Multiple frames of reference for analysing TQM	*44*
TQM and the bureaucratic processes of management	46
TQM and political processes in management	48
TQM and the management of cultures	54
Conclusion: TQM and management theory	57

Part II: TQM in Australian and New Zealand Companies — 59

4 A Processual Framework for Understanding TQM
Introduction — 61
A conventional approach: the example of Lewin's change model — 62
A processual framework for analysing change — 64
The context of change — 65
The substance of change — 66
The politics of change — 66
Conclusion — 68

5 Conceptualising the Need for TQM at Accom Industries Pty Ltd
by Verna Blewett
Introduction — 70
Company background — 70
Quality assurance and accreditation — 71
Conceptualising the need for TQM — 73
The policy and practice of employee involvement — 74
Conclusion — 75
Questions — 75

6 Management Rationale and the Introduction of TQM at the State Bank of South Australia
by Patrick Dawson and Margaret Patrickson
Introduction — 76
Company background — 76
The origins and rationale for a service quality programme — 77
Implementing service quality: a strategy of change — 80
Conclusion — 83
Questions — 84

7 Implementing TQM in Manufacturing: the Route to Change at Tecpak Industries
by Tom Batley and Michelle Andrews
Introduction — 85
Company background — 85
Introducing TQM — 87
External relationships — 90
Human resource implications — 91
Conclusions — 93
Questions — 94

8 Health and Safety, Customer–Supplier Relations and Statistical Process Control: Strategies for Continuous Improvement at Hendersons Automotive (SA)
by Verna Blewett

Introduction	95
Company background and business context	96
Health and safety: managerial strategies for employee involvement	98
Establishing a quality structure and the use of statistical process control	100
The development of external customer–supplier relations	102
Kaizen, quality groups and continuous improvement groups	104
Conclusion: the route to recovery at Hendersons	104
Questions	107

9 The Development of Process Improvement Teams and the Measurement of Outcomes at Alcoa's Kwinana Refinery
by Alan Brown

Introduction	107
Company background	107
The context of change	108
The formation of process improvement teams	109
Initial operation: measuring the outcomes of change	113
Conclusion	114
Questions	115

10 Evaluating Change: Senior Management Assessment of Service Quality at Laubman and Pank
by Patrick Dawson

Introduction	116
Company background	116
Senior management assessment of service excellence	117
Conclusion: an assessment of TQM in the Laubman and Pank Group	122
Questions	123

11 The Process and Politics of Change at Vicbank
by Cameron Allan

Introduction	125
Company background	126
The conception of a need for TQM	126
Period I: the process of establishing TQM	127
The routine operation of TQM	128
A reappraisal of TQM	129

Period II: organisational culture as the pathway to
successful TQM 129
Period III: the use of consultants in the re-establishment
of TQM 132
Conclusion: the politics and process of managing change 135
Questions 136

12 The Context and Substance of Change: the Different
Experience Of TQM at Two Plants Within Pirelli Cables
Australia Limited
by Patrick Dawson
Introduction 137
Company background 137
The shopfloor experience of TQM in cable processing 137
The shopfloor experience of TQM in cable manufacturing 138
Conclusion: questions of culture and communication 141
Questions 144

Part III: TQM in Perspective 149

13 TQM and Managemnt Theory: Some Emerging
Themes and Issues
Introduction 151
The bureaucratic elements of TQM 152
The political elements of TQM 160
Cultural elements of TQM 167
Conclusion 170

14 TQM and Management Practice: the Process of
Change Reappraised
Introduction 174
Understanding TQM: a processual approach 177
Common features of TQM programmes in practice 179
General lessons on the process of establishing TQM 183
Conclusion 190

Appendix I: Guide for Interviewers 192
Appendix II: Deming's Fourteen Points, Juran's Ten Steps and
Crosby's Fourteen Stages to Quality Improvement 199

Bibliography 203
Index 215

List of figures

2.1	The PDCA/SPCA cycles	24
4.1	A processual framework	67
6.1	The State Bank's quality improvement framework	82
13.1	Relationship with suppliers	154
13.2	Employee empowerment strategies	161

Case contributors

Cameron Allan is a PhD student at the University of Griffith in Brisbane.

Michelle Andrews is a postgraduate student in the Department of Management at the University of Otago, Dunedin, New Zealand.

Tom Batley is a Senior Lecturer in Operations Management at the University of Otago, Dunedin, New Zealand. He was trained as a professional engineer in Britain and has acted as a consultant for a number of manufacturing firms. His main research interests include productivity and quality management studies, production planning systems and management skills development.

Verna Blewett is the Managing Consultant of New Horizon Consulting. She specialises in the management of occupational health and safety as a tool for the management of change. Verna is currently enrolled in a PhD in the Department of Commerce at the University of Adelaide.

Alan Brown is an Associate Professor and Head of the Department of Management at Edith Cowan University in Perth. His research, teaching and consultancy work includes quality management and human resource management. He has published and presented a number of papers on quality management both nationally and internationally. Current research interests include the impact of TQM on HRM and industrial relations.

Margaret Patrickson is an Associate Professor at the International Graduate School of Management at the University of South Australia. She has recently edited a book with Greg Bamber entitled: *Organisational Change Strategies*, Melbourne, Longman Cheshire. Her main research interests are in the areas of quality management, change, and strategic human resource management.

Acknowledgments

The research behind the writing of this book was stimulated by an absence of Australian material on the organisational implications of introducing Total Quality Management (TQM). A national programme of research was initiated by Gill Palmer, who was at that time Professor and Director of the Key Centre in Strategic Management at Queensland University of Technology. Funded by the Australian Research Council (ARC), a series of qualitative longitudinal case studies were conducted in a number of different organisations throughout Australia. The project was initially undertaken by two research teams: one was located at the Key Centre in Strategic Management under the direction of Gill Palmer, with research support from Cameron Allan; the other was based at the University of Adelaide under the direction of Patrick Dawson, with research support from Verna Blewett. Additional case studies were later commissioned in Western Australia and New Zealand, and data collection was completed in June 1992.

In carrying out the interviews and compiling case material the authors would like to thank Cameron Allan, Michelle Andrews, Tom Batley, Verna Blewett, Alan Brown, and Margaret Patrickson. Without their participation, the completion of this manuscript would not have been possible. Within the case organisations, grateful thanks must also go to the management, union and employees of: Accom Industries, the State Bank of South Australia, Tecpak Industries, Hendersons Automotive (SA), Alcoa's Kwinana Refinery, Laubman and Pank, Vicbank, and Pirelli Cables (Australia) for their willingness to share their knowledge and experiences of introducing TQM.

In transcribing a vast range of taped interviews of various quality and length we would like to thank Althea Leonard, who has demonstrated considerable skill and enormous patience. We would also like to thank those members of the research team who spent their own time and energies in transcribing taped interviews prior to data analysis. The book therefore involved many people's research and labour. In preparing the final manuscript, Patrick Dawson was initially responsible for Chapters 1, 2, 4 and 14, while Gill Palmer was initially responsible for Chapters 3 and 13. However the final text is the work of both authors and we accept joint responsibility for it.

For commenting on initial draft papers and/or parts of the manuscript, we would like to thank Stephen Hill, Ian McLoughlin, Helen Thorne and Barry Wilkinson. We would also like to acknowledge MCB University Press Limited for granting permission to reproduce part of the article by P. Dawson and M. Patrickson (1991) 'Total quality management in the Australian banking industry', *International Journal of Quality and Reliability Management*, Volume 8, Number 5. Finally, we would like to give thanks to our families, friends and academic colleagues who provided support, relief and encouragement for the completion of this book on quality management.

Patrick Dawson
Department of Commerce
University of Adelaide

Gill Palmer
Head, Department of Management
University of Woollongong

PART *I*

TQM in Context

CHAPTER 1

Introduction

INTRODUCTION

The importance of Total Quality Control (TQC) to the development of strategies for competitive advantage was highlighted by Armand Feigenbaum in 1956:

> Customers—both industrial and consumer—have been increasing their quality requirements very sharply in recent years. This tendency is likely to be greatly amplified by the intense competition that seems inevitable in the near future. (Feigenbaum, 1956:93)

His ideas and those of other popular exponents of quality management, such as Deming (1981) and Juran (1988), have only recently been adopted by Western companies following the rise and dominance of Japanese manufacturing industry within world markets (Schonberger, 1982). The adoption of Total Quality Management (TQM) ideas is now viewed as a competitive weapon for business operations in the 1990s and is bringing about significant changes in the management of human resources (see, Dawson and Webb, 1989; Oliver and Wilkinson, 1989). These new and emerging principles of management have been represented as a new doctrine of work organisation and a more encompassing world view and social philosophy. This managerial philosophy seeks to increase organisational flexibility enabling companies to adapt to changing market conditions and rapidly adjust operations to meet the requirements of on-going and emerging programmes of change. Lowering costs, gaining employee commitment and ensuring continuous improvement in the delivery of services and/or the manufacture of products to meet changing customer expectations, are all part of the modern corporate push for quality management. Since the beginning of the 1990s, the organisational uptake of quality programmes has broadened to include an increasing number of service organisations as well as manufacturing companies (Schonberger, 1992). The widespread adoption of TQM draws attention to many of the competitive pressures now facing companies operating in the dynamic and international markets of North America, the Asia-Pacific Region and Europe (DeMeyer and Ferdows, 1991; Hurd, 1992; and Kanter 1991). Essentially, the aim is to produce quality goods and services at a lower cost which meet or exceed customer expectations.

The growing interest in TQM as a philosophy for achieving continuous improvements in quality and gaining employee commitment, has sparked a plethora of popular articles and texts on how to make more effective use of employees in the pursuit of quality, flexibility and productivity (see, for example, Brown, 1989; Hoernschemeyer, 1989; Oakland, 1989; and Berry and Parasuraman, 1992). The works of Deming (1982), Juran (1991), Ishikawa (1985) and Taguchi (1986 and 1988), have been modified and adapted by a growing number of consultants, who both aid and hinder the organizational introduction of TQM. As Roberts (1990) has noted, too many organisations assume that quality is a 'quick fix' package to be purchased, rather than a transformational change in the nature of organizational operations. The tendency for organisations to be misled by 'flashy presentations and snappy illustrations' has been highlighted by Barnett's (1991) account of the prevalence of the Taguchi approach in Australia. He claims that it is an astounding, if unhelpful, achievement that Taguchi exponents have popularised experimental design even though it is widely known to be 'inefficient and flawed' (Barnett, 1991:11). He concludes that:

> Total quality management must be founded first and foremost on solving people problems and, second, on 'picking the eyes out' of appropriate proven techniques, and using them intelligently. Fadism must be avoided and 'quality hype' replaced by social application and teamwork. (Barnett, 1991:13)

Although the search for 'quality' is often posed as being non-problematic, in practice, there is considerable disagreement as to what constitutes quality and how it can best be achieved. For example, Forker (1991) listed five different approaches to the definition of quality management, namely: innate excellence (transcendent approach), quantity of desired attributes (product-based), satisfaction of consumer preferences (user-based), conformance to requirements (manufacturing-based), and affordable excellence (value-based). For the most part, however, there are two major thrusts in the prescriptive literature, one arguing that companies should restructure to encourage multi-skilling and innovation on the shopfloor; and the other, that companies should develop high-trust co-operative cultures to support process improvement through customer-centred and employee-involvement programmes. Typically, these views are not based on any systematic analysis of empirical data but, rather, on cursory summaries of quality management strategies and anecdotal evidence (Hill, 1991a:398).

There is an absence of detailed empirical data on the implications of TQM both for the theory of organisational change and for theories of management. The ideas behind TQM remain clouded by the hype and gloss of neat prescriptive post-hoc rationalisations and market-driven consultant packages, and as such, they are in need of detailed investigation and critical appraisal. This book attempts to bring empirical case study evidence and theoretical analysis together in a review of the implementation of TQM. It outlines some of the important issues and themes which have emerged from theories of management and of organisational change. It then uses a national case study programme on the introduction of total quality management in Australian and New Zealand companies to analyse the importance of TQM in managment theory, and the lessons that can be learnt on the processes of organisational change.

TQM RESEARCH PROGRAMME

The TQM research programme was carried out over a period of three years and involved detailed case study research on the introduction and effects of TQM on a number of Australian and New Zealand organisations (see also, Dawson and Palmer, 1993). The project was undertaken by two research teams: one was located at the Key Centre in Strategic Management at Queensland University of Technology under the direction of Professor Gill Palmer with research support from Cameron Allan, the other was based at the University of Adelaide under the direction of Dr Patrick Dawson with research support from Verna Blewett. Additional case studies were commissioned in Western Australia and New Zealand, and data collection was completed in June 1992. In all, a total of eight organisations were studied, comprising: Pirelli Cables Australia Limited; State Bank of South Australia; Vicbank; Accom Industries; Laubman and Pank; Alcoa; Tecpak Industries; and Hendersons Automotive Limited.

The main methods used in the study were as follows:
1 indepth interviewing of key personnel
2 management, union, and shopfloor interviews

3 participant observation
4 non-participant observation
5 documentary analysis

The case studies are largely based on qualitative data which have been collected during 1989–92. A longitudinal element was built into the research strategy and, where practicable, repeat interviews have been carried out at a number of different stages during the process of organisational transformation. Each interview lasted approximately 60–90 minutes and covered topics such as: the spread of TQM and the influence of change agents, the employment and industrial relations implications of change, and the process of change (the interview schedule used in the study is outlined in Appendix I).

ANALYSING CHANGE DATA: A PROCESSUAL APPROACH

The problem of analysing a large amount of detailed change data was tackled by adapting Dawson's processual approach to understanding organisational change (see Dawson, 1994). This argues that change does not unfold in a simple linear fashion but, rather, is a complex and dynamic process which rarely has a clear beginning or end point. As such, the routes to change can only be fully appreciated through the collection of longitudinal detailed case material which can note the various changes in direction and the reason why certain decisions are made (rather than relying on retrospective post-hoc rationalisations). For the researcher this form of data poses a problem of analysis and can create a puzzle impossible to solve. Therefore, for analytical purposes, data categories are constructed to represent activities and decision-making tasks (which may occur throughout the period of change) rather than sequential series of stages (which occur in timed sequences during a change programme). The categories we constructed to guide data analysis comprised: identification of type of change; search and assessment of options; system selection; preparation and planning; implementation; initial operation; evaluation and appraisal. In practice, therefore, a company may be evaluating one part of their quality programme whilst they are implementing another element and assessing their options for future or additional quality developments. In other words, these data categories were used for analytical purposes rather than as framework for describing sequential stages in the process of managing change.

The temporal element of managing change is described under three general timeframes. These comprise:

- Conception of a need for a quality initiative
- Process of establishing total quality management

- Operation and on-going change.

It is important to identify and differentiate organisations who are only just beginning to experiment with quality programmes and those who are routinely operating new quality practices and procedures. In our empirical study most of the case organisations can be located within the second general time-frame. However, we did collect some data from an organisation who was only beginning to think about the possibility of introducing TQM (see Chapter 5). In this case, the information was by its nature only partial and therefore we decided to limit our analysis to one company.

In seeking to understand the direction and routes to change, we identify three major groups of determinants, namely: the context, substance and politics of change. The context of change refers to the history and culture of an organisation and the business market environment in which it operates. The substance of change relates to the content and scale of the quality initiative. Finally, the politics of change is used to refer to the power and politics of organisational decision-making which surround these types of large-scale change programmes (see Dawson, 1994:35–47).

ANALYSING MANAGERIAL THEORY: A MULTIPLE PERSPECTIVES APPROACH

Quality management ideas represent the latest in a long history of prescriptions for managerial reform. They can be shown to combine social and cultural ideas from earlier human relations and socio-technical systems theories with technical and administrative prescriptions from scientific management and bureaucratic theories. To analyse the complexity of the ideas within TQM, we make use of a multiple perspective approach to management. Palmer has suggested three perspectives to analyse the bureaucratic, political and cultural elements of management (see Gardner and Palmer, 1992 and Palmer 1993a and 1993b). These perspectives are first used to review the nature of the managerial prescriptions in TQM and later, at the end of the book they are used to review the evidence that the case studies produce on the complexity of management practice, when these theories are put into use.

OBJECTIVES AND STRUCTURE OF THE BOOK

At the time of writing, the majority of quality management books available focus on: the statistical methods for quality improvement (see, for example,

Barker, 1990; Ryan, 1989); the achievements and methods of particular exponents of quality (see, for example, Aguayo, 1991; Ealey, 1988); and the practical guidelines which managers and chief executives should follow if they wish to 'successfully' implement TQM (see, for example, Blakemore, 1989; Fox, 1991; Roth, 1992; Tenner and DeToro, 1992). In this book we set out to break some of the myths surrounding TQM and explain the importance of others through providing new empirical evidence on the conception, introduction and effects of quality management programmes on a number of Australian and New Zealand companies. Our main objectives are to:

1. Locate TQM within the development of other management movements and in the context of management theory.

2. Summarise the main principles of quality management in a way that makes them accessible to management and business studies students.

3. Develop a processual framework for analysing data and explaining the nature of the organisational change processes associated with the introduction of TQM.

4. Present new empirical evidence drawn from eight systematic case studies on the introduction of TQM in Australian and New Zealand companies.

5. Use this case study data on the implementation of TQM to comment on theories of organisational change and on the theory of management and the value of multiple perspectives on the managerial process.

Whilst there are inevitable limitations in a project of this kind—for example, case study data cannot claim to be totally representative of management practice—there is also the challenge of breaking new ground and trying to get behind the gloss and hype of consultant and executive rhetoric. Our approach will be valuable if it is able to increase our critical understanding of the dynamic and complex processes involved in management and associated with the introduction of TQM in manufacturing and service industries.

The book is divided into three major parts. Part I sets out to provide an understanding of TQM. Chapter 2 provides both an overview of the major exponents of quality and a brief history of the emergence of TQM in Australia. The definitional problems which surround TQM are discussed and the common characteristics of total quality management programmes are identified. Chapter 3 is divided into two halves. The first half examines the place of TQM in the more general development of management thought and notes that many TQM ideas have roots in earlier management movements. The second half provides a new way of analysing the complexity of TQM by using three different perspectives to discuss different aspects of management. It introduces the bureaucratic or administrative, political and cultural perspectives on management.

In Part II, a processual approach to analysing data on the process of introducing TQM into organisations is outlined and explained. Chapter 4 briefly sets out a conceptual and analytical framework for describing and explaining the adoption of TQM. In the empirical chapters which follow, a range of themes and issues are discussed through the presentation of analytically grounded case studies. These studies highlight some of the myths of TQM through describing the real experiences of introducing TQM in a number of Australian and New Zealand companies. In Chapter 5, the conception of a need for a quality initiative is examined in the case of Accom Industries Pty Ltd. This chapter focuses on the period prior to the decision to embark on a TQM programme, when senior managers are still collecting information and evaluating the potential costs and benefits associated with change. It illustrates how the size and market position of a small business, in addition to a previous commitment to formal quality systems, can all influence the conception of a need to evaluate TQM. The case also demonstrates the definitional confusion which surrounds quality assurance as compared to and contrasted with total quality management (see also, Chapter 2).

Chapters 6 and 7 examine the implementation of TQM in a manufacturing and service organisation. In Chapter 6, the origins and rationale behind the adoption of a service quality programme at the State Bank of South Australia are analysed and management strategy for implementing change is described. The case discusses the cascade method of introducing TQM and demonstrates the use of a quality improvement framework for overseeing the total service quality effort. In contrast, Chapter 7 analyses the route to change in a small New Zealand manufacturing firm. In this example, Deming's fourteen principles of management are used as the starting point for establishing TQM. Unlike the State Bank, there is little initial planning and no developed strategy for change. After a period of five years the company is still in the process of implementing TQM and yet, they have also been successful in restructuring the social organisation of work. The two case studies provide interesting comparative examples of the problems and practice of implementing TQM.

Chapter 8 examines managerial strategies for continuous quality improvement in an automotive component manufacturing plant. The case illustrates how TQM is part of a series of changes aimed at developing a highly specialised and flexible workforce which can be easily accommodated within rapidly adjusted production arrangements to meet changing market demands. In particular, attention is given to the importance of health and safety at work as a strategy for securing employee commitment, and the use of statistical process control for devolving responsibility for quality to the shopfloor. In comparison, Chapter 9 analyses the development of Process Improvement Teams (PITs) at Alcoa's Kwinana refinery. The gradual emergence and development of group-problem solving teams is described and the obstacles to establishing the new PITs are outlined. The case also addresses the difficult issue of how an organisation sets about measuring the qualitative and quantitative outcomes of change.

Senior management appraisal of change is the main topic investigated in Chapter 10. The case study reports common and competing evaluations on the process of establishing a service quality programme in Laubman and Pank. It is shown how different assessments of change reflect different management attitudes towards the traditional belief and value system rooted in Laubman and Pank as a 'family business'. The case also illustrates how there is no formal evaluation procedure and how executive decision-making on the next phase in the process of establishing a total quality organisation is, in part, based on the informal assessment of the senior management group.

Chapter 11 sets out to re-examine the processual framework of change through examining the political and dynamic nature of company transformation. Vicbank is used to empirically demonstrate the validity of the processual approach developed in Chapter 4, and to highlight how the route to TQM is a complex, temporal and iterative political process which cannot be represented by a straight line or linear pathway. Chapter 12 uses the final case of Pirelli Cables to provide an example of how the substance of change (in terms of the philosophy, principles and managerial strategy for implementing TQM) may have very different outcomes as a consequence of variations in intra-organisational context. Two different experiences of TQM are presented from an analysis of two physically adjacent plants within Pirelli Cables. The gender composition and ethnicity of the workforce are shown to be important factors shaping the outcomes of change, and the voluntary nature of TQM teamwork activities is questioned.

Part III uses the case study data to provides a critical discussion of the implications of TQM for both the management of change and for management theory. Chapter 13 notes that the case studies did not uncover a single or coherent package of TQM reforms. Instead the TQM initiatives undertaken by the companies varied in their scope and focus, the changes introduced were not always coherent or successful, and the experience of the companies was complex. In order to unravel some of this complexity, the chapter uses Palmer's three perspectives on management, introduced in Chapter 3, to comment on the bureaucratic, political and cultural elements of TQM. As part of this analysis, the chapter discusses whether TQM increases bureaucracy or alters its nature. It discusses the extent of employee empowerment, and the nature of the cultural changes advocated by TQM.

Chapter 14 uses Dawson's processual approach to examining the change process involved in TQM. It draws on the empirical material presented in

Part II, to compare and contrast the seven common features of TQM identified in Chapter 2 with company practice. The processual approach is then used to identify eight general lessons on the implementation of TQM. Unlike the blueprints for change offered by writers such as Peters and Waterman (1982), we suggest that whilst there is no one best way to managing change, it is possible to develop a series of guidelines based on the experience of companies implementing TQM in Australia and New Zealand. Each guideline is illustrated by reference to the case material and the main lessons which can be drawn from the study are summarised at the end of the chapter.

CHAPTER 2

Understanding Quality Management

INTRODUCTION

In the minds of some journalists and industrialists, Japan's world leadership in product quality is the result of the lectures given four decades ago by two Americans—W. Edwards Deming and Joseph M. Juran. Had Deming and I not given those lectures, these people would still be of stone-age quality. In my view, there is not a shred of truth in such assertions. Had Deming and I stayed at home, the Japanese would have achieved world quality leadership all the same...the job might have taken longer, but they would still be ahead of the United States in the quality revolution. (Juran, 1993:42)

Total Quality Management (TQM) is a term which emerged in the late 1980s to refer to the strategic and widespread organisational adoption of quality techniques and policies. Unlike Quality Assurance (QA), Total Quality Control (TQC) or Total Manufacturing Management (TMM), TQM incorporates both service and manufacturing industries and is a company-wide change strategy which is no longer the sole preserve of production and/or operations managers or quality assurance departments. It originated in America, was developed in Japan and is now forming a central part of strategic decision-making in companies in North America, Asia, Europe and Australia and New Zealand. Although the extent of the uptake of TQM is debatable, it has been estimated that an average of 90 per cent of companies in Asia, Europe and North America are using TQM compared to 60 per cent of Australian companies (James, 1991).

During the late 1980s and early 1990s, organisations have moved away from Total Quality Control, which, following Feigenbaum (1961), had a strong association with production, towards the management of organisational culture through the enlisting of all parts of an organisation in the systematic effort for quality (Hames, 1991). As such, it has developed from a purely operational technique to a transformational programme which generally forms part of a company's strategy for gaining operational improvements, ensuring employee commitment, and increasing competitive advantage. Furthermore, in the search for quality, corporations are not solely focusing on intra-company relations, but also on the development of collaborative inter-organisational relations with their major customers and suppliers. In this way, TQM is increasingly being used as a cultural control strategy which goes beyond the shopfloor to incorporate strategic human resource management and inter-organisational relations.

In this chapter, an attempt is made to get behind some of the hype and gloss associated with the consultant marketing of TQM as a simple 'competitive' solution to complex organisational problems. It is argued that whilst there is an increasing number of consultant packages and recipes on 'how to do TQM', these have tended to over-simplify the complexity of change and have supported the myth that TQM can be fully embraced within relatively short timeframes. This myth of TQM has been further compounded by glossy presentations and anecdotal evidence of 'honeymoon success stories' which have tended to focus on the initial implementation-and-operations phase of managing change. Consequently, there has been a lack of detailed systematic investigation into the process of introducing TQM from the initial conception of the decision to embark on a programme of change through to a period where working under a new system has become a matter of routine. It is our objective to remedy this imbalance within the literature through presenting a range of analytically grounded case studies (see Part II). In order to set the scene we will first outline the history of the quality management movement and provide an explanation of TQM.

In the section which follows, a working definition of TQM is provided and the historical context from which quality management developed is briefly discussed. The emergence of TQM within the Australian context is then described and the contributions of the major exponents of quality are summarised. This is followed by an examination of the major components of TQM programmes and a consideration of the organisational arrangements required to accommodate the uptake of TQM. The chapter concludes with an overview of the major elements of TQM and a restatement of the importance of contextual factors in shaping the direction and pace of change and, in the case of diffusion agents, stimulating the adoption of particular quality programmes.

QUALITY MANAGEMENT: CONTEXT AND DEFINITION

There remains considerable confusion over what constitutes TQM. In part, this can be explained by the history of quality management and the development of quality programmes. The latter has broadly moved from the establishment of principles of quality assurance to issues of quality control and, finally, to the incorporation of the more behavioural and attitudinal aspects of quality which are intended to be encompassed in the term 'Total Quality Management'. Although some people continue to use the terms Quality Assurance (QA), Total Quality Control (TQC) and Total Quality Management (TQM) interchangeably, there is an important distinction between them (Campbell and Davies, 1992:2).

Quality Assurance (QA) is generally taken to refer to the establishment of documented procedures often based on national or international standards which are designed to ensure that products or services meet specified requirements. The term began to be used in professional journals in 1967 and was used principally in US Military Standards and the NATO allied quality assurance publications (Hunt, 1990:73). In a typical organisation, QA would normally be assigned to a specialist group who would be given responsibility for independent inspection and the removal of items which failed to meet customer specifications. Historically, QA activities have tended to dominate in manufacturing and testing areas and, particularly, in defence-related products. For example, in order to supply military equipment to national defence organisations, a company would first have to demonstrate an ability to meet preset specifications and standards through the use of formally documented sourcing, processes and testing procedures. The need to have full traceability of materials, processing, manufacture and testing of military products would generally be carried out by a QA department. This department would audit the complete production process from reception of raw materials through equipment design and manufacture, and the testing and delivery of the end product to the customer. National governments (the customers) would also normally have a QA department for defence. These governmental QA departments would in turn routinely monitor, audit and document the production of all goods and services purchased by the government from their approved suppliers. The supplier organisation would have to satisfy a continual series of system and process audits in order to remain an approved military supplier. In short, QA operates by the use of documented formalised procedures which can be monitored and evaluated by internal QA inspectors and assessed by external quality agents for local, national and international accreditation.

Total Quality Control (TQC) originated from developments in Quality Control (QC) which were based on the development of statistical techniques for measuring actual quality against established quality standards. In 1924, Shewhart (who worked in the QA department of Bell Laboratories in the US) developed a series of statistical control charts which were able to detect changes in the variability of a production process before defects were produced, rather than separating defects from acceptable components after production (Allan, 1991:24). These early findings were further developed by Deming, Juran and Feigenbaum, but were not widely taken up by industry until the Second World War, when the armed services in America 'adopted the quality control methods designed by statisticians from Bell Laboratories and established widespread training and education programmes for industry' (Allan, 1991:25). In the post-War period, the use of these quality control methods was limited, with American industry placing an emphasis on quantity rather than quality (Walton, 1986:8–9); British management was reluctant to adopt and adapt these techniques (Morrison, 1990:27); and Australian manufacturers were concerned about the cost of preventative quality control practices.

Armand Feigenbaum continued to develop the principle of QC, and in 1956 used the term 'Total Quality Control' to convey the view that quality is the responsibility of all groups within an organisation who should work together in a systematic effort to achieve TQC (Feigenbaum, 1956:93–101). He claimed that improved quality systems would reduce costs in the long term and that quality should be a shared responsibility. In his view, everybody should be involved in the process of satisfying customer requirements, rather than quality being the preserve of a small group of specialists in QA departments (Feigenbaum, 1961). As such, the development of TQC has historical connections both with QA and the more recent developments in TQM. The main difference between TQC and QA is that TQC is about total employee commitment to the achievement of quality from the identification of customers' requirements through to product delivery. QA is about establishing documented procedures to ensure that products or services meet certain specified standards. Moving on to TQM, Jennison (1991) has noted that whilst the measurement functions performed by health care QA departments are likely to continue, there will be a number of marked differences with the adoption of TQM:

> Most QA programs directed individual departments to perform specified functions in order to comply with regulatory requirements…Future iterations of health care quality programs will

integrate these functions under one organisation wide quality program...Measurement will be motivated by an internally driven quality plan, developed not to comply with regulation or accreditation but to meet the needs of internal as well as external 'customers' for information on performance. (1991:455–7)

In comparing TQM with TQC there are numerous similarities, and many of the principles developed under TQC are readily transportable to companies operating TQM programmes. The main difference is largely one of emphasis, that is, TQC programmes have tended to focus on the use of statistical techniques in manufacturing industries, with no attention being given to service-based companies. In contrast, TQM is seen to have a broader application in being based on a general philosophy for involving employees in the pursuit of quality objectives. Another difference is that TQM programmes tend to place greater significance on techniques for achieving an increase in employee commitment and the development of high-trust relationships. The non-tangible and cultural elements become the keystone to strategic change, with the operational statistical techniques and group-problem solving forums being the method for gaining employee involvement.

Within Japan, early attempts to tackle the problem of poor quality were based on the use of 'quality circles'. Essentially, a quality circle is a group of employees who meet regularly to undertake work-related projects designed to advance the company, enhance working conditions and improve quality through the systematic use of quality control concepts (see also, Vries and Water, 1992:33). The 'circle' participants are taught a range of quality control concepts or problem solving techniques, which can be used to identify problems, determine how to rectify these problems and communicate to management and employees the need to resolve these problems.

Although quality circles originated in America, they have not proven to be particularly successful in Western companies (see, for example, Littler, 1985:25–7). This lack of success has been discussed by Stephen Hill, who claims that Japanese companies have used their organisational reward systems to ensure that employees, and particularly managers, (voluntarily) co-operate with circles, and that Japanese QCs were only one part of an organisation-wide system of quality improvement (1991b:550–1). In commenting on the British QC programme he concludes that there was: an absence of top management involvement; a failure to match authority with an increase in employee responsibility for quality; only partial consideration of the cultural change aspects of quality management; and a failure to incorporate middle managers into QC programmes. (Hill, 1991b:556). The essential difference with the Western adaptation of quality circles and the current move to introduce quality management is that the former was introduced as a stand-alone participative scheme, whereas the latter has been used as a total organisational approach to quality improvement through employee participation. Thus, in contrast to both quality circles and quality control, the focus with TQM has shifted from operational techniques for improving quality or employee involvement, towards the strategic management of attitudes and behaviours and the development of collaborative intra-company and inter-organisational relations. In other words, cultural change strategies are combined with operational techniques for enhancing customer–supplier involvement and commitment.

There are numerous definitions of TQM and considerable disagreement on what constitutes a TQM programme. For some writers, TQC is synonymous with TQM (Blakemore, 1989), for others TQM has been redefined as Total Quality Service (TQS) to account for the special characteristics of service organisations (Albrecht, 1992), and for others TQM is seen to be composed of a distinct set of principles (see for example, Fox, 1991; Tenner and DeToro, 1992). What is common among these apparently different approaches is their attempt to delineate a unique methodology for the successful implementation of TQM in manufacturing and/or service organisations. This 'product' differentiation is not surprising when one considers that the published material on TQM has generally been written by consultants with a vested interest in promoting their own 'distinct' ideas. As Dobyns and Crawford-Mason have commented:

> The Japanese had learned how to produce quality from Sarasohn, Protzman, Polkinghorn, Deming, Joseph Juran, Armand Feigenbaum, and others. Kaoru Ishikawa and Genichi Taguchi would add their own quality wrinkles in Japan over the years, just as Phillip Crosby would in the United States beginning in 1979. What is interesting years later is that no two of those men—indeed, no two people we've talked to anywhere—agree precisely on how to define quality. (Dobyns and Crawford-Mason, 1991:20–1)

The problem of defining a total approach to quality also stems from the development of TQM as a more general philosophy of change. Although it has its roots in many of the principles of total quality control, it now encompasses a broader and more strategically oriented change management model aimed at revising existing organisational attitudes and belief systems. This cultural dimension of TQM is often heralded as the 'unquantifiable heart' of modern quality programmes and yet has proven very difficult to identify and define. For example, Philip Crosby (1984; 1988), through presenting a simple definition of quality based on 'conformance to requirements', has been successful in formulating a common language which has facilitated attitudinal change within organisations (Dobyns and Crawford-Mason, 1991:64–71). However, whilst he has been described as an evangelist he has also been criticised for a lack of practicality on the 'nuts-and-bolts' of change (see for example, Macdonald and Piggott, 1990:97–101). Once again, this highlights how the breadth and scale of change now associated with TQM makes it difficult to capture the meaning of TQM within a single definition.

From this discussion it has been illustrated how the definitional problems which surround TQM are unlikely to be resolved in the immediate future. The vested interests of competing consultant groups, the incorporation of service industries into TQM programmes, the long-term nature of transformational change strategies, and the growth in the application of TQM to include cultural and attitudinal change—as well as the more conventional application of statistical process control techniques to shopfloor operations, all render it difficult to construct a single definition for TQM. For our purposes, TQM is broadly defined as a philosophy of change which centres on the management of continual improvement through involving employees (and external customers and suppliers) in the group problem-solving of processes, rather than end-product quality issues, in order to meet changing customer expectations. Although the initial focus of TQM programmes is generally on employee involvement in quality improvement activities, it is important to remember that TQM is, in the longer term, about improving 'external' as well as 'internal' customer–supplier relations. Furthermore, by defining quality on the basis of customer expectations rather than developing quality systems on established specifications and standards, the on-going dynamic of continuous improvement is built into the TQM approach and contrasts with traditional conceptions of quality based on the setting of internal standards and measurement (Dawson, 1994a). It should also be noted that there are clear overlaps between various quality developments and that these are likely to continue and generate further confusion over what QA, QC, TQC and TQM mean in practice.

The confusion which surrounds quality management is also evident in the response and concern for the various national quality award programmes, as illustrated by Garvin's (1991) article on the Malcolm Baldridge National Quality Award. This prestigious American quality award originated from the 1987 Malcolm Baldridge National Quality Improvement Act, which advocated that awards for quality improvement be given to appropriate companies in manufacturing, service and small business (Garvin, 1991:81). Although the legislation mentioned elements such as worker involvement and management-led and customer-oriented programmes, little attention was given to the criteria for evaluation. This has led to criticism of the award, particularly in view of the poor financial performance of past winners, such as Motorola, Federal Express and Cadillac. Garvin claims that this is not and should not be, the focus of the Baldridge Award, rather, he highlights the importance of the award in stimulating greater inter-organisational co-operation:

The award has created a common vocabulary and philosophy bridging companies and industries...Benchmarking is by definition a cooperative activity, and it is an award requirement. Even warring factions of the quality movement have united under the Baldridge banner. To become more competitive, American companies have discovered co-operation. (Garvin, 1991:93)

In some cases, award winners have set about documenting their processes to gain international accreditation and hence, combine formalised procedures with a broader philosophy of continuous change and employee involvement at work (Hill and Freedman, 1992:81). In short, the current drive for quality has its roots in both traditional quality assurance practices for setting standards and the more philosophical approach which emphasises continual employee involvement in process improvements to meet changing customer expectations.

THE EMERGENCE OF QUALITY MANAGEMENT IN AUSTRALIA

The emergence of TQM in Australia followed in the wake of the American and European interest in Japanese manufacturing practices which were proving to be so successful in the world product markets of the 1970s. At this time, quality management was identified as a major contributing factor to Japan's competitive advantage and, as a consequence, the Japanese model of quality management began to diffuse into Western nations. The original American quality control experts, Juran and Deming, became major agents for the diffusion of quality management to international management audiences (Allan, 1991:34). Ironically, Deming, who had been invited to Japan in 1947 to assist in the Japanese population census, had, through a series of executive seminars, been a primary figure in the development of the Japanese model of quality management (Gabor, 1990). In 1987, his acceptance by Western management was illustrated by the attendance of some 50 000 executives to a series of four-day seminars in America (Allan, 1991:30). Similarly, Juran attracted thousands of managers to his seminars on quality management in the 1980s, and both Deming and Juran visited Australia several times during this period (Allan, 1991:31). The 1980s also witnessed the emergence of a number of consultancy groups which formed around these 'new' quality management principles (for example, Crosby, Conway, Joiner and Scholtes) and acted as diffusion agents in stimulating interest in quality management programmes. These individual quality leaders and consultant groups became the main vehicles for the diffusion of quality management in Britain, America and Australia.

In the early 1980s, the Australian concern with quality management became the focus of attention at the 53rd Annual Convention of the Federation of Australian Radio Broadcasters (FARB) in Perth, Western Australia. At this conference the Federal President and Director of FARB and Jack Keavney (representing Enterprise Australia) were able to get the support of the delegates to mount an Australia for Quality Campaign (Sprouster, 1984:17–18). The campaign was officially launched by the Australian Prime Minister Bob Hawke on the 2nd April 1984 and was a major vehicle for initiating the introduction of TQM into Australian manufacturing industries (Dawson and Patrickson, 1991:67). At this stage, Enterprise Australia acted as a catalyst and promoter of quality management and provided free seminars to Australian managers.

On 25 September 1986, the Minister for Industry, Technology and Commerce, Senator John Button, made a news release to announce the formation of a 'Committee of Review of Standards, Accreditation and Quality Control and Assurance in Australian Industry'. The review was conducted over a six-month period, and an advertisement inviting submissions from interested sources was placed in all the major Australian newspapers. In response, a total of 197 submissions was received and, in conjunction with information collected from a further 199 organisations, the committee prepared a final report. The report was presented to John Button on 26 June 1987, and claimed that there was a plethora of public and private sector organisations with little effective co-ordination and no national strategy (Foley, 1987). The report recommended that the Government assist the development of quality management in Australia, which was accomplished through using the National Industry Extension Service (NIES) (which had been established in March 1987 as an agency to promote process and product innovations). NIES formed a Quality Forum with representatives from industry, unions, government and academia, and through Aptech (a consulting firm) designed a TQM implementation package (Allan, 1991:48). A further recommendation of the Foley Report was that an Australian Quality Authority (AQA) should be established to co-ordinate a national strategy on quality management (Foley, 1987). However, the response and activities of both Enterprise Australia (EA) and the Australian Organisation for Quality Control (AOQC) proved instrumental in reshaping the direction of the Australian quality movement in the late 1980s.

One of the main activities of EA which brought about a shift in emphasis in the quality movement occurred in the mid-1980s when John Sprouster, Managing Director of Nashua Australia, and Bruce Irvin, Managing Director of the Australia for Quality Campaign (both Directors of EA), proved successful in developing an Australian Total Quality Management Institute

(TQMI). TQMI was launched by the Minister for Industry, Technology and Commerce on 10 April 1987 and was set the objective of promoting the diffusion of TQM in Australia (Allan, 1991:39). In 1988, an annual Australian quality award for outstanding achievement in TQM was established and awarded to organisations who could prove that the principles and practices of TQM had been incorporated into daily operations (Sohal, 1991:7). Over the past few years, EA and TQMI have continued to work closely together and, by the early 1990s, were promoting a TQM perspective which emphasised cultural change and the importance of senior management commitment.

In the case of the AOQC, which had its roots in quality assurance and espoused an engineering model of quality management, attempts to influence Federal Government were largely unsuccessful until the mid-1980s. At this time, the public inability to differentiate between QA and TQM combined with a growing national awareness of quality as a world manufacturing issue (in part, resultant of the 'success' of the Australia for Quality campaign), led to the growing success of AOQC as a diffusion agency. For example, Cameron Allan, in describing the way in which the Queensland Division of the AOQC influenced State Government, states that:

> The AOQC successfully convinced the Queensland Government to make the adoption of QM systems mandatory for those firms which wish to supply to Government...This policy stipulates that government suppliers of manufactured goods, and services related to those manufactured goods, must possess a certified quality management system to the Australian Standards, AS 3900 series. (Allan, 1991:45)

In 1990, AOQC set up the Quality Society of Australasia (QSA) with the aim of providing recognition and professional status for quality practitioners. Among others, this organisation is supported by Standards Australia, the Institute of Quality Assurance and the National Association of Testing Authorities (Sohal, 1991:7). Today, EA and AOQC act as the main controllers and founder member organisations (with the Total Quality Management Institute (TQMI) and the Quality Society of Australasia (QSA)), of the new umbrella organisation, the Australian Quality Council (AQC), established in 1990 (Sohal, 1991:8). This new peak body for quality has incorporated AOQC/QSA and EA/TQMI into its new offices at St Leonards in Sydney, and represents an attempt to unify the two major opponents in the diffusion of quality management in Australia. It is within this historical context that the quality movement has developed within Australia and particular models of TQM implementation have been taken up by industry and commerce. In the sections which follow, the main contributions of the popular exponents of quality management are discussed and the main elements of a typical TQM programme are identified and explained.

POPULAR EXPONENTS OF QUALITY MANAGEMENT

The number of popular exponents of quality management has been increasing with the growth in the application and uptake of TQM across manufacturing and service industries worldwide. They include Armand Feigenbaum who championed the phrase 'Total Quality Control' (1961 and 1991), Tom Peters who has called for a managerial revolution (Peters and Waterman, 1982; Peters, 1987), Richard Schonberger who has outlined an action agenda for manufacturing excellence (Schonberger, 1982 and 1986), and Karl Albrecht who has advocated the need for a Total Quality Service model to accommodate the special requirements of service industries (Albrecht and Zemke, 1985, Albrecht, 1992). There has also been an increase in the number of Japanese international quality experts, such as: Kaori Ishikawa (1985), Genichi Taguchi (1986 and 1987), and Masaaki Imai (1986). Ishikawa is recognised for his seven tools for workers engaged in TQC (namely: Pareto charts, cause-and-effect diagrams, histograms, check sheets, scatter diagrams, flow charts, and control charts) and for originating the fishbone or Ishikawa (cause–effect) diagram (Brocka and Brocka, 1992:77–9). Taguchi developed a sophisticated set of statistical methods, which have been recognised as being difficult to assimilate 'even for reasonably sophisticated engineers' (Macdonald and Piggott, 1990:120). His main contribution to quality has been to focus practitioner attention on the design phase through highlighting the value of design experiments prior to full production (see Ryan, 1989:285–345). The essential Taguchi concept is that quality should be built-in during the design phase of a product, process or service in order to prevent future problems during the production stage (Barker, 1990:103). Finally, Masaaki Imai has elaborated the Japanese management strategy of Kaizen, which stresses that incremental improvements are equally as important as radical (break-through) innovations in securing and maintaining competitive success (Imai, 1986). In summing up, Imai describes this philosophy of continuous improvement as follows:

> KAIZEN is a humanistic approach, because it expects everybody—indeed, everybody—to participate in it. It is based on the belief that every human being can contribute to improving his workplace where he spends one-third of his life. (Imai, 1986:227)

More detailed accounts of the main contributions of these exponents of quality have been usefully summarised elsewhere and are not dealt with here (see for example, Oakland, 1989:281–93). Rather, this section summarises the work of three popular and widely acclaimed American experts on quality management, namely Juran, Deming and Crosby. These three exponents of quality management have been referred to as 'the quality masters', 'the gurus', and the 'charismatic pacesetters', of quality management development (see Brocka and Brocka, 1992:55).

The first of these popular exponents of quality management, W. Edwards Deming (1981 and 1982), studied under Walter Shewhart, a statistician employed by Bell Laboratories, and was interested in Shewhart's sampling and control charts for monitoring and evaluating process operations. He later became known as an expert on sampling and, in the 1930s, was recruited by the US Department of Agriculture to work within the Census Bureau and help establish a new sampling approach. In 1947, he was invited to Japan to assist in the Japanese population census. In a series of seminars to Japanese executives, Deming applied and developed his systematic approach to productivity and quality management. He argued that the commonly accepted levels of product mistakes and defects highlighted a problem of poor quality and that, through improving quality, a 'chain reaction' would be instigated resulting in: improved productivity, and decreased costs and prices, which would in turn increase market share, stimulate employment growth and provide return on investment (Macdonald and Piggott, 1990:102–3).

According to Deming, poor quality is generally 85 per cent a management (or systems) problem and only 15 per cent a worker problem. He advocated that whilst good quality does not necessarily mean high quality it always means a predictable degree of uniformity and dependability at low cost with qualities suited to the market (Sprouster, 1984:54). In explaining the route to quality, Deming formulated his famous fourteen points (see Appendix III), and seven deadly diseases and obstacles to achieving a quality culture (see Walton 1986:34–6), the former of which has been summarised by Gabor (1990) as consisting of the following six principles:

1. Quality is defined by the customer.

2. Understanding and reducing variation in every process is a must.

3. All significant, long-lasting quality improvements must emanate from top management's commitment to improvement, as well as its understanding of the means by which systematic change is to be achieved.

4. Change and improvement must be continuous and all-encompassing. It must involve every member in an organization, including outside suppliers.

5. The on-going education and training of all the employees in a company are a prerequisite for achieving the sort of analysis that is needed for constant improvement.

6. Performance ratings that seek to measure the contributions of individual employees are usually destructive.

Lloyd Dobyns and Clare Crawford-Mason—who introduced Deming to the American public through their NBC television documentary (*If Japan Can, Why Can't We*, on 24 June 1980)—compare Deming to the other popular quality management exponents in the following way:

> Deming is the philosopher; the others are more pragmatic, telling managers what to do—specifically, to make things better. Deming does not. People who believe in his method have been known to compare it to religion because, they say, it not only improves quality in manufacturing, service government, and education, but it also makes their lives better...Dr. Deming reaches people through the heart. It is hard to imagine any of the other quality experts hammering away, as Deming does at his seminars, at the right of all people to have 'joy in their work'. (Dobyns and Crawford-Mason, 1991:56)

They note that whilst Deming has been closely associated with statistics and Statistical Quality Control (SQC), he also advocates that statistics should be used as a tool for highlighting 'manufacturing as a system' and should be combined with other on-going interactions and communication between research, design, production and sales. This cycle (also known as the Shewhart–Deming wheel) has been recast as the Plan-Do-Check-Action (PDCA) and Standardise-Do-Check-Action (SDCA) cycles (see Figure 2.1). The PDCA cycle commences with the collection of data through the use of statistical tools for the purpose of formulating a plan for improving present practices (Plan). When a plan has been agreed it is implemented (Do) and

Figure 2.1: The PDCA/SPCA Cycles

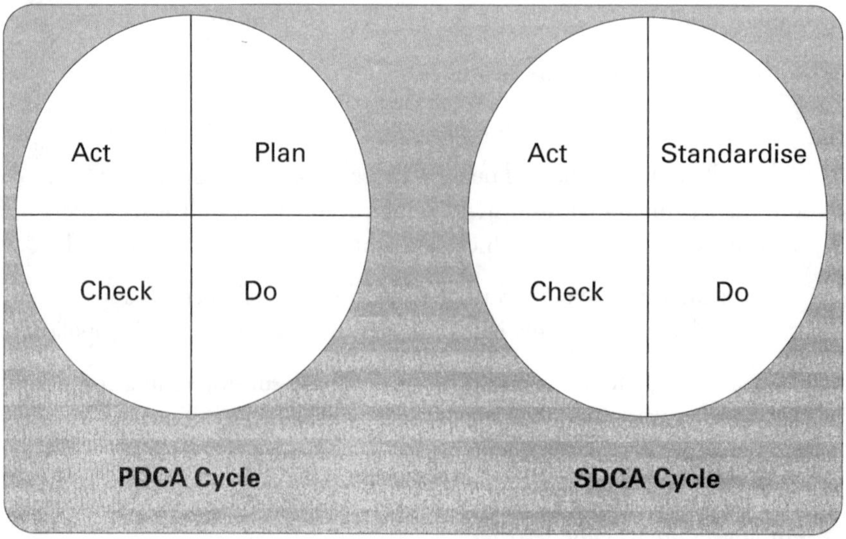

Act	Plan	Act	Standardise
Check	Do	Check	Do

PDCA Cycle   **SDCA Cycle**

then the results are evaluated to assess whether the change has brought about the desired improvement (Check). Once a change has proven successful, then steps are taken to prevent the recurrence of old ways of working and to 'institutionalise' the new practice (Action). The process of stabilising standards is accounted for by the SDCA cycle (Blakemore, 1989:20). Once the new practices have become established and stabilised as new standards, they then become the operating practices which may be challenged with new plans for further improvement. Thus, SDCA is used for stabilising and standardising operations and PDCA for improving them (Imai, 1986:63).

Another popular American exponent who has influenced the development of quality within the Japanese business community is Joseph Juran (1988 and 1991). Like Deming, Juran was familiar with Walter Shewhart's work and during the 1950s assisted the Japanese in restructuring their industries (Berry, 1991:41). His contribution was formally recognised in 1981, when Emperor Hirohito awarded him the Order of the Sacred Treasure.

One of Juran's major contributions was his early emphasis on management as a process and the importance of people and communication to the achievement of quality. Although a statistician by training, Juran pointed out that statistical control techniques would not help a company manage quality. On this count, he argued that managing for quality involves three basic managerial processes which comprise:

1 *Quality planning*: the process by which customers are identified, their requirements clarified and the operating practices necessary for the delivery of customer goods or services are defined and communicated to production.

2 *Quality control*: the process by which a good or service is evaluated against customer requirements and detected problems corrected.

3 *Quality improvement*: the process by which new organisational arrangements are put into place to ensure the pursuit of quality on a continuous basis.

In pursuing this 'trilogy' of managerial processes, Juran advocates the need to: establish policies and goals for quality, formulate plans for meeting quality goals, provide the necessary resources to evaluate progress and take appropriate action, and provide motivation to ensure that people meet the desired goal (Macdonald and Piggott, 1990:110). He maintained that many of the serious quality problems are systemic and interdepartmental, requiring the involvement and commitment of senior management. This approach thereby highlights the inappropriateness of systems which delegate responsibility for quality to the workforce and by so doing sidestep managerial responsibilities. Although Juran is a strong supporter of employee participation and self-directing teams of workers, he nevertheless stressed the need for management to be an integral part of any quality improvement programme. His ten steps to quality improvement are listed in Appendix II and his twofold definition of quality is quoted in Brocka and Brocka:

> One form of quality is income oriented, and consists of those features of the product which meet customer needs and thereby produce income. In this sense higher quality usually costs more. A second form of quality is cost oriented and consists of freedom from failures and deficiencies. In this sense higher quality usually costs less. (Brocka and Brocka, 1992:80)

From this definition, it is clear that Juran is also concerned with the quantifiable costs of quality and elsewhere, he has argued that project teams can, on average, return approximately $100 000 in cost savings (Tenner and DeToro, 1992:20). Moreover, whilst Juran supports the view that closer relationships should be built with suppliers, he also believes that single sourcing for key purchases may reduce the supplier's quality commitment (particularly in an environment where quality is a competitive issue). Thus for Juran, quality improvement rests on the development of management processes which are able to motivate employees in the pursuit of quality through the formation of project teams.

The final exponent of quality management discussed here is Philip Crosby (1980 and 1988). He has been described as an 'evangelist' and charismatic leader of the quality movement, in gaining and holding the attention of thousands of business executives and committing them to the 'quest for quality' (Macdonald and Piggott, 1990:97). Crosby created the idea of 'zero defects' and argues that quality is conformance to requirements which can only be measured by the cost of non-conformance. In this sense, there is either conformance or non-conformance, with nothing in between, and hence the appropriate goal to set for performance is that of zero defects. As Crosby states:

> Quality is free. It's not a gift, but it is free. What costs money are the unequality things—all the actions that involve not doing jobs right the first time...Zero Defects is a standard for management, a standard that management can convey to the employees to help them to decide to 'do the job right the first time'. (Crosby, 1980:2 and 145)

Crosby received international recognition as a quality expert in the 1980s following the success of his best-selling book *Quality is Free*, which was published in 1979. The book is written in a clear, readable manner which made it instantly accessible to the general public, and has since sold two million copies in several different languages (Dobyns and Crawford-Mason, 1991:64). His quality programme is centred on four absolutes of quality management which comprise:

1. *Quality is conformance, not elegance.* This differs from conventional definitions as the emphasis is on customer expectations rather than process methods or technical specifications. Crosby has estimated that only about 10 per cent of the requirements for an automobile rest on internal technical specifications, with the remainder largely being determined by the external expectations of customers (Dobyns and Crawford-Mason, 1991:67).

2. *The quality system for meeting customer expectations should be based on prevention (do it right the first time) and not inspection.* A system which does not require mass inspection will produce quality products at far less cost.

3. *The only performance standard is Zero Defects.* Crosby argues that any tolerance for defects is unacceptable and is an ardent critic of statistically based quality methods, which he claims perpetuate the myth that the laws of variation are inviolable (on this count, Deming and Juran would strongly disagree with Crosby's approach to quality management).

4. *The only performance measurement is the cost of quality.* Poor quality reduces bottom-line performance and may threaten customer–supplier relations. Crosby claims that it costs less to produce quality than not to produce it, and that quality does more to increase profits than anything else.

Crosby's fourteen steps towards the attainment of quality management are outlined in Appendix II (see also, Crosby, 1980:149–222). He sets out a pragmatic programme for practitioners to follow in 'the art of making quality certain' and argues that terms such as 'quality control' and 'quality assurance' are no longer relevant as they 'identify relatively insignificant and minute differences in approach' (Crosby, 1980:58). Crosby suggests that the success or failure of quality programmes rest on the ability of quality managers to interact, communicate and discipline other management groups without antagonising them and yet ensuring that quality is embraced by all functions. He claims that quality managers should direct actions at preventing problems and that this cannot be achieved by simply revising or restructuring existing organisation charts:

> Successful quality managers know that the way to make people quality conscious is to make them comfortable with the concepts of quality, and show them how to recognise what they can receive from loy-

alty to the concept. The art must be practiced in most functions. But quality is unique in that all the successes as well as failures are caused by people in other operations. The product or service is quality because of other people's fingers and minds, and the quality managers must be able to work with those people in order to handle the function properly. (Crosby, 1980:59)

Deming, Juran and Crosby all agree that quality is an essential requirement of modern business and a key to reducing costs and increasing profits. Whilst Deming is more of a philosopher, who argues that quality requires a transformational change in the management and operations of an organisation, Juran claims that the introduction of quality programmes requires the time and support of senior management, although such programmes need not necessitate a radical change in a company's strategy and structure. Juran also places less importance than Deming on the use of statistical methods for quality management. Control charts and the like are identified as useful tools which are made useless without the support, education and involvement of employees in identifying and meeting the needs of customers.

In promoting quality, Crosby has been very active in America and he has set up his own quality college with a staff of about 325 (see, Crosby, 1980:137–48); in contrast, Deming teaches four-day seminars and works out of a basement office with his secretary Ceil Kilian in Washington; and the Juran approach to quality has largely be promoted through the Juran Institute in Wilton, Connecticut (Dobyns and Crawford-Mason, 1991:67–71). Through their writings and associated teaching practices these three have become the 'charismatic pacesetters' of the so-called 'quality revolution' and have motivated individuals and companies to follow the high, low or middle course to the establishment of a quality organisation. All three agree that poor quality is a management problem which should be tackled by examining existing processes and identifying routes to improvement so that defects can be prevented (Crosby) or reduced (Deming and Juran). As Brocka and Brocka describe:

> Deming, Juran, or Crosby are often identified (or even equated) with the Quality Management movement. Their magnetism has resulted in passionate devotees and 'disciples' of the various masters, each proclaiming their pundit to have revealed the one true path to total quality enlightenment. The squabbling that occasionally occurs between each guru's camp sometime resembles religious 'heresy' disputes, where much arguing proceeds over differences without distinction. (Brocka and Brocka, 1992:55)

COMMON FEATURES OF A QUALITY MANAGEMENT PROGRAMME

There are a number of common characteristics which tend to be present in discussions and debates on TQM and these will serve as a useful starting point for explaining the core principles surrounding mainstream total quality management programmes. For our purposes, the seven main elements of TQM are seen to comprise:

- A management philosophy of change
- An emphasis on continuous improvement
- Application of appropriate quality control techniques
- Group problem-solving of process operations
- A focus on 'internal' and 'external' customer–supplier relations
- A commitment to employee involvement
- A climate of trust, co-operation, and a non-adversarial system of industrial relations.

The first key feature of TQM is that it is a *total management approach* to quality improvement which involves all aspects of internal operations and every employee of the company, as well as external operating practices and customer–supplier relations. This holistic approach to quality management and change differentiates it from historically earlier attempts at quality control (through quality assurance departments) and employee involvement programmes (through the use of quality circles on the shopfloor). In essence, it is a management philosophy of change which is based on the view that change is a necessary and natural requirement of organisations wishing to keep pace with dynamic external business market environments and continually improve existing operating systems. Those organisations embracing this new management philosophy support an ideology of participation and collaboration through involving employees in certain managerial decision-making processes. The philosophy is based on an approach to quality which incorporates the skill and expertise of employees in group decision-making exercises which have the backing and commitment of senior management. The total approach requires the involvement of chief executive officers (who are expected to strongly endorse the programme and align themselves with the objectives), other managerial groups, supervisors and shopfloor and branch level personnel. In other words, it is a philosophy of change which centres on the management of continual improvement through involving employees in group problem-solving of processes, rather than end-product quality issues.

The second main characteristic of TQM is its emphasis on *continuous improvement* or incrementalism. Unlike typical operational change programmes, which often seek to remodel established working procedures, relationships and practices, and to stabilise operating systems through instituting a new and clearly prescribed set of processes, the TQM change strategy is based on institutionalising a system of continuous process improvement. The principle of on-going change in process operations is established as normal operating practice. Minor developments and changes in process operations are no longer viewed as a threat to established working relationships but, rather, become an employee expectation and form part of a new routinised way of working based on incremental change and process improvement.

The principle of continuous improvement has also been employed by consultants in their formulation of implementation strategies. However, as Susan Whittle has noted:

> This stop–go model for implementing TQ, alternating between action and reflections, contradicts orthodox images of TQ as continuous improvement and suggests a less planned and more chaotic process of change than many consultancies would advocate. (Whittle, 1992:9)

The organisational adoption of TQM is often marked by a radical departure with previous methods of working and requires a significant shift in employee attitudes. Once this transformational change is achieved, incrementalism then becomes the order of the day for further process changes. The aim is to utilise the skills and experience of everyone in continually adjusting operations with the aim of achieving major long-term competitive advantages through employee-generated innovations in the manufacturing of products and the delivery of services. In Japan, the term Kaizen has been used to refer to a system which supports gradual, unending improvement for achieving ever-higher standards in meeting changing customer and market requirements. In the words of Masaaki Imai:

> The essence of KAIZEN is simple and straightforward: KAIZEN means improvement. Moreover, KAIZEN means on-going improvement involving everyone, including both managers and workers. The KAIZEN philosophy assumes that our way of life—be it our working life, our social life, or our home life—deserves to be constantly improved. (Imai, 1986:3)

Kaizen (and the principle of incremental innovation in process operations) has been the basis from which many Japanese systems have been developed. It is an essential characteristic of TQM programmes which seek to make top management and all other employees 'Kaizen conscious' in being committed to continuous process improvement (see also, the Shewhart or Deming wheel of Plan-Do-Check-Action (Merli, 1990:17)).

This leads to the third element of TQM programmes, namely the *application of appropriate quality control techniques*. Although some commentators have argued that 'sustained quality improvement without the use of quality measurement techniques is impossible' (Fox, 1991:7), with TQM the emphasis is not on systematic measuring techniques per se, but on the use of statistical methods to support the objective of continuous process improvement. Traditionally, quality control has been the concern of quality inspectors who monitor and evaluate finished products against a set of requirement specifications. Those products which meet the specifications are sent on to customers and those which fail are either scrapped or reworked. In practice, there may also be a degree of adjustment and revision to product quality standards in response to such factors as: market demand, type of customer and perceptions of customer dissatisfaction. Thus, under this conventional quality control system, problems of poor quality are addressed with the end product or service rather than at the stage in which the fault in producing the good or service actually arose. Dealing with quality issues after the event can add considerable costs whilst at the same time decreasing productivity, whereas improving the process may eliminate the problem at its source and result in lower costs through the reduction of scrap and rework (Crosby, 1980:101–7; Tillery and Rutledge, 1991). Under a TQM system, the aim is to identify and solve process problems and eliminate the need for 'armies' of inspectors. This is achieved in groups (see below) and through the use of various statistical tools. Statistical tools are used to provide a simple way for monitoring and evaluating process operations (Newton, 1990:243–85). Some of the more common statistical techniques include: control charts, statistical measures and sampling, design of experiments, evolutionary operation, and Pareto analysis (see McConnell, 1988:3–134). For example, a shopfloor operator may be trained on how to take a sample of items from a production line and then to measure and record these items on a control chart. The charts would normally have two lines which set the upper and lower control limits, indicating whether the process is in control (that is, within these parameters) or whether corrective action is required. However, it should be noted that in the TQM studies carried out by the author, there has been little evidence of the on-going use of statistical process control by shopfloor operators (see also, Dawson 1994a).

The fourth and related characteristic of TQM, is the use of *group problem-solving techniques* to process operations. There are a number of different techniques which are used to facilitate team problem-solving activities. A good illustration of some of the more prominent methods is provided by

Blakemore's steps in problem-solving and decision-making (Blakemore, 1989:73). Step one involves selecting a process which requires attention through drawing on the knowledge and experience of all members of the TQM group. Brainstorming is a common tool used at this stage where each member is asked for suggestions until all ideas have been exhausted. The aim is to maximise the number of suggestions through encouraging participation and ensuring that no evaluations are made during the brainstorming session. Following this, the team identifies a few important items and eventually a decision is made about which process should be the focus of the group's attention. The next step centres on increasing group understanding of the process in question. This may be achieved through the use of flow charts which will help break down the problem into smaller parts and simplify complex structures and inter-relationships. The third step involves measuring the process through collecting various data which can be represented on simple run charts and histograms. The group may then decide to run a further brainstorming session to identify the range of problems generated by the data. This would be followed by the need to list the problems in rank order and may involve the use of a Pareto chart (a bar chart arrayed in descending order listing the category and frequency of factors that contribute to the total problem). Essentially, a Pareto analysis reveals which causes are responsible for the greatest effect and is based on the principle that few of the causes often count for most of the effect. On the basis of these results a problem is selected and the nature of the causes identified. At this stage an Ishikawa or fishbone diagram may be used to clarify cause-and-effect relationships. Kaori Ishikawa argued that symptoms are usually the first indication of a problem and that it is important to differentiate between different levels of causes and to take action on root causes rather than surface indicators. Tenner and DeToro use the example of a car not starting as a symptom of a problem, with a dead battery or broken fan belt being two possible causes, and the root cause of the problem being inadequate preventive maintenance (Tenner and DeToro, 1992:119). Once the cause has been identified, the TQM group must then select a solution, implement the change and monitor the outcome to evaluate the effectiveness of the solution. Once again, the use of process control charts provide a useful statistical indicator which allows TQM team members to detect any abnormality in process operations. The TQM team may then seek to make further refinements to the process (Kaizen) and may redirect their attention to another process 'problem'.

A fifth major component of TQM programmes is the *focus on 'internal' and 'external' customer–supplier relations*. The internal customer is the next person or group in the process of manufacturing goods or providing services. Apart from those involved in external customer–supplier relations, everyone should have an internal customer and, under TQM, should aim to meet the requirements and expectations of that customer. In order to meet customer needs it is first necessary to clarify what those needs are and this requires open and regular communication between the various customer–supplier groups. In stressing the importance of these internal relationships, TQM highlights the importance of teamwork and communication, and illustrates how external customers' requirements cannot be achieved if each output passed between employees within the company is deficient. Quality as defined by the customer is central to TQM (Albrecht, 1992:1–22). Consequently, whilst it is expected that internal suppliers focus on meeting the needs of their immediate customers, an overview must also be maintained of the expectations and requirements of the external customer. In some cases customer requirements may be vague and in others they may be unrealistic, in either event TQM provides the vehicle for developing stronger links with external customers and clarifying requirements. This is particularly important within service industries where the quality of the service may occur during service delivery and cannot be assessed in terms of whether a tangible product accords with a precise set of manufacturing specifications. For example, Zeithaml, Parasuraman, and Berry (1990:68) claim that in cases where quality evaluation occurs during service experience, a discrepancy can often occur between what customers expect and what management perceives that they expect. This is further complicated by the fact that customers' service expectations may comprise both the service the customer hopes to receive (the desired level) and the service the customer deems acceptable (the adequate level), and these expectations may change over time (Berry and Parasuraman, 1991:58–63). Thus, the concept of internal as well as external customers cannot only be used to encourage greater inter- and intra-organisational communication, but also as the starting point for wider customer–supplier participation in decision-making about process improvements to meet product and service requirements.

The sixth element associated with the principles of TQM is based on *a commitment to employee involvement.* In discussing the other elements above, it should already be clear that changes, such as the development of TQM problem-solving teams and the concept of internal customers, all form part of a programme of change which emphasises employee involvement. However, the extent to which TQM can in practice achieve total employee involvement is questionable (see Part II). The aim of TQM is nevertheless to achieve 'unified purpose via extensive sharing of information and involvement in planning and implementation of change' (Schonberger, 1992:83). Through training programmes, education, multi-skilling, cross-career developments and multi-function project teams, employees are actively encouraged to be involved in current organisational problems and the future competitive success of the company.

The seventh and final element, centres on the *building of high-trust relationships, and the development of non-adversarial systems of industrial relations.*

Through the development of stronger internal relationships and the implementation of policies which seek to devolve greater decision-making to operative level employees, TQM programmes aim to create and sustain greater employee commitment and trust. Communication is identified as the main vehicle for building trust between senior management, middle management and other employees within the organisation. The objective is to bring about a shift in existing attitudes and remodel adversarial systems of industrial relations through a more open and participative management approach which actively seeks and places a premium on the knowledge and experience of all employees. Unions are identified as 'critical players' and 'partners' in the process of establishing a total quality organisation. The aim is to replace large bureaucratic contracts and elaborate grievance procedures with a more collaborative system where unions act to facilitate employee involvement in a quality programme. As Bowen and Lawler point out, if union support is absent then employees may distrust the objectives of TQM and reject activities associated with a total quality program (Bowen and Lawler, 1992:39). The questions of whether TQM is a system for by-passing shop stewards in introducing shopfloor change, whether it undermines the power of trade unions, and whether it ultimately increases the demands placed on workers, are central union concerns (see for example, Parker and Slaughter, 1988). Roth notes that in America some union leaders have embraced various quality initiatives whilst other have strongly resisted attempts by management to introduce change (Roth, 1992:154). Within Australia, workplace resistance emanating from changes in work rules and job restrictions is largely being dealt with under other change programmes, such as award restructuring. Moreover, the other key issue of job security is being addressed through highlighting the need for company quality initiatives in order for businesses to prosper and survive. The economic imperative argument for more collaborative systems of industrial relations is in evidence in the Australian and New Zealand context, and, in the cases reported in Part II, there were no major industrial relations problems associated with the introduction of TQM. Essentially, change is being initiated through TQM teams and supported by management and unions, rather than being imposed by management on the workforce.

Finally, it is worth noting that organisations operating under a management philosophy of TQM would normally have introduced new organisational arrangements to accommodate such a change. The organisational structure for TQM is likely to vary between organisations, although it would generally mirror rather than supplant existing reporting and command structures. Typically, there would be a steering committee formed by the executive of the company who would set policies and quality programme objectives, recommend and approve TQM quality groups, monitor and evaluate progress, and ensure that the TQM programme fitted with the overall strategic direction of the company. Below the steering committee, there may be a number of quality groups located in different plants or assigned to different functions, such as manufacturing, research and development, finance and administration, and sales and marketing; and there may be a number of quality teams tackling different quality problems (Oakland, 1989:27–48). In addition to this basic structure, there would normally be a TQM co-ordinator with responsibility for directing and evaluating the implementation of quality programmes and recommending new TQM initiatives. The TQM co-ordinator would also provide support to the various quality groups and teams, and assist in the training, development and education of employees and external customers and suppliers.

CONCLUSION: QUALITY MANAGEMENT

Total Quality Management (TQM) is being introduced and used by a wide range of companies—in the Asia-Pacific region, North America and Europe—who are seeking to improve their national and international competitive position through developing inter-company and intra-organisational systems of collaboration. The focus is on the integration of new operational techniques with strategic management, and the development of policies and practices centred on 'internal' and 'external' customer–supplier co-operation and engagement. This involves the management of belief systems and the enlisting of all levels of employees in the systematic search, assessment and adaptation of organisational processes for the strategic objective of gaining efficiencies, cost reductions, and better quality products and services. In the monitoring and evaluating of existing operations, companies have also turned their attention to improving inter-organisational systems and relationships with their major customers and suppliers. Whilst this chapter has indicated that there can be no single definition of TQM, it was nevertheless advocated that there are a number of common characteristics between the various TQM programmes found in industry and commerce. These were seen to comprise: a management philosophy of change, an emphasis on continuous improvement, the application of systematic measurement techniques, group problem-solving of process operations, a focus on 'internal' and 'external' customer–supplier relations, a commitment to total employee involvement, and the development of high-trust relationships and a non-adversarial system of industrial relations.

Through examining the emergence of TQM in Australia it was demonstrated how the original American quality exponents, Deming and Juran, acted as major agents for the diffusion of TQM within the international management arena. Within Australia, quality management was shaped by a range of factors, including the activities of two influential organisations—the Australian Organisation for Quality Control (AOQC) and Enterprise Australia (EA)—who had very different perspectives on what constituted quality. The AOQC acted as a promoter of quality assurance principles and was the major protagonist behind the creation of the Quality Society of Australasia. In contrast, EA promoted employee involvement programmes and developed the Australian Total Quality Management Institute. AOQC and EA have now established closer links under the peak umbrella organisation of the Australian Quality Council founded in 1990.

Although there is an ever-increasing number of quality experts, this chapter has focused on the work of the three influential quality exponents: Deming, Juran and Crosby. Deming argued that poor quality is generally a management problem, that individual rating systems should be abolished and that understanding and reducing variation in every process is central to producing a predictable degree of product uniformity and dependability at low cost with qualities suited to the market. The heart of quality improvement is people, emanating from top management commitment and being secured and maintained through the on-going education and training of all employees within an organisation.

Similarly, Juran emphasised the importance of senior management commitment. He identified three managerial processes of quality, consisting of planning, control and improvement. He claimed that it is possible to gauge the financial cost savings of quality programmes, that training programmes should be used to change behaviour rather than educate, and that upper management should retain responsibility for quality within a system where employees are trained to control the quality of processes to which they are assigned. He also believed in combining the devolution of quality control to work teams with the centralisation of decision-making within senior management (who would maintain overall responsibility for quality developments), and thereby argued that the introduction of quality programmes need not necessitate transformational change.

The third major quality exponent, Crosby, has done a lot to popularise quality and make the concepts accessible to a wide range of management groups. Through his concept of zero defects he emphasises the importance of doing things right the first time so that they do not have to be fixed or redone. He believes that quality is free, and that it is non-conformance to requirements which wastes company assets. All three exponents agree that poor quality is a senior management problem which should be tackled by examining existing processes and identifying routes to improvement so that defects can be prevented or reduced.

Finally, it is worth restating that TQM is a philosophy of change which seeks to secure a cultural shift in attitudes among all levels of employees and cannot be explained as simply an operational technique for increasing control over shopfloor operations. As a cultural control strategy, TQM goes beyond the shopfloor to incorporate strategic human resource management and inter-company relationships. It is a new and emerging manufacturing and service strategy which remains clouded by the hype and gloss of neat prescriptive post-hoc rationalisations and market-driven consultant packages, and, as such, is an area in need of further detailed investigation and longitudinal critical appraisal.

CHAPTER 3

TQM and its Place in Management Theory

INTRODUCTION

This chapter is designed to suggest different ways of analysing Total Quality Management (TQM). Chapter 2 discussed the prescriptions advocated within the Quality movement, and in the next section, Part II of the book, we analyse the companies that were studied. Before we move from the prescriptions to the empirical case studies, this chapter introduces a discussion of different ways of analysing TQM in order to clarify the place of TQM within the development of management theory.

There have been several previous movements for managerial reform. These earlier management theories were also formulated to help management improve performance and organisational effectiveness. We can contrast TQM with the earlier ideas for management reform, in order to see how it builds on, or differs from, the past. By noting the impact that prescriptions for reform have had in the past, we are in a better position to judge the influence that TQM is likely to have today. The first half of the chapter therefore sets TQM in the context of the historical development of ideas about management.

Any review of the development of managerial ideas only serves to emphasise the complexity and diversity of the management process. The second half of the chapter investigates this complexity within management processes. Within organisational theory, a multiple-perspective approach is currently being advocated as a way of gaining insight into the many different aspects of organisational life (Morgan 1986, Palmer and Dunford, 1993). In this chapter we use a multiple-perspective approach to distinguish between bureaucratic, political and cultural aspects of management. We then relate these perspectives to TQM in order to identify issues relevant to our study of the implementation of TQM.

PART ONE: TQM AND THE HISTORY OF MANAGEMENT THOUGHT

Histories of management thought are often presented in terms of a linear development. Managerial prescriptions and ideas for action are assumed to rest on rationality and logic, and in simple histories of management thought there is an underlying assumption that there is a straightforward and continuous improvement over time. Many textbooks describe the transition from one set of managerial prescriptions to the next in terms of simple progress. Consultants are likely to present the latest ideas that they wish to sell as a rational improvement on the ideas of the past, and academic work on managerial techniques is often associated with a search for improved methods of working. As a result, notions of progress usually underlie discussions of new managerial theories, and are particularly important for practitioners implementing change.

Such a history of events is important if people believe it to be true, and we sketch a 'rationalist' history below. However, as we shall see later in this first part of the chapter, the development of management thought is more complex than this and we will need to consider more than the simple development of improved, more rational ideas.

A rationalist history of management theory can be briefly described as follows (see also, Brown, 1992). At the beginning of the twentieth century, *Scientific Management* popularised the important notion that the management process could be understood through study, and that managerial skills could be learnt. It had previously been a common assumption that managerial skills and competences were associated with particular personalities, or with dominant social classes or castes. Scientific management put the argument that managerial authority could be developed, and should rest on scientific, systematic decision-making.

Scientific or systematic managerial decision-making could be achieved by the measurement and the collection of data on the inputs, processes and desired outputs of production. This data could then be used by industrial engineers to work out the most efficient design for materials, mechanical tools and work processes. As the ideas of Scientific Management spread, industrial engineers and work study experts used their work study and measurement skills to rationalise and standardise the work process. They designed carefully specified, standardised jobs. They time-studied and streamlined work processes and they developed effort-related payment systems to reward individual workers.

As Taylorism spread, certain problems became associated with the ideas of Scientific Management. The main problems were seen to be the impersonality of its scientific approach to job design, and the coldness of its strictly economic approach to human motivation.

Human Relations was developed by psychologists in the 1930s to improve upon the managerial prescriptions of the original school of scientific management. The ideas of the Human Relations school sought to add an understanding of human needs and motivation to supervision and job design. Supervisors were taught to recognise the importance of non-economic, social rewards and motivators. Jobs were enriched to add variety and a sense of responsibility to the performance of work.

The profession of personnel management developed from this time and carried ideas about human motivation into the growing industrial organisations. However, from some parties, criticisms were heard that scientific management had deskilled the workforce by systematically restricting decision-making to higher levels in the organisation, and that Human Relations policies had done little or nothing to restore responsibility or the use of intelligence to employees at the bottom of the hierarchy

Socio-technical Systems Theory was developed from the 1950s by academics in Europe who sought to combine some of the social and technical prescriptions of the earlier schools. Their main recommendations sought to redress the imbalance of the non-participative hierarchies of authority established by the earlier schools of management thought. They called for the involvement of employees in group decision-making on the management of their jobs. Socio-technical Systems Theory recommended the creation of autonomous work groups in order to add democracy and flexibility to over-specialised and over-standardised work processes. These new ideas were promoted in industry by academic institutes such as the Tavistock Centre in London, and the Quality of Working Life Institute in Scandinavia. They backed some famous experiments such as the innovative design of Volvo's Kalmar plant in the early 1970s. However, despite the academic backing and research in the area, autonomous workgroups did not become widespread. Unlike the earlier schools of thought, they were not extensively adopted by industrial consultants. Autonomous workgroups did not replace conventional methods of working.

Academics from the 1960s were also producing studies which showed that managerial structures and behaviour appeared to vary in different contexts, and as a result of different contingencies (Burns and Stalker, 1961; Lawrence and Lorsch, 1967; and the Aston studies, Pugh and Hickson,

1976). The main message of these studies was that there was no one best way to manage, and that the economic, social and sectoral context had a major impact on the adoption and success of different managerial policies. *Contingency Theory* was to have a major impact on academic work, but, as with Socio-technical Theory, it did not have an immediate impact on the spread of prescriptive managerial ideas, through the management consultancy industry (Grint, 1991:139)

How does TQM relate to these earlier ideas? As we saw in Chapter 2, TQM combines the use of computerised data collection and statistical experimentation with a focus on teamwork, group participation and a culture of continuous improvement in operating systems. It therefore combines the human-centred concerns of Human Relations and Socio-technical Systems Theory with Scientific Management's use of statistically manipulable data to enable the use of standardised monitoring systems. In many ways it can be seen as a synthesis of earlier theories and ideas.

Does TQM combine the best of earlier movements for reform? Will the new package provide the most rational management techniques? Such questions assume a rational progression in managerial improvements. Although rationalist history may provide some understanding of the development and acceptance of new managerial theories, history based on dogmatic beliefs in rationality can promote major misconceptions. A rigid belief in rational progress presupposes that ideas can be universally applied in every context, or that no rational manager will have difficulty in successfully implementing the latest ideas of best practice. The evidence of the contingency theorists does not support these propositions. Instead, cross-cultural studies show significant variations in the adoption of managerial ideas. Early studies noted major differences in Japanese and Western management (Dore, 1973) and many recent researchers have noted the impact that national culture, time of industrial development, and economic and political environment have on the adoption of different managerial practices (eg. Hofstede, 1990). In the Quality management area, Bemoski (1991) reports on a survey of 500 companies in Canada, Germany, Japan and the United States and notes significant differences in the ways the Quality Management ideas of employee involvement, business evaluation, customer focus and strategic planning have been adopted.

CONTEXTUALISING THE DEVELOPMENT OF MANAGERIAL IDEAS

Ideas are not universally applied in every context. The latest ideas of good practice may be inoperable, or have different effects, in different situations. What is seen as rational appears to vary in different contexts.

We can examine the influence of context and environment on the development of managerial ideas through the twentieth century. If we study the industrial, social and political contexts in which particular ideas have developed we can add analytical depth to the history of management thought, which may influence our interpretation of the impact of TQM.

A history which considers the context in which ideas spread might note that the prescriptions of *Scientific Management* were associated with the development of bureaucratic, large-scale, mass production in the USA. In the USA at the turn of the century, the cheapest and most tractable labour available was often migrant, unable to speak the language of their host nation, and previously socialised to accept a great diversity of behavioural norms. The pre-existing culture of social cohesion was weak. Scientific Management's detailed, formalised specifications were used to emphasise the very clear enunciation of management's requirements for the performance of basic, generally unskilled tasks. The highly structured and mechanistic methods of Taylorism were used to build the mass production industries with a workforce made up of culturally heterogeneous, isolated and ethnically segmented workers.

Systematic methods of work were analysed by Max Weber in the context of the development of a professional civil service in Prussia in the nineteenth and early twentieth centuries (see, Weber, 1947, 1948 and 1976). Weber studied the developing systematisation of white-collar, office work and used the concept of 'bureaucracy' to label the formal organisation and rationalised office procedures that he analysed. In his view, bureaucratic management techniques had a frightening power because they enabled modern rulers to build efficient, highly centralised, administrative machines to fulfil whatever purpose they intended. Although Weber was aware of the dangers inherent in the bureaucratic centralisation of power, his comments on the superiority of bureaucracy over earlier methods of administration are often quoted with the assumption that he did not see an oppressive downside to the development of modern bureaucracy (see Clegg, 1993). It needs to be emphasised that Weber was aware of the dangers inherent in the bureaucratic centralisation of power.

Weber did not analyse shopfloor or industrial work, however, the prescriptions of F. W. Taylor can be analysed as an attempt to use Germanic ideas of bureaucratic, rational administration to increase managerial control of work processes in industrial organisations. Cross-country comparisons suggest that Taylorism was introduced in different ways in different countries and had different effects. For example, in the USA it was associated with the expansion of mass production. The managerial techniques were widely seen to contribute to the expanding labour market. The rationality of improved production was widely accepted and many unionists and workers accepted the value of more rational management. In contrast, in the UK, Taylorism was introduced several years later in the context of job loss. The rationality of the new managerial techniques was fiercely contested by those threatened by the changes they brought. For many years, British industrial relations carried the scars of a growing mistrust between management and labour (Littler, 1982; Palmer, 1983).

Human Relations concern for the complexities of human motivation developed in the context of economic depression and the rise of mass unskilled unionism in the USA of the 1930s. Industrial psychology developed within the universities and the human needs of employees became the focus of many studies designed to improve managerial supervision and job design. This focus on the need to build employee commitment and loyalty to supervisors remained a strong theme in the post-War years of economic stability and prosperity, and neo-human relations added a concern to give employees intrinsic, as well as extrinsic satisfaction in their work (for a discussion of the context in which Human Relations developed, see Rose, 1988).

The ideas of Socio-technical Systems Theory were developed in the context of the full employment and democratic idealism found in Europe after the Second World War. The American individualism of the earlier movements was rejected in Europe by theorists with a concern to re-create cohesive, self-directing work groups. Experiments in Britain, India and Scandinavia provided much scope for academic debate on the problems and possibilities of teamwork and self-management by work groups. However, semi-autonomous work groups did not become widespread.

A contextual analysis of the history of developments in management thought suggests that we should expect context to affect the development of new managerial ideas, and the acceptance and influence that those ideas have in different situations. For example, ideas to empower employees in the past have often failed to generate the widespread changes that their supporters desired. Some of the current advocates of TQM do worry about such historical evidence. Danjin, a union representative from the United Auto Workers, and Gershenfeld, an academic from Michigan State University, share a concern that the employee participation of TQM may prove as difficult to implement as the similar ideals of earlier movements (Danjin and Gershenfeld, 1992)

At a general level, the rise of TQM can be linked to the trauma experienced by the old industrial nations since the 1980s as competition, first from Japan and then from the newly developing countries, eroded their dominance in world markets. The globalisation of business, and the evidence of Japanese success in coping with economic crises have stimulated an interest in Japanese managerial controls and an appreciation of different cultural assumptions underlying working relationships. In addition, the democratic idealism that followed the Second World War and gave support to pluralism, and the collective representation of different interests as a means of managing conflict, has weakened. Organisational change in many of the large-scale bureaucracies in the public and private sectors has shaken confidence in centralised organisational structures and in the old prescriptions. In this context, assumptions of rational management practices are being recast to build flexibility and an easier response to continuous change into organisational life.

TQM appears to offer an opportunity to combat the Japanese threat by adopting Japanese managerial methods. From studies of Japanese management has come the concern to develop a strong culture of organisational commitment, the use of teams for the extensive discussion of process improvements and the development of deeper and more sophisticated relationships with customers and suppliers.

The impact of information technology provides the second major stimulus to the development of TQM ideas. Computer software permits the development of new methods for calculating and disseminating performance indicators. Information technology can be harnessed to eliminate much of the personal supervision once exercised by supervisors and middle managers. It provides the opportunity, both for more stringent monitoring of performance by senior management and for the clearer communication of managerial expectations and requirements to workers. In this context, the greater involvement of employees in the management of their own work-processes can be seen to involve less risk for management. With concrete and statistically available performance indicators, the squandering of organisational resources should be apparent, and constant review should guard against the subversion of managerial intentions.

At the particular level of different countries, industries, companies or enterprises, many factors may have an impact on the implementation of TQM. Our case studies will seek to explore the impact of varying contexts.

To summarise, the development of managerial ideas needs to be set in context, and there is no inevitability about the acceptance or rationality of new managerial ideas. Any study of the implementation of managerial theories will need to consider a wide range of factors that may determine the outcome. To provide an overview of the range of variables that may need to be considered, in the second half of this chapter we make use of different perspectives in order to give a broader view of the complexities involved in the managerial process.

PART TWO: MULTIPLE FRAMES OF REFERENCE FOR ANALYSING TQM

Recent organisation theory has noted the value of multiple perspectives to the analysis of organisations (see Morgan, 1980). As Morgan states elsewhere:

> Any realistic approach to organisational analysis must start from the premise that organisations can be many things at one and the same

time. A machinelike organisation designed to achieve specific goals can simultaneously be: a species of organisation that is able to survive in certain environments but not others; an information-processing system that is skilled in certain kinds of learning but not in others; a cultural milieu characterised by distinctive values, beliefs, and social practices; a political system where people jostle to further their own ends; an arena where various subconscious or ideological struggles take place; an artefact or manifestation of a deeper process of social change; an instrument used by one group of people to exploit and dominate others; and so on. Though managers and organisation theorists often attempt to override this complexity by assuming that organisations are ultimately rational phenomena that must be understood with reference to their goals or objectives, this assumption often gets in the way of realistic analysis. If one truly wishes to understand an organisation it is much wiser to start from the premise that organisations are complex, ambiguous and paradoxical. (Morgan, 1986:321–2)

Morgan used metaphors to view organisations from a number of perspectives, and he analysed organisations as machines, as organisms, as brains, as cultures, as political systems, as psychic prisons, as logics of change of flux and transformation, and as instruments of domination. This approach has been reinforced by others who have used a multiple perspective approach to understand the *managerial* processes within organisations. For example, Bolman and Deal (1991) claimed the use of multiple perspectives would contribute to 'both personal freedom and organisational prosperity' by giving managers greater effectiveness, power, creativity and communication skills (Bolman and Deal, 1984 and 1991).

If the reframing perspective is to be used to give a new approach to management theory, then several 'frames of reference' have been proposed. Bolman and Deal (1991) distinguished between structural, human resource, political and cultural perspectives on organisations. Talking more specifically of management, Reed (1989) contrasted technical, political and critical perspectives on management. Palmer and Dunford (1993) studied the extent that managers valued reframing as an analytical tool, and concluded that it was not the use of *particular* frames of reference, but generic use of a multiple perspective approach, that was useful.

In this book we distinguish between bureaucratic, political and cultural aspects of management (see also Gardner and Palmer, 1992:195–200). We use these three quite different perspectives on management to discuss the managerial processes affected by TQM, and the likely effects of TQM's implementation.

TQM AND THE BUREAUCRATIC PROCESSES OF MANAGEMENT

The bureaucratic perspective on management focuses on the establishment of administrative controls. Such controls lie at the heart of our ability to build formal organisations with the capacity to co-ordinate the activities of large numbers of people to achieve specified goals. Reed (1989:2–6) referred to this aspect of management as the 'technical' side, which defines management as a formal structure of rationally designed technical, bureaucratic and financial controls. His technical theoretical perspective saw management as an instrumental tool, a means to obtain the efficiencies needed to achieve organisational goals. Morgan's organisational metaphor of a machine, and Bolman and Deal's structural perspective also relate to these ideas. We prefer to use the concept of 'bureaucracy' to explain this perspective, because it can be discussed in terms of the long tradition of organisational analysis stimulated by Weber's analysis of rational administration.

Arising from Weber's analysis, bureaucracy can be seen as a set of organisational controls designed to make explicit and to formalise structures of organisational responsibilities and their rewards. Weber discussed various bureaucratic techniques, which we can divide into two sets. First are those which establish hierarchies of work responsibilities, specialised work roles and detailed systems of supervision and performance monitoring. Second (and often ignored in later organisational theories) are those which specify equitable and meritocratic policies on recruitment, promotion, and the rewarding and disciplining of employees. The first set can be seen to bureaucratise task control, and the second to bureaucratise personnel policy (see Littler, 1982, Palmer, 1983).

As noted earlier in the chapter, the practices of Scientific Management were designed to develop bureaucratic techniques which extended and centralised managerial controls over tasks performed at work. However Scientific Management did not introduce many bureaucratic personnel policies. Bureaucratic personnel policies were given to government public servants in Europe and some white-collar but not shopfloor workers in the old world. However bureaucratic personnel policies were used for the regular industrial workforce of Japan (see Palmer 1983, 41–45).

In relation to TQM, this therefore raises a number of questions. For example, how should we view the development of TQM in terms of the concept of bureaucracy? Does TQM develop the types of administrative control that have helped build large formal organisations through the twentieth century, and if it does, does it focus on task or personnel bureaucracy? Or is TQM quite different—is it the antithesis of bureaucracy?

The view that TQM is anti-bureaucratic is analysed by Tuckman (1994).

He suggests that TQM can be seen as a new managerial ideology which offers a critique of bureaucracy—or more precisely its dysfunctions—and presents a set of market-oriented metaphors to replace the bureaucratic reliance on hierarchies of authority. TQM helps to conceptualise organisation in non-bureaucratic terms by focusing attention on market and customer relationships, rather than hierarchical administrative ones. It serves to legitimate pseudo-market relations within the organisation by creating internal customers and markets. In this way it seeks to dissolve rigid organisational boundaries and end the distinction between the extra-organisational world of markets and the inter-organisational world of administration, it seeks to muddy the classic distinction between markets and hierarchies (see Williamson, 1975).

However, although TQM is often presented as a means of overcoming the problems of the over rigid structures of bureaucracy, Tuckman notes a paradox: 'far from being an alternative to bureaucracy *per se* TQM extends a bureaucratisation process while challenging some of its dysfunctions'. TQM contributes to the bureaucratisation process, for example by promoting standards like BS5750 and ISO9000. TQM's concern with statistically based measurement of variations in performance and with performance indicators which can be used to monitor system performance, are all direct descendants of the bureaucratic techniques of task control that have been used throughout the twentieth century.

The collection of data to give a basis for judgements about the most effective methods of work directly parallels the techniques of Scientific Management. There are, therefore, clear bureaucratic elements within TQM even though certain new dimensions have been given to the data collection and statistical analysis.

One significant difference between the bureaucratic task controls of TQM and the older methods of measuring performance, is in the use of electronic information processing technology. The greater flexibility and power of computer technology extends the types of data that can be collected and distributed for monitoring performance. Another significant difference between the data collection of Scientific Management and that of TQM concerns the type of decision-making process into which the data collection is fitted.

Scientific Management was based on the assumption that there was always one best, most scientific way to perform work. This method was best determined by specialists—the industrial engineers and work study experts. Their scientific expertise gave them the authority to design management processes. TQM is based on very different assumptions. It assumes that there is no one best way to work, and that any system is capable of continuous improvement. It also puts the case that in order to uncover suggestions for improvement and gain employee commitment to the need for continuous change, employees should be closely involved in the processes used to identify problems and solutions. They should be involved in data collection and evaluation. Instead of relying on experts, TQM recommends employee participation in the study and design of improved working procedures.

The significant difference in the role of employees in the scientific, data-based decision-making processes, links in with next perspective on TQM, which is concerned with the political relationships at work.

TQM AND POLITICAL PROCESSES IN MANAGEMENT

Bureaucratic perspectives ignore or simplify issues surrounding the exercise of power at work. The bureaucratic perspective concentrates on power as formal and legitimate authority, associated with position, rationally determined objectives and organisational rules. Other power bases, and other forms of influence are either ignored, or seen as problematical. Typically they are regarded as illegitimate power plays, verging on disloyalty or corruption, which correct administrative procedures are designed to eliminate. As a result, the bureaucratic frame of reference carries a moral preference for certain forms of power, and this closes off any analysis of the full range of political activity that is usually found in organisations.

A political frame of reference focuses on all forms of power. It does not assume that organisational objectives are unambiguous, or that those at the top of the hierarchy automatically have the political resources they need to implement these goals. A political perspective on management focuses on the political processes involved in establishing negotiating positions and gaining support for different policies. 'In this view management is concerned to resolve conflicts between stakeholders in an organisation in a situation where there is considerable uncertainty about the criteria used for judging organisational effectiveness. In place of the rational, co-ordinated machine this perspective sees a plurality of competing groups and coalitions.' (Gardner and Palmer, 1992:196). It looks for a plurality of interests and assumes the different interests will have a variety of resources with which to press their claims.

If we use a political perspective to study the implementation of TQM, several issues are thrown into focus. In this chapter we raise three. We first address the question of whether TQM changes the power relationship between employees and their managers. Does TQM's 'employee empowerment' increase the power that employees exercise over the management process? If so, does this increase or threaten total managerial control? Secondly, we comment on the role of trade union power in the context of TQM.

Finally we look at the level of the state, and the relevance of TQM for government and national politics.

The politics of employee involvement

TQM is often represented as the opposite of Scientific Management in terms of the power it gives employees at work. Scientific Management is seen as centralising decision-making power away from employees whereas TQM empowers and reskills them. An alternative view is that TQM is similar to Scientific Management because it takes knowledge held by workers, and makes it available to management. Knowledge is a source of power, and whereas Scientific Management centralised knowledge about existing materials, work methods and possible speeds, TQM makes available employees' knowledge about improvements in work processes (see Tuckman, 1994a).

Does the involvement of employees in quality improvement activities represent empowerment or exploitation? L. Holpp (1992), as a consultant, expressed concern about the ambiguity of employee participation under TQM and contrasted quality circles with self-directed teams. Under TQM, employees work within traditional job descriptions, meeting as teams only for problem solving. Problem solutions are not necessarily linked to overall business strategy and the traditional supervisor–employee reporting relationships remain in force. In contrast, in what he regarded as the more genuine involvement of self-directed work teams, employees control their own work situations, deal directly with people at all levels of the organisation, vendors and customers, manage a team budget, and take responsibility for productivity, cost and quality. Holpp argues that in genuine self-directed teams, work roles should be more flexible and team members should be able to make major changes in their work processes without going through levels of approval.

Any assessment of the employee involvement that occurs in TQM needs to be related to the extensive literature on employee participation (Lansbury 1980, Gardner et al 1988). Employee participation can vary by the structures established for employee involvement, by the issues on which participation occurs and by the level of influence employees can gain. Employees may become involved in managerial decisions as individuals, or as groups, their involvement may be direct (as in face to face interactions, or referendums), or indirect (electing representatives to sit on works council, boards or decision-making bodies). The issues on which they participate may be limited to the conduct at their own work stations, or it may range across a variety of economic, strategic and policy-making issues. Their influence may range from the right to be informed, the right to voice an opinion, the right to negotiate, to veto or to decide. The range of possible forms of participation is wide, and TQM makes no pretence to cover this range.

Does the 'empowerment' of TQM represent a genuine increase of power?

and if so is this at the expense of existing managerial power, or is there a mutual gain in control by employees and management? Sewell (1992) and Sewell and Wilkinson (1992a, 1992b) have produced a case analysis of TQM which discusses the question of employee empowerment and management control. Sewell starts from the position that Scientific Management was designed to establish more direct managerial control over the work performance of employees through the use of careful work specifications, the monitoring of performance output and a hierarchy of supervision. However, as organisations have grown larger, supervision became more important and more difficult.

Extended supervisory hierarchies became necessary to relay managerial controls down through the organisation, but each level of the relay was always a potential source of resistance (Clegg, 1988). Each new level of the supervisory hierarchy represented a new frontier of control for workers to contest. The traditional, bureaucratic organisation could establish fixed controls over work speeds and repetitive tasks but these standards were not flexible. Problems of inflexibility and supervision developed with size, and Human Relations and Neo Human Relations policies did not provide a remedy.

TQM is designed to overcome these problems by 'empowering' employees to play a more active role in process improvement and quality monitoring. Sewell (1992:15) suggests that 'for use of the term "empowerment" to be meaningful there must be a genuine shift in the locus of power away from management and to the shop floor'. An alternative view is that it is possible for managerial power to be increased and for employees to be given more participation at the same time. Pluralists would argue that under certain policies, management can regain control by sharing it, and it is possible to negotiate win–win as well as win–lose deals (see Palmer 1983, Chapter 2).

In what ways does TQM solve the managerial control problems not solved by the older bureaucratic techniques? Sewell suggests that TQM's promotion of a supportive and common culture is not the main mechanism. Instead the use of monitoring of performance, using sophisticated information technology and employee involvement serves as the main and most effective control. He describes a Japanese-owned plant, manufacturing consumer electronics, in Britain. The Kay plant used advanced TQM and Human Resource Management (HRM) policies to empower employees and increase managerial control. Team meetings met each morning to allocate members to different stations. A concern for continuous improvement was encouraged by constantly reminding team members that performance targets represented minimum standards that could always be improved. The manufacturing standards for the entire plant were set at corporate headquarters in Japan and non-Japanese plants were obliged to achieve these standards within a 5 per cent variance. Several methods of quality review were combined to give detailed information about the quality performance of the team and its individual members. This information was prominently displayed to be visible to all members in the team.

At the time this case study was conducted, specialists from corporate headquarters spent a month implementing a system of visual displays which would show the levels of error or incorrect insertion of components in the assembly process. The displays took the form of 'traffic light' cards suspended from the production line superstructure. The cards were green (no misinsertions in the previous shift); amber (between one and four misinsertions) and red (four or more misinsertions). The levels of performance enabled management to see if the production line was too fast or too slow, or if particular members were under-performing or could cope with a faster output. The amber zone appears to have 'been set by management to represent a level of performance where the number of errors are acceptable but which also creates a climate where all members are constantly made aware of the need to make improvements—an approach which Slaughter (1989) describes as 'management by stress' (Sewell, 1992, p. 18).

In his analysis of this case, Sewell uses Foucault's notion of surveillance to discuss the relationship between knowledge and power in formalised social systems. In *Discipline and Punish*, (1977) Foucault emphasises the importance of surveillance, using Bentham's conceptualisation of the Panopticon. The Panopticon was developed in the eighteenth century and was regarded as the ideal or model prison. It consisted of a central observation tower surrounded by a concentric ring of peripheral cells. The architecture ensured that all inmates would be continuously watched from the centre but would have limited visual contact with each other. This served to 'induce in the inmate a state of conscious and permanent visibility that assures the automatic functioning of power' (Foucault, 1977:201–2) Sewell suggests that TQM's methods of involving team members in the vetting and monitoring of performance can be associated with this type of monitoring. As with the Panopticon, people are placed in a situation where their own perceptions encourage them to play a role in maintaining the social order required. The architectural apparatus of both the computerised monitoring systems of TQM and the physical observance of the Panopticon alters the relationship between the observer and the observed. On the periphery, one is totally seen, without ever seeing; whereas in the centre, one sees everything without being seen.

However the factory is not a prison. Whereas the prison, like Scientific Management, seeks to separate workers in order to reduce their impact on decision-making and control their time and space, such direct controls are not part of TQM. Sewell discusses the role of the Electronic Panopticon of TQM's performance review. He suggests it enables top management's disciplinary gaze to be extended, but that this is done in the context of job enlargement and empowerment. The teams involved in TQM act to reinforce the disciplinary message. Why do they support rather than subvert the disciplines involved? In this case, Sewell suggests that the HRM focus on participation and a culture of involvement gained acceptance for the increased electronic supervision. Management did succeed in reinforcing its control, by sharing certain managerial responsibilities with employees (Sewell, 1992:20).

In summary, whereas Scientific Management and, later, HRM protected the right of managers to control decisions on the best way to design and operate work processes, this managerial prerogative is not an aspect of TQM. Instead of managerial control of the processes to design and improve operating systems, employee involvement contributes both employee knowledge and greater acceptance of managerial controls. This focus on the importance of employee involvement represents a shift from a technicist, rational approach to managerial problem solving, to an approach that is sensitive to the political power that employee acceptance can bring.

TQM's prescriptions for employee involvement represent a sharing of managerial power on matters concerning improvements in work flow and operations management. However this form of employee involvement cannot be regarded as a major extension of industrial democracy. Under TQM policies, employees are not necessarily involved in strategic decisions or major areas of company policy-making. Managerial prerogative is still retained on issues such as the mission or direction of the enterprise, the strategic use of resources and basic conditions of employment. TQM allows employee participation in low levels of decision-making, primarily in an advisory rather than a deciding role. However the 'empowerment' involved may be significant to the company in terms of commercial costs, and significant to employees in terms of their own work practices.

TQM and trade union power

On the question of trade union power, does TQM's 'employee empowerment' conflict with the representation of employee interests though trade unions? TQM allows participation through methods that do not provide for the pluralist representation of competing interests. There is no system of group representation or election to represent different employee voices in the decision-making process. Instead there is the assumption of an underlying common interest in outcomes. With this 'unitary' as opposed to 'pluralist' assumption in the participative process, there is no formal allocation of sanctions to back the participation of the different interests involved. As a result, some commentators suggest that TQM is anti-union because unions represent a pressure for pluralistic decision-making. In the UK, in particular, TQM has been associated with a drive to extend non-unionism at work. However, in Australia and New Zealand, many unionists take part in TQM activities, and many schemes have been endorsed by official union representatives.

It is possible that the apparent paradox arises because, in Australia, TQM introduces a degree of employee involvement in an area of decision-making that has not previously been the subject of arbitration or industrial relations negotiation. In the UK, employees would previously have had some involvement on work issues through union negotiation of enterprise collective bargains. However, in Australia, arbitral awards tended to exclude formal employee participation on all managerial issues. TQM may be more acceptable to unions in Australia because it helps to introduce formal employee involvement where there was none before (Palmer, 1989).

TQM and the politics of government

The final political issue takes the study of TQM outside the boundaries of the organisation to the level of government action. What role have governments played in the promotion of TQM? What change agents have helped to promote its spread, and what interests are served by this external activity?

Tuckman (1994a) notes that governments in Britain and the United States have played a central role in introducing quality management approaches. In Britain this has come through strategies of denationalisation as well as though the promotion of enterprise-based employment relations. In the United States, governments have used both the powers of military procurement and the *National Quality Improvement Act* of August 1987 to promote TQM. The Malcolm Baldridge Awards were developed in 1987 by major business and congressional leaders. Baldridge had been Secretary of Commerce, and the awards were administered by the Department of Commerce with evaluation by the American Society of Quality Control. The American Federal government also sponsors the 'national quality month' and the Federal Quality Institute sponsors Quality Management in government administration, especially in the military and environmental protection agency (see Garvin, 1991; Zeitz and Mittal, 1993).

In Australia the available evidence, as noted in Chapter 2, points to the extensive use of government support for TQM. In Queensland, State government procurement policies are used. Nationally the main mechanism is the National Industry Extension Service (NIES) subsidy for companies using consultants to introduce approved Quality Management programs.

Why do governments intervene to support the adoption of particular managerial techniques? In Australia the rationale given relates to governmental concerns to promote industry restructuring to better equip the economy to meet increasing competitive challenges from abroad. NIES involves employer and union groups in an extension of the tripartism that characterises the neo-corporatism, or co-ordinated interventionism of the Australian Labor Party's labour-management policies.

Given the liberalism of British government's recent policies and their non-interventionist stance, state support for TQM in the UK might seem more surprising. Tuckman suggests that TQM links with a general political strategy which accords with the political ideologies of the new right. The empowerment of the individual through TQM at workplace levels has become equated with their active involvement in the market. The release of markets from the constraints of administrative control was a major tenet of Prime Minister Thatcher's politics.

There are other elements of TQM that have a power-related, or political aspect. The participative processes within TQM can also build flexibility into existing organisational structures. In establishing quality teams, people may be chosen from different departments, different occupational or skills groups and different levels in the status hierarchy. The purpose of this mixing of participants does not seem to be intended to represent different interests. Instead it may serve to weaken political loyalties to the old structures, for example to vested interests in departments. Teambuilding may be used to homogenise the organisation, overcoming perceptual differences between different groups. It can create new alliances in support of change, encouraging attitudes that support organisational goals for improvement, rather than sectional goals for the status quo.

TQM AND THE MANAGEMENT OF CULTURES

Our final perspective on management is concerned with culture. A cultural perspective emphasises moral order. Instead of management being concerned to establish systems of bureaucratic administration or political accommodation, managers of culture are involved in the construction of moral systems of meaning and value. Images and assumptions come under review, for the cultural perspective encompasses Bolman and Deal's 'symbolic' frame of reference (Bolman and Deal, 1991). In the 1980s and 1990s prescriptions for managing or changing organisational culture have become a major feature of management thought. These prescriptions emphasise the importance of creating supportive, positive, cultures that emphasize organisational rather than sectional goals (Peters and Waterman, 1982; Kanter 1983 and 1989).

The recent managerial interest in culture has been stimulated by two challenges that have encouraged the questioning of traditional values, assumptions and beliefs. The first challenge is competition from newly developing nations with the increased globalisation of world markets. This stimulated comparative studies of Western and Japanese management (for example see Abbeglen, 1974; Abbeglen and Stalk, 1985; Dore, 1973 and Ouchi, 1981) which threw into relief the importance of cultural differences between different organisations and nations, and their impact on economic performance. The second challenge is the movement of women into non-traditional work areas, particularly management. Problems surrounding women in management raise the possibility that traditional images, expectations, assumptions and beliefs about management and managerial authority may need to be changed (Kanter, 1983; Aburdene and Naisbitt, 1992).

TQM is the first managerial movement that has specifically considered culture and the values that develop in an organisation (Rieley, 1992; Sashkin and Kiser, 1992). What type of culture, what beliefs does TQM legitimise? TQM values the continuous improvement of systems and warns against valuing or judging individual performance. It advocates the use of employees to suggest and implement improvements, rather than leaving managerial problems to be owned to by top management alone. These practices are intended to build a more positive and unified culture, embued with common values of commitment to continuous change. The intention is to create a homogenous culture which supports managerial innovation, an integrated culture in which distrust and segmentalist competition within the organisation is overcome.

The attempt to emphasise a homogeneous collectivity, rather than a collection of plural interests, links the culture-creation aspects of TQM with the prescriptions of Human Resource Management that developed in the USA. The creation of a positive, homogeneous culture is not an easy process and it does not automatically follow from TQM. For example, a recent study in an Australian manufacturing company found the introduction of information from Deming's PDCA feedback cycle, on the performance of work processes, generated attitudes of concern and resistance among supervisors (H. De Cieri, D. Samson & A. Sohal, 1991).

One recent study focuses on cultural aspects of TQM in terms of the extent that TQM has influenced dominant managerial cultures. Zeitz and Mittal (1993), discuss the spread of TQM as a case example of the social institutionalisation of ideas and values They are concerned to judge whether TQM has itself become an institutionalised or formal part of our society, ingrained in our cultural expectations and beliefs. They argue that Scientific Management has been the dominant, institutionalised, management philosophy in the United States since the 1920s, but that TQM is now replacing it. They see similarities and differences between TQM and Scientific Management but on the whole believe the institutionalisation of TQM involves the de-institutionalisation of scientific management. In order to study the acceptance of TQM's ideas into the general culture, they compare the implementation of TQM against various indicators of acceptance and institutionalisation. They note that TQM has been adopted by many organisations and they give particular attention to state authorisation and the development of a professional support network as indicators of the social strength of TQM in the US business community.

Endorsement by powerful organisations like Ford, GM, IBM, Motorola, and ITT gives TQM a significant symbolic presence. In 1987 the unknown US company, Florida Power and Light, won Japan's prestigious Deming Award. It attracted pilgrimage visits from 500 organisations in 1987. Harley Davidson became a major symbol of quality management from the mid-1980s. In this way, the quality movement not only creates symbols in terms of the successful firms to emulate, it also establishes new training networks as companies compare information on management techniques. TQM builds new networks in which managers from different industries and environments can exchange experiences and learn from each other.

TQM has also established an institutionalised support network through professional associations, which ensures that any organisation establishing a quality co-ordinator has access to extensive external support and training. Quality Assurance was supported by professional institutions from the early days of Scientific Management. The American Society for Quality Control always supported the development of the more human resource-focused TQM in addition to the more numerically focused quality control approach. With Juran as founder and Crosby and Feigenbaum as presidents the ASQC grew to 55 000 members in 1988 and to 120 000 in 1993. In the 1980s it made a major commitment to quality management and launched the journal *Quality Progress*. A new Association for Quality and Productivity was started to focus on employee empowerment and teamwork. This professional support network, like that of the early Scientific Management movement, is seen by its members as a social movement dedicated to significant organisational and managerial change. The social and cultural impact and acceptance of TQM is evidenced by the spread of many education and training courses, new university certificates and so on.

Zeitz and Mittal (1993) therefore use aspects of institutionalisation theory to suggest that TQM is now so accepted as a cultural phenomenon in management, that its implementation can often be explained in terms of a desire to gain cultural legitimacy, rather than any particular desire for improved quality or organisational performance. As they state:

> Institutional theorists argue that organisations adopt practices for efficiency reasons at early stages of the institutionalisation process, while later on they adopt standardised practices merely to gain legitimacy. Thus early adoption of a practice is likely to be based more on specific measures of benefit and thus will be more predictable by some antecedent conditions (Tolbet & Zucker, 1983). At later stages

it becomes more difficult to predict adoption based on specific functional benefit (Zeitz and Mittal, 1993:17)

They go on to suggest that research is needed to see if later adoptions of TQM have been less concerned to test or justify the adoption by measuring the impact or output of the initiative. It is possible that more rigorous assessments of the value of TQM were undertaken in the earlier manufacturing-based implementations. More recently, in government, service and non-profit sectors there seems to be less assessment, and implementation of TQM in these areas may have been influenced by the desire to gain cultural legitimacy.

Zeitz and Mittal conclude that TQM is replacing scientific management as the dominant, institutionalised set of ideas surrounding management. TQM is not just a 'flavour of the month', but is part of the broad shifts in management and organisational design identified with 'post modernism'. Like Scientific Management before it, TQM represents a broad shift toward greater rationalisation in the management of organisations, and is not the only expression of this broad movement. Both Scientific Management and TQM, unlike the other major managerial philosophies of the twentieth century, have served to institutionalise new philosophies of management. Among all the important indicators of the success of TQM, Zeitz and Mittal suggest the main evidence of successful institutionalisation is found in the existence of a vibrant group of professionals committing their careers to the values and practices of quality management.

CONCLUSION: TQM AND MANAGEMENT THEORY

Quality management is the latest in a long line of different managerial prescriptions in the twentieth century. All have been associated with extravagant claims made by people with an interest in their promotion. All have had some impact on the development of managerial practice, but some appear to have had more impact than others.

In this chapter we have placed TQM within the context of management theory, in order to highlight several analytical approaches to TQM. The first part of the chapter focused on the history of management thought, and the second part used the theory of 'reframing' and discussed multiple perspectives on management. The history of the development of managerial ideas is often presented in terms of a straightforward progression towards universally ideal solutions. However, contingent factors in the social, political and economic environment can affect the spread of particular ideas at particular times. There is no inevitability in the development or rationality of management ideas. Indeed, comparative evidence suggests that the managerial process is very complex.

To gain an insight into this complexity, several perspectives or frames of reference can be used to analyse the likely impact of TQM. This chapter uses the lenses of bureaucracy, politics and culture to discuss the different elements of the management process that are affected by TQM. Bureaucratic, political and cultural perspectives highlight many different factors that can influence both the implementation and the impact of TQM. In Part II of the book which follows, we examine the organisational processes associated with TQM in a number of Australian and New Zealand companies.

PART *II*

Quality Management in Australian and New Zealand Companies

CHAPTER 4

A Processual Framework for Understanding TQM

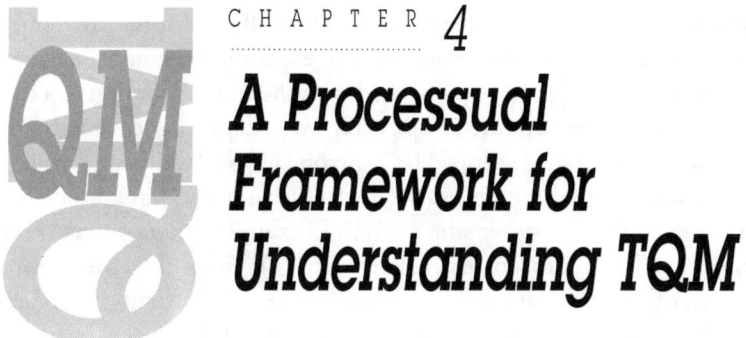

INTRODUCTION

The principles of Total Quality Management (TQM) and the context of its historical development and emergence within Australia have been described in Part I. It was argued that TQM can be located within the development of management thought and represents a new and innovative approach to achieving some long-established aims in the control and management of organisations. The emphasis on continual improvement through employee (and external customer and supplier) involvement and the formation of group problem-solving teams is at the heart of TQM. Quality is defined on the basis of customer expectations and represents an on-going dynamic rather than any end state. It is best understood and examined as a long-term change strategy which seeks to institutionalise employee commitment through the management of belief systems and the establishment of more participative operating procedures. However, as yet, there is little detailed empirical evidence on the complex processes associated with the organisational introduction of TQM on which critical assessments can be made. It is our intention to rectify this shortfall through presenting a series of analytically grounded case studies which focus on particular elements of TQM at various historical timeframes in the process of change.

We aim to highlight the weakness of conventional frameworks of organisational development rooted in Kurt Lewin's unfreezing, changing, refreezing model, and to present new empirical data on the introduction of TQM in

Australian and New Zealand companies. Essentially we argue that linear models of change are no longer appropriate to explaining the non-linear and complex organisational processes associated with the transformation to a total quality organisation. In support of our claim, we adapt a processual framework for analysing change developed by Dawson (1994). Whilst we recognise that this framework has limitations, we contend that it also has considerable strengths in enabling the systematic analysis of complex change data. From our perspective, it has proven particularly useful in informing the research design, in clarifying the data collection requirements of distant researchers, and in enabling the case studies to be analytically grounded.

A CONVENTIONAL APPROACH: THE EXAMPLE OF LEWIN'S CHANGE MODEL

Kurt Lewin has been a major influence on research within the behavioural sciences and on the development of tools for the effective management of change within organisations. As a German Jew, Lewin was forced to leave Germany in 1933 and this early experience of anti-Semitism, is shown in his concern for democracy and participation at the workplace (Board, de 1978:50). His work on intergroup dynamics and change has proved to be particularly influential on those practising within the field of management known as Organisational Development (OD), and many theories of organisational change originate from his landmark work on planned change (see, Kreitner and Kinicki, 1992:723–61). Essentially, Kurt Lewin argued that in order for change to be successfully managed it is necessary to follow three general steps (Robbins, 1991:646). These three steps identified by Lewin (1951) comprise: unfreezing, changing, and refreezing. Unfreezing is the stage in which there is a recognised need for change and action is taken to unfreeze existing attitudes and behaviour. This preparatory stage is deemed essential to the generation of employee support and the minimisation of employee resistance. According to Lewin's technique of force-field analysis (1947:5–42), there are two sets of forces in operation within any social system; namely, driving forces that operate for change and restraining forces which attempt to maintain the status quo. The example of smoking illustrates this where, although there may be strong driving forces to stop smoking, such as social pressure, cost, fear of cancer, new laws, disapproval of children and the concern of others, the restraining forces of habit, camaraderie, relief of tension, spouse smoking and the dislike of coercive methods may act to maintain the status quo (Weisbord, 1988:79). If these two opposing forces are equal in strength, then they are in a state of equilibrium. Consequently, to bring about change you either need to increase the strength of the driving forces or decrease the strength of the resisting forces. Furthermore, as these two sets of forces are qualitatively different it is possible to modify elements of both sets in the management of change. In practice, however, the emphasis of OD specialists has been on providing data that would unfreeze the system through reducing the resisting forces rather than increasing the driving forces (Gray and Starke, 1988:596–629; Weisbord, 1988:94). Once these negative forces have been reduced through disconfirming information, then the consultant embarks on moving the organization towards the desired state. This is the second general step of changing or moving an organization, and involves the actual implementation of new systems of operation. Once this has been complete, then the final stage of refreezing occurs which may involve the positive reinforcement of desired outcomes to promote the internalisation of new attitudes and behaviours. An appraisal of the effectiveness of the change programme is the final element used in the last step to ensure that the new way of doing things becomes habitualised.

This three-phase model of change is currently an integral part of the conventional orthodoxy taught in business departments and management schools around the world. Whilst the strength of the model lies in its simple representation (which makes it easy to use and understand), this is also its major weakness as it presents an unidirectional model of change. The linearity which this three-stage model suggests is not supported by the empirical evidence on the introduction on total quality management (see Chapter 11). In addition, this approach adopts a normative framework and assumes that there is one best way to manage change that will increase both organizational effectiveness and employee well-being. In managing large-scale change, there is often a need to revise implementation strategies to overcome or tackle unforseen contextual difficulties. Organisational change is a complex and dynamic process which is also influenced by powerful coalitions within organisations and the history and context within which change is taking place. This is illustrated in Chapter 12 where the same strategies for change resulted in very different outcomes for employees working within two different plants on the same manufacturing site. Finally, in assuming that there is an uncontested and clear view of the desired consequence of change, this model has a tendency to overlook organisational politics and to solidify (through the concept of refreezing) what is a dynamic and on-going process. From our research into TQM, the change process can more aptly be described as an odyssey, which whilst generally being planned, requires the continual revision of navigational decisions to meet unpredictable and unfolding conditions.

A PROCESSUAL FRAMEWORK FOR ANALYSING CHANGE

Time was used as a major frame of reference in our empirical case studies of the introduction of TQM in Australian and New Zealand companies. A central aim of the studies was to monitor organisational changes over a period of time in order to identify and describe the pathways of TQM programmes. From these temporal descriptions of change, we then sought to explain why organisational experiences of change followed a particular pace and pattern. However, we were unable to monitor the change process over several years and had to contend ourselves with data collected from an examination of organisations at different timeframes in the process of establishing TQM. For example, whilst our main focus rested on the organisational implementation of TQM, we also sought to include organisations who had only just begun thinking about TQM, as well as those who had been involved with TQM for a number of years. By so doing, we have been able to collect data on company experiences at different timeframes during the process of change.

For research purposes, we constructed a processual framework for analysing change based on three general timeframes. These comprised:

- Conception of a need for a quality initiative
- Process of establishing total quality management
- Operation of total quality programme and on-going change

In practice, we discovered that even those organisations who had introduced TQM a number of years prior to our investigation were still developing their strategies of change, involving other sections of the company and, in some cases, re-implementing TQM throughout the organisation. Furthermore, whilst we did not find it difficult to identify companies who were considering TQM but had not yet embarked on a programme of change, we found that they had little to say about TQM and, in some cases, were threatened by our unveiling of their lack of understanding. Consequently, only one organisation is used to describe this conceptual period prior to the decision to adopt a TQM programme (see Chapter 5).

For the most part, the organisations we studied fell into the second and third general timeframes associated with the process of transformation from the initial decision to invest in a TQM programme through to the implementation and operation of quality-based initiatives. Moreover, whilst we wanted to avoid any implication of a rational linear path for the adoption process, we did feel that it was important for analytical reasons to construct data categories around the various activities and tasks associated with the management of change (see also, Dawson, 1994:35–47). In other words, to increase our understanding of the process of establishing TQM, a number of categories for locating and analysing data were defined. The seven data categories employed comprised:

Evaluation and appraisal

Identification of type of change

Implementation

Initial operation

Preparation and planning

Search and assessment of options

System selection

During the process of establishing TQM, organisations would not normally progress through these stages in any linear fashion but, rather, would occupy a number of different categories at the same point in time. In addition, there may be distinct time periods over which various change management tasks and activities are played out, only to be re-enacted at later timeframes (an example of this is provided in Chapter 11). For our purposes, the framework provided a useful analytical tool for aiding our understanding of complex organisational processes.

In using Dawson's (1994) processual approach for examining organisational change, we would argue that there are three major dimensions which shape company transitions; these are: the context, the substance and the politics of change.

THE CONTEXT OF CHANGE

Starting with the context of change: this is taken to refer to those factors in the present and past which form a part of the organisational life of employees. The external environmental context would include factors arising from the political, social and economic environment in which a company operates, and the internal organisational context would include administrative structures, technology, human resources, and the product or service of an organisation. Administrative structures is taken to refer to the allocation of tasks in the design of jobs and work structures. The context of technology is used broadly to refer to the plant, machinery and tools and the associated philosophy and system of work organization which blend together in the production of goods or services. Human resources refer to the individual members and groups of people who constitute an organization. Finally, the primary product or service of an organization refers to the core business, whether this is providing a banking service, baking biscuits, or manufacturing cables.

In examining the context of an organisation, it is also important to incorporate an historical perspective which is able to account for the influence of past events on present activities. For example, in the case of TQM, previous experience with other quality initiatives may influence employee attitudes to future quality change programmes. Moreover, there often exists a number of competing individual and group beliefs about past events which may be said to constitute socially constructed organisational histories. These histories of change may serve to reinforce the belief systems of dominant coalitions within a company and promote the adoption of particular routes to change over other potential avenues. Thus, the history and culture of an organisation is also an important contextual factor which is likely to influence the process of establishing total quality management.

THE SUBSTANCE OF CHANGE

The second major dimension to our processual framework centres on the substance of change, or the principles and practice of a total quality management approach. As outlined in Chapter 2, TQM is a management philosophy of change which: emphasises continuous improvement; focuses on 'internal' and 'external' customer–supplier relations; develops and applies systematic measurement techniques; uses group problem-solving teams to tackle process issues; and is committed to employee involvement and the development of high-trust relationships through the maintenance of a non-adversarial system of industrial relations.

These principles of TQM are further refined, interpreted and developed during their introduction into organisations. As can be seen from the case study chapters which follow, the practice of TQM does not always accord with the principles espoused by a management philosophy of TQM. For example, the notion of 'continual TQM improvement' is in many ways a misnomer. In practice, TQM group-based activity is by its very nature temporary in being project based, of a fixed duration, and aimed at solving discrete operational problems. Hence, it is important to take account of the substance of TQM both as it is espoused by the various quality exponents and how it is practiced within organisations operating under a TQM regime (see Chapter 7).

THE POLITICS OF CHANGE

The final dimension relates to the politics of change. As Clark et al. have noted:

In any process of change a number of substantive issues arise which require decisions to be made by actors, either by conscious choice and negotiation or by omission (non-decision). These include not only traditional collective bargaining issues such as pay and grading, staffing levels, and the selection and training of staff, but also 'control' issues such as skill, job design, supervision, and the organisation and control of work. (Clark et al., 1990:31)

In their study of telephone exchange modernisation, they argue that these substantive issues become particularly pertinent at critical junctures during the process of change, where organisational actors are able or seek to intervene to influence a particular issue or outcome (Clark et al., 1990:32). Whilst we would support this view, we would argue that this also highlights the importance of power and politics in the organisational decision-making surrounding change programmes. In referring to this form of political organisational activity we use the term the politics of change. Examples of political activity outside of an organization would be governmental pressure, competitor alliances or the influence of overseas divisions of Multi-National Corporations (MNCs). Internal political activity could be in the form of shopfloor

Figure 4.1 A Processual Framework

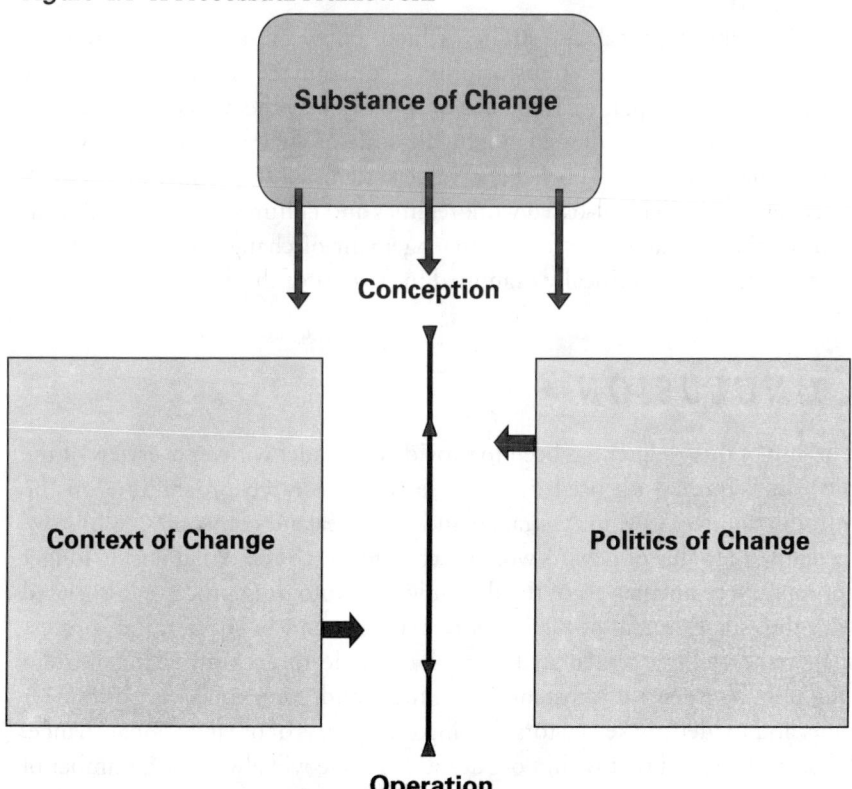

negotiations between trade union representatives and management, between consultants (working within the organization) and various organizational groups, and between and within managerial, supervisory and operative personnel. In short, certain well-placed individuals, groups or powerful coalitions can influence decision-making and the setting of agendas at critical junctures during the process of transformational change.

By combining these three dimensions (the politics, substance and context of change) with our three general timeframes on the process of organisational change (conception of a need for TQM, process of establishing TQM, and operation and on-going change), it is possible to construct a processual framework for understanding the process of transformation through the adoption of TQM. This alternative model is presented diagrammatically in Figure 4.1.

The diagram above is intended to convey the inter-connectedness and complexity of dynamic processes of change through combining a threefold classification of factors shaping the process of organizational transformation with a clear representation of the temporal nature of large-scale change. As a diagrammatic representation of the processual framework employed in the case studies presented in Part II, it should be referred to by the reader whenever necessary.

The eight empirical case studies, which follow, all illustrate the strategic and long-term nature of transforming a company towards a total quality organisation. Although each focuses on a particular theme, issue or stage in the process of change, they highlight the scale of change programme which seek to change traditional belief and value systems and introduce group work practices into individual-based work regimes and cultures. What the implications of these findings are for the management of change and employment relations at work, is critically examined in Part III of this book.

CONCLUSION

The aim of this chapter has been to provide the reader with an overview of the processual framework used in our case study research programme on the introduction to TQM in Australian and New Zealand companies. Whilst we recognise the value of Lewin's work on change, we contend that it is no longer appropriate to an analysis of the dynamic and unfolding processes associated with the establishment of total quality management. In contrast, our processual framework presented in Figure 4.1 is able to accommodate shifts in emphasis between the substantive, political and contextual categories over time, and to identify key factors shaping the process of organizational change. It has been argued that within organisations there will always be a number of periods (sometimes overlapping and rarely distinct) associated with any major change programme. In retrospect, every successful TQM programme will have a beginning, a middle and an end. What the analytical framework allows us to do is to analyse the dynamics of change through identifying and explaining factors which shape outcomes during the process of managing organisational transitions.

CHAPTER 5

Conceptualising the Need For TQM at Accom Industries Pty Ltd

Verna Blewett

INTRODUCTION

Accom Industries is a small company in the anti-corrosion engineering industry. The company has three main areas of business: it sells its technology and engineering expertise in anti-corrosion, it provides a specialised blasting and coating service, and it custom builds Fibre Reinforced Plastic (FRP) items, principally for industrial use. As such, it has both service and manufacturing sides to its operation, and work is carried out both at the Accom facilities in Salisbury and on-site at its customers' premises.

In 1991, Accom was considering the need to establish a quality programme in order to enhance the marketability of its products and services. At this conceptual stage in the process of change, a lot of attention is given to gathering information for the purpose of assessing the meaning of quality initiatives and their applicability and potential consequence for a small anti-corrosion business. Unlike larger organisations, Accom could not afford to employ management consultants to implement change, and therefore set about comparing and contrasting the principles of TQM with the more conventional quality assurance techniques. This case examines the pre-TQM stage of organisational transition in a brief account of the early experiences of Accom Industries.

COMPANY BACKGROUND

Accom was founded in 1982 by entrepreneur Charles Figallo (the current Managing Director) and it has few competitors in the niche market in which it operates. Although the workforce fluctuates with workload, at the time of writing, it employed approximately thirty-five people. It has a management philosophy based on:

> The provision of competent and responsive management, an integrated project team, an accurate, efficient and timely internal management information system and a high intensity effort on project commencement. (Accom Industries P/L marketing document, 1991)

The company is highly innovative in its application of technology and in its readiness to grasp new products and materials as they become available. For example it has developed a highly sensitive blasting operation which can remove one layer of paint at a time without altering the profile of the layer beneath, a technique of interest principally to the defence industries that are located nearby. It has incorporated new coating and reinforcing products into its stocklist as they become available, acquiring expert knowledge of the products and their application. A number of manufacturers recommend only Accom to apply their products in recognition of the company's professionalism.

Herein lies the strategic advantage of the company. It markets its specialised engineering knowledge and at the same time manufactures and sells finished products, custom-made to meet the particular needs of each customer. Corrosion protection is a specialised area of engineering with general application across industry. Accom provides custom-made solutions for problem areas from protective coatings under bridges, on floors and plant in breweries, and on hospital floors, to the manufacture of pipework and tanks for use in highly corrosive environments.

QUALITY ASSURANCE AND ACCREDITATION

Total Quality Management has only become an issue at Accom in the last two to three years. This is not to say that quality has only just become important; the provision of quality service and product has been one of the reasons for the company's success. However, it is only relatively recently that it has become necessary to document the process of Quality Assurance in the company because of customer demand. Several large contracts have been won on the basis of the Quality Assurance systems that Accom employs and each of these projects was closely monitored by the client throughout the term of the project.

The growing need to be able to show clients (by the documentation of processes) that quality is managed and is regarded as an important issue for management led Accom to the decision to seek certification with Standards Australia. In mid-1991, the company was determining its strategy for achieving certification. This came at a transition stage in the life of the company. Since 1982 it had been managed very successfully in an entrepreneurial style. There had been a close and casual working relationship between the Managing Director (MD) and the employees in the company. During busy times it was not uncommon to see the MD working on the factory floor. This willingness to 'get his hands dirty' helped to establish his close understanding of the business and his employees. As a growing company with a bright future, the old, casual management style became difficult to maintain. The question the management of the company faced was: What systems will support and assist our growth?

The entrepreneurship of the founder of Accom had without doubt led to the rapid growth of the company. The next step, from Mr Figallo's perspective, was to use the appropriate tools to consolidate the growth of the company using its existing business, while always being on the alert for new business opportunities. He and his management team recognised the importance of developing a formal approach to quality management. Inherently suspicious of consultants, and believing their industry to be unique, the company was, in mid-1991, beginning to develop its own methodologies based on the Australian Standards.

Accom's reputation as a manufacturer of quality product was responsible for repeat business from many of its customers. Stringent quality assurance procedures that could be closely supervised at the factory were made available to those customers that demanded them. In fact, the procedures themselves contributed to the winning of new contracts. However, the story was not the same for work done on site. There, although the actual work was considered to meet specifications, cleaning up was often attended to in a sloppy fashion or not done at all. The Managing Director recalled one example:

> I visited one site at the end of a job which had been done extremely well. There was this terrific complex; I felt really proud and so did the men. Then I came around a corner and one of our blokes was cleaning his brushes and flicking paint onto a cement path. I was furious. I said, 'That'll be the first thing they notice—they won't even notice your work—after all that good work.' Sure enough the CEO came around the corner and saw the paint on the path—you can imagine what he said. (Executive Interviews, 1991)

Management were seeking a system to cope with quality and to identify methods to bring attention to quality at all stages of the work as a basic tenet of each employee. Achieving accreditation by Standards Australia and maintaining a high level of customer service was important in winning new clients and repeat business. The company was market-driven and the management believed that the company's growth would be enhanced by a TQM system. In other words, whilst management generally accepted that TQM extended beyond Quality Assurance for products and processes, during this period their thinking was largely directed towards formal accreditation.

CONCEPTUALISING THE NEED FOR TQM

The major reason for Accom's commitment to quality was the recognition of the huge cost of ignoring it. Quality is sometimes seen as an alternative to low cost, as if there were some kind of trade-off decision to be made between the two. However, Accom recognised that it is a myth that good quality has to cost more than bad quality. When jobs have to be done again there is a very real extra cost that highlights the benefit of doing it right the first time.

The management of Accom had carefully dissected the internal costs of failure of their product and services (including scrap, rework, lost production time, correction time, inspection and re-inspection time, and the overhead costs that result) and added these to the costs of external failure (customer dissatisfaction, lowering of reputation, costs of on-site product repairs, returns and replacements) and could see the vital importance of quality.

Quality was not regarded as a problem at Accom; rather it was regarded as the solution to a problem. The difficulty the management believed it faced was having the attitude to quality permeate the culture of the organisation in order that it be an effective tool. The General Manager saw that it was not something that could be acquired by sending people to a quality training seminar, it needed to be an all-embracing philosophy that must infiltrate the company so that every member of the company could see the importance of satisfying the customer as being the ultimate priority.

The competitive importance of quality was recognised at Accom and some jobs had been undertaken that had required the development of stringent quality assurance programmes. These had been achieved and Accom was building a reputation for quality service and product. However, quality performance had not been consistent, particularly in on-site work and especially in remote locations. There were problems associated with the communication between sales and the shopfloor, with the supervision of casual employees in remote locations, with the development of commitment to the company by employees, and with communication between the General Manager and the shopfloor. All of these areas impacted on the company's capacity to deliver consistently high-quality services and products.

For Accom to work towards TQM status the management understood the need to focus on occupational health and safety, communications within the firm, employee involvement, industrial relations, training, customer service and marketing. In mid-1991 the management was planning ways to improve the company performance in these areas. Quality Assurance was seen as the first stepping stone to achieving TQM; establishing employee commitment to quality was regarded as the second. In other words, Accom's management considered TQM as something that would be a future focus of the firm after the Quality Assurance strategies were well understood.

THE POLICY AND PRACTICE OF EMPLOYEE INVOLVEMENT

The acceptance of responsibility for quality by its on-site workers was identified by management as one of the most crucial issues facing Accom. The close relationship that had existed between the MD and the shopfloor could have been expected to facilitate this and be the foundation for the company structure, but in this transition stage considerable authority had been devolved to the General Manager (GM). The GM lacked the shopfloor experience of the MD and did not have the same easy relationship with the employees. He made no attempt to devolve responsibility for quality to the shopfloor, rather he assumed responsibility himself. He showed no inclination to release control in order to allow workers to take responsibility and seemed to deny even highly skilled tradespeople the capacity to make decisions about their work. His attitudes were quite incongruous with those of the MD.

In mid-1991 the senior management of Accom used a weekend away from the workplace to consider the company's future development and write the business mission and business plan. These documents were regarded as highly confidential by the GM and under no circumstances would he allow them to be shown to people on the shopfloor. As he expressed it:

> In this industry there's no need to talk about this stuff with the shopfloor. They're not interested in this type of thing. It would be different in a high tech industry. But frankly, in this place the shopfloor people are there to do a job and the job is what we give them. They are unskilled people, or at best semi-skilled. They're only there for the money, nothing else, they're not interested in the company. If they were offered $20 extra down the road they'd be off, and they'd take our company ideas with them if they had them. (Executive Interview, 1991)

Understandably, the level of trust between the shopfloor and the GM was low. However, despite this lack of trust, he attempted to retain a stable group of skilled workers through ensuring the availability of work:

> If they run out of work on [that] project we find other work for them. We don't want to lose that group. It's a way of keeping a stable workforce on the job. (Executive Interviews, 1991)

CONCLUSION

Accom Industries was a company on the verge of exponential growth in an enormous local and domestic market. Noted for the quality of its work, it was about to break new ground by contributing to the development of training courses for the industry. There was recognition that TQM was both achievable and important to the strategic thrust of the company and that it could be reached by an extension of the work done on quality assurance. The managing director had identified several potential blocks to achieving TQM: the maintenance of on-site quality, the development of teamwork, and improving communication. However, the General Manager was inherently distrustful of the workforce, although this attitude was at odds with that of the Managing Director. The incongruity in their attitudes to the shopfloor not only contributed to the problems the company faced but was also the potential key to their resolution. Thus, the importance of individual managers in not only setting policies but also implementing change is highlighted in the case of the small business. Although Accom had embraced Quality Assurance they remained at the conception stage of a possible journey towards Total Quality Management.

QUESTIONS

1. What is the difference between QA and TQM?
2. What was the context that influenced Accom to consider the need for a TQM strategy?
3. Was a concern for quality new at Accom?
4. What problems might you predict with the implementation of TQM?

CHAPTER 6

Management Rationale and the Introduction of TQM at the State Bank of South Australia

Patrick Dawson and Margaret Patrickson

INTRODUCTION

This case examines the rationale behind the introduction of a service quality programme in the State Bank of South Australia. Attention is given to the origin of TQM and the influence of American business practice in stimulating the uptake of a quality management programme. The process of introducing change and the development of a quality improvement framework are discussed, and the need for a conceptual shift in the strategic and operational management of the bank's financial services are highlighted.

COMPANY BACKGROUND

The State Bank of South Australia was established on 2 July 1984, following the merger of the Savings Bank of South Australia and the former State Bank. The new Managing Director, Tim Marcus Clark, announced that the bank would: be a catalyst for change; adopt a competitive stance in the market place; and develop and enhance the skills of its staff required to achieve these objectives. Up until the early 1990s the bank pursued a vigorous acquisition policy aimed at horizontal expansion across the full range of financial supply services and acquired an interest in a number of other institutions in the financial sector. There was also a consolidation of the number of branches in South Australia with the closure of one branch in areas where both banks were located prior to merger, and a rapid expansion of additional branches interstate and overseas.

By 1989 the bank had branches in every mainland state in Australia and was represented in New Zealand, the United States, Hong Kong and the United Kingdom. By 1990, the State Bank employed 3 600 full time staff, with a further 2 800 staff located in other subsidiaries and affiliates.

This rapid growth in the size of the organisation and financial service market penetration, was also associated with rapidly rising profits. For example, from an initial profit of $12 million at the end of the financial year in June 1985, consolidated profit increased to over $90 million by 1989 (State Bank, 1984 and 1989). Thus, one of the two major goals which management policy had stressed from the beginning of the merger—namely, the necessity to grow profitably—had largely been achieved by the end of the 1980s through a programme of diversification and acquisition. Unfortunately, these achievements have not been maintained into the 1990s (Ward, 1989) and the State Bank Royal Commission's final report into the $3.15 billion State Bank fiasco (released in September 1993) criticised the bank's purchase of Oceanic Capital Corporation and the acquisition of $250 million worth of receivables from the New Zealand merchant bank Equiticorp. In November 1993, the State Bank announced the winding up of its New Zealand operations and their general withdrawal from the trans-Tasman market—with the consequent loss of jobs in Auckland, Wellington and Christchurch (Read, 1993:7). The bank's other goal—to expand its customer local base—has, however, received strong and vigorous support throughout and has become the bottom line of the bank's operating policy aimed at maximising customer satisfaction through an emphasis on service quality. This is the focus of the sections which follow.

THE ORIGINS AND RATIONALE FOR A SERVICE QUALITY PROGRAMME

The rationale for change stemmed from the belief held by the bank's executive that customer satisfaction was the way to achieve competitive advantage because it would help maintain their customer base. This was viewed as essential if the bank was to compete in the new banking arena of the 1980s following the Federal Government's decision to float the dollar and to allow foreign banks to operate in Australia. These two financial moves had major implications for the business practice of all Australian financial institutions, and were moreover followed up by a rise in the services provided by building societies and credit unions. Given all that, it is perhaps not surprising that there was a consequent market push for survival via policies of growth which would simultaneously increase the range of services offered and attract new customers. However, the option of offering financial incentives alone was not enough to secure new customers and retain existing clients. The bank also needed to develop a clear competitive strategy on customer service if it was to survive in what had become a highly competitive financial market.

In 1986, the executive team developed the State Bank's core values comprising: customer satisfaction, respect for the individual, and performance and profit. Whilst these core values are interdependent, the first two were identified as the key to sustainable competitive advantage and in order to acquire this knowledge the bank undertook a number of surveys of existing customers. The results from these studies indicated that the major source of dissatisfaction among customers was the poor level of service being provided, this included such things as: lengthy queues, long delays on loan decisions, and staff being guided by bank rules to such an extent that they often failed to see matters from the perspective of the client. However, although improving the quality of customer service was readily recognised as the road to expansion of the bank's customer base, how this was to be accomplished was less straightforward. Throughout 1987 the executive team actively searched for a strategy for implementing a programme of service improvement. They were equipped with a new set of core values which they believed expressed the new direction of the bank (for example, in July 1988 the movement towards a performance-based culture was supported by the Bank and by Union agreement on a new system of payment based on performance rather than seniority). However, how to make these core values part of a new banking culture was a far harder issue to tackle. Initially, P. A. Management Consultants were engaged to undertake a survey of employee opinion in order to assess the congruence between existing employee values and those of the management team. The results showed that the existing bank culture was geared more to financial matters than to customer service and that any programme of service improvement would need to confront this issue either at the outset, or as part of a service improvement strategy. They also found that there was little awareness of the four core values outside of the senior ranks. Whilst this indicated the importance of changing conventional banking philosophy and practice, the problem of how to implement this new customer service philosophy continued to frustrate the executive and acted as a barrier to change.

Against this background a member of the senior executive group (whilst on a study tour in the United States) met Dr Karl Albrecht, a management consultant in the field of service quality management and author of a number of influential books (Albrecht and Zemke, 1985). During this meeting the problem of implementing a service quality programme was discussed and information was exchanged about other organisations who had successfully implemented such programmes. On returning to South Australia and following discussions with other members of the executive team, it was decided that

Karl Albrecht should be brought to Adelaide to participate in a weekend seminar in which the bank's senior executive would confront the problem of strategic innovation and change in customer service. As a State Bank executive described:

> ABC had met Karl Albrecht during a tour of the United States and Karl Albrecht (was recognised) as a service management guru. ABC came back with...religion and said that if you guys want religion you must meet Albrecht, and so the bank invited Dr Albrecht out. He came and spent a weekend with the executive team, including TMC (the Managing Director). Just espousing the philosophies and methodologies of service management. The objective from that weekend was for the executive to make a decision as to whether they would develop (an) implementation plan. At the end of those two days they made that commitment even though there were one or two reservations within the group as to the possible success of it. But they made that decision and they committed themselves to it on that Sunday night. (Senior Management Interview, 1990)

The input of Karl Albrecht over the weekend (and during his talks with groups of Senior Management over the following week) was decisive in several ways. First, in his ability to identify with, understand, and analyse the problem facing the State Bank. Second, in being able to compare and contrast State Bank issues with similar problems in other well-known overseas service organisations which had successfully managed change. Third, through convincing the group that, although an expensive exercise, introducing a culture of service quality was achievable and that the anticipated benefits would outweigh the costs incurred.

As illustrated in the quotation above, discussions with Karl Albrecht resulted in a commitment by the senior executive to implement a programme of service quality throughout the State Bank. As part of this commitment and with the assistance of Albrecht, the group produced a series of written documents which incorporated their vision of the future direction of the bank. The three main documents comprised: a mission statement, a service strategy, and a management strategy. The mission statement outlines the importance of keeping in touch with customer needs, of providing a reliable and responsive financial service, and of ensuring controlled growth while maintaining a sense of social responsibility to the local community. Within the context of these more global statements, the service strategy provides a seven-point list on how to attract and retain customers for life through improved service provision, and the management strategy outlines ten good practices for sustaining staff commitment to a programme of continual process improvement.

By March 1988, the executive had allocated a substantial budget to the programme and appointed one of its internal managers, NH, to head it up. After initial orientation, NH's first activity was a service leadership tour to the United States where he immersed himself in learning about the emerging service culture (which had a longer history and greater visibility in America). On his return a contract was awarded to P. A. Management Consultants to help set up a pilot programme. By August 1988, following the success of the early pilot activity, the programme had entered a critical phase with the executive team meeting to assess the budgeted costs for a full-scale exercise and whether it was worthwhile continuing. The programme was approved and managerial commitment to the project was reaffirmed through the production of Best Management Practices (BMPs), a code of conduct for senior managers. Whilst BMPs were never formally measured or appraised, they did signal a significant change in the organisational expectations of managerial practices and standards. This reinforced some earlier changes in the system of payment and rewards, which, since July 1988, had moved from a seniority- to a performance-based system. The major block to employee acceptance of the new system can best be described as a 'cultural barrier', in that the change undermines the traditional status hierarchies associated with a career in banking. Although the changes in the selection and appraisal systems for career advancement were never a direct part of the Service Quality Programme (SQP), they were a part of the context in which SQP was being introduced. Thus, a major challenge facing the implementation team was how to manage a change in operating practice which demanded a further shift away from conventional banking belief systems, and hence, necessitated further changes in employee attitudes and behaviours. How the service quality group tackled this issue is described below.

IMPLEMENTING SERVICE QUALITY: A STRATEGY FOR CHANGE

The implementation team comprised four key people covering four key functional areas with a number of associated support staff. First, there was a culture and development programme with the remit to establish and maintain a new service culture. Second, an assessment and measurement function to focus on what 'internal' and 'external' customers require and how to measure the delivery of those requirements. Third, process analysis, with the objective of analysing all of the bank's internal processes for the purpose of setting up a structure for continual process improvement. Fourth, a communication function to ensure that employees are informed of all new activities and changes.

The main implementation strategy adopted by the State Bank for training and educating their staff about service quality centred on a cascade process. This process utilised a top-to-bottom approach whereby employees at lower levels in the bank's organisation structure were progressively introduced to the philosophy and practice of service delivery. Within each level of the cascade training programme, participants were made aware of the values, the mission, the strategy and the management principles which form the core of new service arrangements. Each of these was presented in small group sessions where new concepts were introduced and discussed. On returning to their sections, staff behaviour which reinforced the developing service culture was encouraged and rewarded by those in senior positions. Communication networks were also set up which publicly recognised and rewarded new behaviours either through including details of individual activity in staff publications or by recognition in more concrete ways through assignment to more challenging opportunities.

Four levels were included in the cascade training process. The top twenty members of the executive team comprised level one. The second level involved some 200 members of the senior management group. Level three comprised some 700 managers and supervisors, and level four comprised the remaining 2,500 staff members employed by the bank. This last level in the training programme was preceded by a large-scale staff function designed to impress all potential participants with the seriousness with which senior management regarded the process. Known as the 'One-Day Event' the function involved bringing every employee in Australia to a fanfare presentation at the convention centre in Adelaide where the concepts were introduced in an atmosphere of gaiety and entertainment. The aim was to convey the message that senior management is committed to the programme and prepared to devote considerable time and effort to ensure employees understand its importance.

Although by the beginning of 1990 the cascade process was almost concluded, it quickly became evident that the senior cascade workshops for managers had brought to light a number of other issues. Many service problems, for example, were as much a function of system deficiency as they were of inappropriate cultural attitudes. Hence, it was not enough to introduce staff to the new concepts involved in promoting a service culture and then expect them to have the necessary skills to introduce change effectively at their own workplace. There was a need to revamp system procedures, to develop some additional training courses in leadership skills which would complement the new culture, and to set up a specially dedicated structure which would continue to support the newly emerging service culture.

A (corporate) Quality Council (QC) was set up which consisted of executive committee members with the portfolio of overseeing the total service quality effort and proactively planning, building and driving quality improvement throughout the State Bank. Reporting to the council were a

82 QUALITY MANAGEMENT

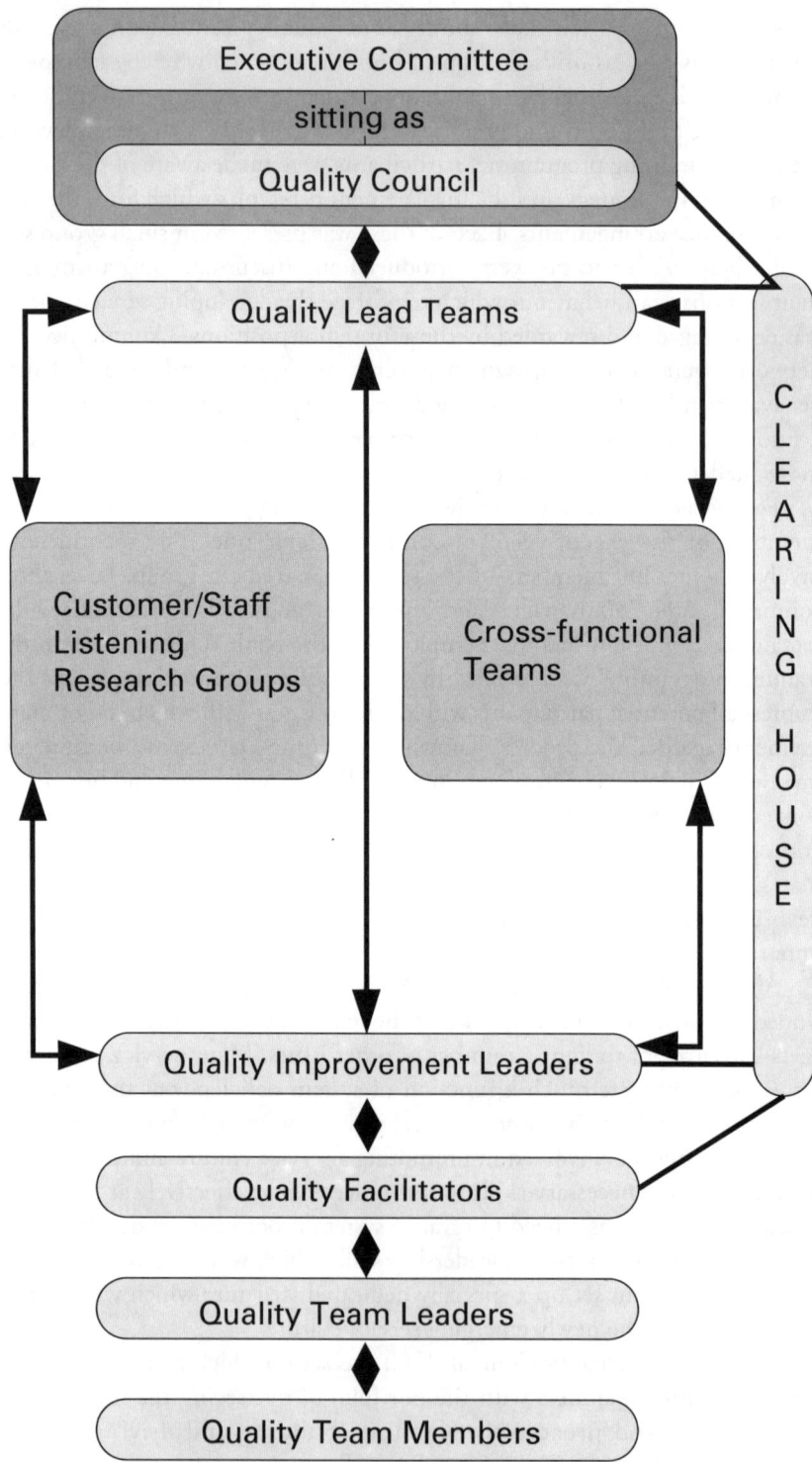

Figure 6.1. *The State Bank's Quality Improvement Framework*

number of (divisional) Quality Lead Teams (QLT) who ensured that divisional quality improvement objectives were consistent with QC policy. Their responsibilities included: leading the divisional quality effort and reporting progress to QC; providing guidance and direction to Quality Improvement Leaders (QIL); setting guidelines for the establishment of the network of process facilitators and Quality Improvement Teams (QIT) within the division. The QILs were to assist their QLT and to accept divisional responsibility for the effectiveness of the quality improvement structure in terms of: training team leaders and facilitators; monitoring team performance and quality results; and translating the findings from the customer and staff listening research groups into improvement action. The difference between Quality Team Facilitator (QTF) and Quality Team Leader (QTL) is that the former is more involved in monitoring, liaising, and assisting QITs; whereas the latter is directly involved in the leadership and management of a QIT in participative problem-solving and quality improvement.

The basic structure of the State Bank's quality improvement framework is shown in Figure 6.1. This framework was developed and superimposed over the existing line structure to support, encourage and enhance their SQP. The other elements in this framework not yet discussed comprise: the Quality Clearing House (QCH), and the Quality Teams (and cross-functional teams). The main function of the QCH (later known as the QTS or Quality Tracking System) was: to identify service complaints or issues raised by staff or customers, to assign responsibility for fixing the problem, to monitor problem-solving, and to ensure that it is resolved within a specified period of time. An on-line computer system is used to track the progress of Quality Teams (QTs) throughout the State Bank. The main objectives of these teams are to find lasting solutions to recurring problems and to help meet and exceed customer expectations. These teams are voluntary and provide: 'An opportunity for staff to use their own experience, knowledge and imagination to find better methods to improve the service (provided) to customers.' Problems which require multi-disciplinary skills to resolve are tackled by cross-functional quality teams. Unlike QTs, these teams are not voluntary.

Each quality team is led by the QTL, whose role is to chair weekly team meetings, stimulate quality thinking through assisting the team to define problems, seek out underlying causes, develop, test and implement solutions and co-ordinate team effort (the QTF oversees the process for *all* of their teams).

CONCLUSION

The process of changing established procedures and systems of operations; of redesigning reporting-and-command structures; of reappraising recruitment, evaluation, reward and promotion policies; and of replacing an entrenched system of beliefs with a new philosophy and approach to work was all part of the implementation of a service quality programme in the State Bank of South Australia. This change represented a strategic innovation in the organisation and the management of the bank, which sought to improve the bank's competitive position through gaining market recognition as the best bank in Australia for satisfying customers (State Bank, 1989).

The process of bringing about this change has involved a major long-term commitment to rearranging the bank's operations in total (see, Dawson and Patrickson, 1991:74–5). A measure of the bank's commitment to the process is that this programme has not been subjected to the same level of budget cuts as those which were made elsewhere in the structure following the 1991 report of the bank's financial problems. Whether this transformation to a total quality organisation can be maintained in the light of the current financial problems which the bank is experiencing is, at this stage, still problematic. The bank is currently under pressure to reduce its entrepreneurial thrust and this may give some support to those staff pushing for a return to the previous operational philosophy (see Patrickson and Dawson, 1994). For our part, we would conclude by stressing the importance of senior management commitment, of a cross-functional implementation team, of a total organisation approach to change, a devotion of resources sufficient to support the planned programme, and the adoption of a long-term processual model of change, within the context of maintaining effective on-going operations.

QUESTIONS

1. What shaped the decision to implement a service quality programme within the State Bank and how was the programme influenced by external events and/or change agents?

2. Describe the processes used to introduce new quality-related decision-making processes at the State Bank.

3. Discuss the arguments for and against establishing a quality council to oversee and drive organisational quality improvement programmes.

4. What is culture and what constitutes a change in culture?

5. Examine the conditions under which the successful implementation of a quality programme may not result in commercial success.

CHAPTER 7

Implementing TQM in Manufacturing: the route to Change in Tecpak Industries

Tom Batley and Michelle Andrews

INTRODUCTION

Tecpak Industries is a small New Zealand manufacturing firm in Dunedin making plastic containers, mainly for the food industry. The two Directors in the firm became interested in quality management after attending seminars on the Deming quality management philosophy and decided that the principles could be usefully applied in their firm.

The company is too small to justify the employment of management consultants for planning and implementing a quality improvement programme. The Directors decided to make the quality changes themselves and employ outside help as and when required. They did not start with a Total Quality Management implementation plan but decided to improve quality of operations in the firm step-by-step through pragmatic problem solving. After several years of promoting teamwork, quality problem solving, communications improvements and organisation development they now understand that they have been following the elements of a TQM programme.

After a series of organisational changes and quality improvement challenges in the last few years, some of which were successful and others not, the main questions now are where and how to direct the future improvement programme.

COMPANY BACKGROUND

Tecpak Industries Limited was formed in 1981 by two Directors, Tom Begg responsible for production management, and Steve Olds, responsible for sales and marketing management. They saw a market opportunity to supply plastic containers made by an injection moulding process. The oyster industry was at that time looking for an alternative to tin containers which were expensive and had problems with the seal. Tecpak's plastic containers had the advantages of being both nestable (able to be stacked inside each other for travelling empty) and cheaper than tin. Their first range of products was 'seal-pack', a composite plastic container with an aluminium top, which provided the same security as tin but at a lower cost. From there they began producing plastic containers for the food industry, to which 95 per cent of their business is now directed. They supply packaging for a wide range of different food industries, including aquaculture, honey, pet food, dry goods and salads.

For the manufacturing process, plastic bought in bulk is heated and squeezed through dies on injection moulding machines to form the shapes of the containers and the lids. Moulds for these machines are expensive and require skilful maintenance to produce consistently high-quality products. Moulds are maintained and some made in the company's machine shop. Others are bought from specialist toolmakers. Containers and lids can then be printed with instructions, company logos or whatever, on automatic printing machines. Setting up and adjusting these printing machines is a highly skilled process.

The standard range of products includes many sizes which Tecpak can supply quickly, for example salad or coleslaw containers and honey pots. These are often printed with the customers requirements. Special sizes or shapes are made to order for customers, and arrangements then have to be made for the manufacture of moulds to suit the order.

The company gradually expanded as business volume increased. Then in 1985 the market increased substantially when Tecpak produced the first clip-top containers for yoghurt (previously sealed with foil). The company then introduced shift work, employing fifteen people to cope with the demand. Staff skill levels increased noticeably from that time due both to recruiting skilled people, and to increasing the skills of the original staff through training programmes. The company now employs forty-one staff operating a three-shift system. Tecpak are known for their willingness to supply short runs of products, which is their biggest marketing strength. Some of their clients are small food companies who previously had trouble sourcing suitable packaging from suppliers that were both geographically suitable and willing to supply small numbers.

Although there has been an increase in competition in the last few years, with major companies bringing out direct equivalents of Tecpak's patented products, the company believes that present competitors are unlikely to take business away from them because of their competitive price and service. Most competitors appear to be production driven, concentrating on long runs and container lots with bulk discounts. Tecpak has left some market sectors to these competitors, particularly large volume products, as the company is in a good position in the industry with their ability to produce short runs profitably.

INTRODUCING TQM

As the company grew the two Directors began to feel more and more that they were continually 'fire-fighting' rather than managing. The Directors and several other members of management attended various management development courses including a course in 1987 on Edward Deming's quality management principles. Both Directors felt comfortable with the Deming philosophy since the company had always been people orientated. The company needed to change, and both Directors agreed it would be worthwhile implementing Deming's fourteen principles of management to achieve an overall improvement in quality throughout the system (see Appendix I). This should result in a more motivated workforce and improved management and staff relations which should be reflected in increased customer satisfaction and a stronger position in the marketplace.

No comparison was made between the Deming quality management principles and any other approach to improving the organisation. The Directors understood that Deming had heard of Total Quality Management but felt that Deming had written proof of his success and several local companies had adopted his Quality Management approach and were achieving good results. Tecpak was having some problems with product quality, and feedback from customers indicated that products were not always meeting their requirements. At this point the company had no quality control procedures for checking what was produced and there were a number of product quality problems, a major one being difficulties with sealing.

After floundering for two years trying to implement Deming's principles without success the Directors decided to enlist outside help in seeking improvements. Their initial approach was to a Quality Manager in a large local manufacturer of whiteware products, asking him how to overcome the barriers to successful implementation of TQM. He suggested a communications consultant who was also at the Deming seminar, which the Directors had attended, and could provide assistance in training staff to accept change. Without improving communications within the organisation, no other changes could effectively take place. The management team was told about the proposed communications training, but although their opinions were often sought on an informal basis, the decision-making power rested solely in the hands of the partners. The communications consultant was employed in 1988 to help the company write a mission statement, stating the company's objectives, and focus on what they were in business for. They also worked through how they should achieve these objectives. They then attempted again to implement Deming's fourteen principles for transformation of company practices.

As a means of communicating the philosophy of TQM to the staff and to improve communications, Tecpak introduced 'Roadshow Meetings' on Saturday mornings in 1989. All staff were invited to attend in order to discuss company operations, make observations or complaints and to hear any management changes or recommendations. The Directors hoped to educate the staff in the Deming philosophy through these meetings, and to improve internal communications between staff.

Unfortunately the 'Roadshow Meetings' did not overcome communication problems as intended. Cliques of staff members soon formed with different points of view and this lead to a number of confrontational arguments. The staff did not trust the Directors' reasons for seeking changes and many negative attitudes emerged. The meetings were also hindered by the lack of communication skills among the staff. The meetings provided more open communication between the staff but brought out negative feelings and resistance to change.

The Directors then felt that things weren't progressing as they should and they looked for outside advice on the next step to take. The same communications consultant was recommended to help improve internal communications and to improve the staff attitudes towards change. Discussions between the Directors and the consultant resulted in a 'Talk Skills' seminar being held in February of 1990. The objectives of the seminar were to improve communication between staff and management, which would hopefully result in each gaining more understanding of the other's point of view. With more open communication, it was hoped that the staff would more easily accept change. Another aim was to provide to all staff the skills for running meetings. These included the use of whiteboards which were installed in all departments. Staff were given exercises in personal and interpersonal communication, and video cameras were used to provide analysis of individual performance.

The communications course helped to make people more comfortable when contributing to group discussions and made internal communications more effective. Management still found that one of their major problems was in justifying their actions and many staff thought that quality management changes were just a 'fad' and would not become a permanent part of the organisation.

Tecpak put the newly acquired communication skills to use immediately, both through the Roadshow Meetings and by initiating team meetings throughout the factory. All staff became members of at least one group consisting of people involved in their work area (for example, Moulding Department group). In the first six months of these groups' existence, most effort was put into determining and solving the 'I wants' (identifying all the things people said they needed). One department identified 264 'I wants' in the first month. Most of the 'I wants' were dealt with satisfactorily and resulted in some departmental changes, for example, work method changes, placement of machinery and flow of work. The groups provided a regular forum for discussing problems and introducing any ideas the members had for improvement.

By late 1990, some processes were being examined by the groups in the hope that this would highlight problems and record how the work was actually carried out. Recording the work procedures would help to establish standard methods of work, and enable the group to co-ordinate their activities better and eliminate slack time. One of the first areas to be put under more detailed observation was Inwards Goods. This was a difficult area for group discussion and recording because it involved people from more than one department, and it was selected as an appropriate problem for a project team. Project team members were chosen during Saturday morning meetings, the main criteria for inclusion being knowledge of areas involved. There have been approximately seven projects since then and these have taken anything between one week and five months to complete. This analysis of processes and problem solving was considered by the Directors to be one of the key stages in the implementation of TQM at Tecpak. This process has encouraged teamwork as they uncover problems and work to improve the processes, and necessitates improved communication both within and between departments.

The Tecpak Directors felt that a sound knowledge of statistical process control was necessary to monitor and improve some processes, and the company needed some people with these skills. They decided to employ an external Quality Manager to provide training in statistical quality control. The five most appropriate staff members were selected and trained at a weekend seminar. The training included check sheets, Pareto charts, flow charts, fishbone diagrams, histograms, distributions from samples, run charts and machine process control charts. Staff were then requested to introduce these tools in their work and whenever appropriate in group meetings and project team meetings.

As a result of all the different types of training in the group meetings and project teams many changes have been made in processes, machinery and layout. Consequently there have been many improvements and some problems of staff settling into new routines but there have also been many positive reactions. Staff attitudes have become visibly more positive as internal communications have improved. Staff have focused on improving work processes and procedures and encouraged consistency in their activities. Both management and staff have become more focused on attitudes and the need for explanations before actions, encouragement of positive motivation, and setting objectives to provide direction.

Some people continually refused to accept the reasons for change and were a negative influence on those around them. One such person in a key technical position was required to leave the firm. Unfortunately the knowledge he held about the process and machinery was not recorded and the remaining people in that area had many problems keeping the process running smoothly. A full two months elapsed before all the problems resulting from his dismissal were alleviated. The Directors tried to work with this technician and others that were recognised as a negative influence, but reached a point where no improvement was forthcoming and the only alternative was to terminate employment. Their policy is to try to work with all problematic staff for a reasonable period of time (in the technicians case, two months) although the push for termination often comes from staff members involved with the problem employee. Other staff were reassured, in order to reduce any feelings of insecurity, that improvements in the company would not result in staff reductions. The technician has since been replaced by two well-qualified people.

Further training was carried out in Tecpak in 1991 when the Directors decided that staff could benefit from a Personal Development Course. The benefits from this were seen to apply outside the workplace, so staff members' partners were also invited. The course was run by the New Zealand Institute of Management and attended by all staff. It was based on self analysis, personal motivation and achievement of personal objectives. A similar course of leadership training was also held for all supervisors and members of the management team.

Steadily increasing work orders during the last few years have been tentatively attributed to an improvement in the quality of products and service to customers. While there has been an increase in staff in many areas there is also intermittent use of casual labour. This is to ensure on-going staff job security as management is unwilling to hire permanent full-time staff until they are assured they really need them. This avoids having to lay-off people at a later date if improvements in processes reduce the work required. This has caused some product quality problems with less skilled temporary staff, and management is looking into the possibility of having a trained pool of people available for temporary work in the future. This will entail new recruitment and selection procedures to ensure appropriate staff attitudes and values are introduced, and on-going training to include trained temporary labour. Management are now involved in designing new recruitment and selection procedures.

External relationships

Tecpak managers have been most focused on improving internal customer relationships, attitudes and communications but the services offered to external suppliers and customers have also changed. Suppliers and customers have been told of Tecpak's changes in quality management. There have been informal discussions with suppliers, and written information sent out, along with a copy of Tecpak's mission statement, philosophy and principles. Some suppliers have shown their willingness to co-operate with Tecpak, recognising that the company is interested in developing long-term relationships and trying to minimise variation. Many have shown a willingness to negotiate, and are responsive to ideas to improve their service. Some have shown trust and confidence in the company by improving delivery contracts. Tecpak now receives a consignment of materials from one supplier, but only pays for the number of items used in any one period, rather than the value of the total consignment. This has advantages for both companies. Tecpak has immediate access to materials but pays only for the exact amount used, while the suppliers cut down on warehousing and transportation costs and have satisfied long-term customers. While Tecpak has always had a policy to help solve any problems with suppliers (and customers), there is now more reciprocal exchange of information and fostering of long-term supply relationships.

There is also a conscious effort to link customers into Tecpak's system. Most respond favourably as the service Tecpak offers is not available from other suppliers. It has always been Tecpak's policy to solve customers' technical problems and minimise causes of dissatisfaction with products and services, but recently they have spent considerable time helping to sort out some customers' processes—an exercise which has benefited both companies. None of the 450 Tecpak customers contributes more than 5 per cent of their turnover, but all are regarded as important and extended the same service. Not all customers and suppliers have perceived the changes, however, since some of the services have not needed to be changed.

HUMAN RESOURCE IMPLICATIONS

Tecpak has always used the national awards for the Engineers, Printers and Packaging Unions as a guide for their payment systems. Any increases and benefits above the national minimum were settled informally with what is now viewed as rather haphazard negotiations. Grievance procedures were also guided by national regulations.

There were few personnel procedures formalised at Tecpak. Recruitment and selection took the form of hiring anybody that turned up looking for work, provided there was a vacancy, and the applicant had the required skills. There were few recognised career routes, people were promoted through grades, promotions being tied to length of service. Dismissal followed the normal course of verbal warnings, followed by three written warnings before termination of employment.

The introduction of Total Quality Management has had a huge impact on many practices within the organisation. The way the work is carried out has changed in many areas, and this has resulted in changes in roles and responsibilities. Work has generally intensified and skill levels have increased, along with opportunities for training and skills development.

There have been few problems with management–staff relations, with Directors trying to foster 'family'-type relationships. Unionisation has been actively discouraged and since 1984 there has only been one trade union member on staff. There have been few problems and staff have not looked to a union for support. Job security has been maintained, with low labour turnover, and intermittent use of casual labour. During busy periods people have always been called in to supplement permanent staff, and this has continued.

The new Employment Contracts Act in New Zealand has necessitated individual or group contracts of employment to be negotiated. Employees have been asked to nominate several representatives to negotiate the new contracts with management. The improved attitudes and communications training should help to provide more effective negotiations. The employees are using some of their new skills in organising representatives and objectives for the upcoming negotiations with management. They are setting up formal meetings to cover these negotiations, and management hopes to tie in an appraisal system to the reward system. This will also include the new training system, and pay people on the basis of both skill and performance. Attaining certain skill levels promotes an automatic pay increase with a performance portion based on team work, resulting in a three-tier wage structure. This has highlighted the need for an improvement in recruitment procedures, possibly introducing interviews, character references and contacting previous employers. There will be an emphasis on potential employees' attitudes and personalities, ensuring that these are consistent with the company. An induction programme will be put in place to ensure new employees are aware of the company's philosophies and policies, and educate them in TQM. Training will be given when required to ensure that people can be fully functioning members of the organisation.

The dismissal and grievance procedures will also be formally defined in the new Agreement, with dismissal procedures probably remaining similar to those at present, with verbal and written warnings. Dismissal is unusual but may result from rejection by the team of which the employee is a member, on the grounds that their behaviour or attitude is no longer acceptable.

By law, all employees, union or non-union, have access to the Personal Grievance procedures that previously were offered to union members only, but internally Tecpak will also have three channels to air grievances so as to try to resolve any problems before they need to go through outside channels. They may take grievances through team meetings, going to a supervisor, or by going directly to the Directors, all of which are equally acceptable to management.

CONCLUSIONS

Tecpak is still in the process of implementing TQM, defining tasks and responsibilities and further work processes. There have been many changes in the social organisation of work, however, in the last few years. Every employee is now a member of at least one work group and may participate in project work to handle specific problem-solving tasks. There is normally full attendance at the Saturday 'Roadshow Meetings'. These meetings are more structured since the communications training courses and every person has the opportunity to speak or lead the meetings.

There is also better communication and more co-ordination and flexibility between departments, and better understanding of quality problems in different work areas. Quality of service and information flows between internal customers in Tecpak has been enhanced. Job rotation and a policy of increased skills training has improved staff motivation and flexibility.

Once the present procedures have been more fully analysed and documented the company hopes to move on to some 'Just-In-Time' (JIT) improvements. Management understands the principles of JIT but are unsure if these should be implemented to enhance the TQM programme. There have already been decreases in buffer stocks between processes and these are expected to reduce further as current problems are solved. The maintenance department have increased their skills in toolmaking and now make many tools which were previously sub-contracted out. Tooling has been improved and produced more specifically for Tecpak's machinery.

There has been only a small amount of financial monitoring of waste reduction in terms of cost savings, labour and time saving. Downtime in the moulding shop has reduced and productivity of the print shop has improved in terms of output units per week. Managers are aware that there is a need to further improve their statistical recording in order to show the benefits of TQM practices.

Managers' perceptions of the effects of implementing TQM principles have brought about a change in the focus of their work. They now recognise that management's responsibility is to monitor and improve work systems and to provide the right resources and training for people to carry out their own work effectively. This change of focus has resulted from the identification and recording of tasks at all levels of the organisation. Managers are now more involved in project teams and feel that they are consciously more competent in most practical aspects of the company's work.

Supervisors expressed similar feelings about the change in emphasis of their work. Responsibility has moved downwards. Previously the supervisors may have taken responsibility for the way their staff carried out the work. Now the operators are more responsible for the way work is carried out and for suggesting improvements. This is seen by some as a loss of power and status. Responsibility has shifted towards supervisors as team leaders, staff trainers and problem solvers.

The Directors believe that although there have been many problems in changing the company's policies and procedures towards higher quality, they have made some mistakes but also done some things well. There are many problems left unsolved but their main dilemma now is where and how to best direct their efforts for further improvements.

QUESTIONS

1 Communication is often seen as being at the heart of TQM programmes. In what ways are communication issues highlighted by the Tecpak case example?

2 Evaluate the importance of training in statistical techniques to the successful management of quality programmes.

3 Describe the changes that were made in internal and external relations.

4 Identify three problems which faced Tecpak and discuss their relevance to other types of small manufacturing companies with which you may be familiar.

5 In what ways were communications changed at Tecpak?

CHAPTER 8

Health and Safety, Customer-Supplier Relations, and Statistical Process Control:
Strategies for Continuous Quality Improvement At Hendersons Automotive (SA)

Verna Blewett

INTRODUCTION

Significant changes to manufacturing and management processes have occurred at Hendersons Automotive (SA) (HASA) since the beginning of 1986. In 1985 the automotive industry took a downturn that affected all components manufacturers, including HASA. Even so, the plant was not achieving its full business potential. It was operating less efficiently than it could have been and there were concerns about morale, absenteeism, and labour turnover and the high cost of workplace injuries. In a climate where the market was unpredictable it was clear that HASA needed plans in place to ensure its survival into the future.

In early 1986 a new management team was appointed. Some of the members were brought in from outside the company while others in the organisation were given new roles. The ability to manufacture quality products for an increasingly discerning world market was identified as the key to the company's long-term survival. A planned approach to management was introduced to the company. A cohesive management team developed and consultation with the shopfloor was used to help produce a company philosophy with emphasis on safety, quality and productivity. By 1991, the firm was profitable and placed a strong emphasis on consultative management, occupational health and safety, training, and quality management. The formulation of policies and their implementation had as their foundation close consultation between management and the shopfloor and their representatives.

The success of the organisational change programme was demonstrated by the observed outcomes of the process: namely, an increase in shopfloor productivity, outside recognition of quality improvements, a reduction in the incidence and severity of injuries, and a reduction in labour turnover and absenteeism. The company was heading towards achieving 'Best Practice' by using a planned approach to World Competitive Manufacturing and Continuous Quality Improvement.

This chapter examines a number of key elements in this process of organisational recovery, with particular attention being given to customer–supplier relations, occupational health and safety, and statistical process control as important strategies in the development of an ethos of continuous quality improvement.

Company background and business context

HASA is the South Australian manufacturing division of Hendersons Industries Pty Ltd, a fully owned subsidiary company of National Consolidated Limited (NCL). NCL is a highly diversified, publicly listed company which has interests in the building and air conditioning industries as well as in the automotive industry.

In 1985 the total number of vehicles built by Australian car assemblers dropped significantly. This downturn in the industry affected all components manufacturers, and HASA was no exception. Along with the downturn in the market, the company faced some hard decisions.

HASA was operating at less than its full efficiency. Workers' Compensation was a major expense at that time with an average of 218 hours per month lost to injuries. The factory environment was cluttered and there was room for improvement. High labour turnover and absenteeism and poor worker morale were concerns that needed to be dealt with. There were also concerns about the level of product quality and about existing re-work levels.

The appointment of the new management team in early 1986 gave the company an important opportunity for change. Their prime objective was to manage a route to recovery. By mid-1991 the company had developed a reputation for quality products amongst its customers—the Australian automobile assemblers and first-tier suppliers in the USA. For example, it had achieved Ford's audited quality standard, Q101, and had a programme for achieving the next level in the standard, Q1. It had also been awarded the National Safety Council of Australia 5-Star Award for the third year in a row in recognition of its achievements in the occupational health and safety arena and had been granted exempt status from the South Australian WorkCover system on the basis of its near exemplary occupational health and safety management performance. In addition, it had fostered a co-operative relationship with the unions that represented its employees and it had developed mechanisms to encourage employee participation. Moreover, significant resources, both in-house and external, had been used to increase the skill level of its employees and provide career paths, succession training and secure employment.

A culture in which change is the norm had been developed through the processes of consultation, Kaizen groups and Quality Circles. Cultural change had fostered a climate in which internal customers were regarded as being as important as external customers and responsibility for quality had been delegated to the shopfloor. Sophisticated quality systems had been introduced including the Statistical Process Control system, numerical co-ordinate measuring equipment and the Manufacturing Resource Planning II (MRPII) system. The company monitored the performance of its suppliers with respect to quality, productivity and competitiveness, and had made quality a cornerstone of the company culture and imbued its personnel with it. It was for this complex range of reasons that HASA was regarded as a leader in the field of automotive seating.

The Australian automotive seating market which had formed the base of HASA's operations had benefited from being unattractive to potential importers because of its small absolute size, fragmentation and distance which exacerbated communication problems and lead times. Within the Australian market, HASA had managed to build a well-established position. With the adoption of Supplier Pre-selection by most of the Australian Automotive manufacturers, Hendersons had elected to base its operations on those processes and products in which it considered it would be competitive in the world market.

HASA's consolidation in the niche market of automotive seating had been a deliberate, strategic move into a market not easily entered by other, overseas competitors. A physical barrier to entry to the Australian market was the shipping costs associated with the cubic size of the product. There were technical barriers to entry for competitors because HASA held certain key licences and technical agreements with global-level automotive seating manufacturers. HASA was the major manufacturer of seating components in Australia outside the Automotive Manufacturers. It was the vision of the company that it would be the sole manufacturer of fully trimmed seats for the Australian market, including the Automotive Manufacturers. Although opportunities for export of fully trimmed seats were unlikely to occur (the physical barrier to entry applied in the export market as well as the import market), there was potential in the seating component market, particularly in lumbar supports and seat slides in which HASA had world renown expertise. Two significant export contracts were finalised at the end of 1991 and more were expected. This marked the entrance by HASA into the fiercely competitive US market. The company had a good past and present record for performance in meeting its Australian customers' requirements and it had a strong financial position, providing resources for company initiatives with additional support available from the parent company.

In late 1991 the automotive industry and the automotive components industry were both suffering from the effects of severe recession. The decline in demand for product both on the domestic and international markets had adverse effects on the operations of enterprises in this industry. Many enterprises had reduced employee numbers through passive means (natural attrition) or active means (retrenchment). For many enterprises the economic climate had resulted in a curtailment of activities that were not directly associated with production.

HASA had also suffered during the recession. Rapid fall-off in the demand for product reduced profitability in the 1990–91 financial year and threatened the security of jobs. However, sensitivity analysis was done in August 1990 in anticipation of the recession deepening. It was based on declines in sales of up to 20 per cent (although 22 per cent was experienced). HASA had plans in place to cope with the effects of the recession. In consultation with the employees the company developed a workable scheme of reduced working hours amongst both direct and indirect labour.

It was within this business-economic context that the key issues of quality and employee training were seen as critical to the long-term viability of the company. These are examined in the next two sections.

HEALTH AND SAFETY: MANAGERIAL STRATEGIES FOR EMPLOYEE INVOLVEMENT

In early 1986 the emphasis was placed on the working environment and on occupational health and safety; matters of vital, personal concern to the workers at the factory. Housekeeping was improved throughout the plant but was especially noticeable on the factory floor. As one leading hand put it:

> This place used to look like a dungeon but now its really clean and neat. That's one of the reasons there aren't many accidents now. (Shopfloor interviews, 1991)

At the same time a health and safety representative was appointed by management from the factory floor. Within twelve months the number of health and safety representatives had increased to four and they were elected by the shopfloor rather than appointed by management. An occupational health and safety committee, consisting of management representatives and the elected health and safety representatives, was established. This group prepared the company's occupational health and safety policy. The finished policy document was signed by both the Divisional Manager and the Shop Stewards. Systems were set in place to devolve the responsibility for health and safety to supervisors and training was provided to enable them to be accountable for it. These systems included procedures for monitoring accidents and injuries, housekeeping checks and the training of their workers. All procedures and policies were developed and endorsed by the health and safety committee. Time during the shifts was set aside to allow training of employees to take place for a few minutes each week. These 'Five Minute Safety Talks' proved most popular and it was not long before elected Health and Safety Representatives and other shopfloor people were leading the talks and the ensuing discussion. Before long, one half-hour each fortnight was allocated to the talks.

The accent on health and safety had several advantages for the company. There was an immediate fall in the number of lost time injuries with a corresponding fall in the costs associated with accidents and illness in the workplace. These included workers' compensation, rehabilitation and the so-called 'hidden costs' of accidents; personnel time, loss of product, damage to equipment and so on. The emphasis on the people and their well-being helped to develop a sense of confidence in the new management and provided a springboard for other changes.

With respect to the management of people, the major shift in emphasis was away from an autocratic style towards a democratic and consultative style. The new management system incorporated formal ways for management and employee representatives to meet and discuss issues in a non-confrontationist manner. Although the Them/Us barrier still existed in late 1991, it was not as impenetrable as it once was and it was expected to crumble further.

Not all supervisors and managers were comfortable with the changes that were expected from them. Although none was fired, some chose to leave. Others found the transition easy. They saw it as an opportunity to work in the way they had always wanted to but had never been able to achieve under the old management systems. As one of the senior managers commented: 'it was like a breath of fresh air'.

These 'people-changes' were the foundation for the push for product quality improvement and they were regarded as a legitimate part of the quality programme. From the time the change programme began to be implemented, the role of people in achieving quality performance was recognised. As the Quality Assurance Manager put it:

> The main thing is people involvement, because no single person can do it. It's got to be a total effort and that effort is being pushed right

down to the shopfloor—they're the people who can best respond. (Executive Interview, March 1991)

The package of changes to the management style with the enhanced emphasis on quality was expected to result in an organisation that would be noted for its product quality, its reliability and its customer focus.

ESTABLISHING A QUALITY STRUCTURE AND THE USE OF STATISTICAL PROCESS CONTROL

The new company strategy was to focus on the customers of the company; to be 'customer-driven'. This was to be achieved by satisfying the internal customers first to allow sufficient energy for people to focus on the needs of external customers. After investigating the state of the business in late 1985, the new Divisional Manager concluded that the workforce was a strength of the company rather than a weakness and that it could be used more effectively with a different management style—one that considered the needs of employees.

Once the changes in the management of people began to take effect, more effort could be put into quality by using the workforce. In mid-1991 the quality infrastructure of the company was multi-tiered. There was a Quality Assurance Manager, one of the senior executives of the company, who led the Quality Assurance Department. He developed the *Defect Prevention Strategy*, outlined clearly in the Quality Policy Statement, that had been disseminated to all employees. Quality Inspectors worked on different facets of the quality programme. Some worked on customer–supplier relations, some worked on the shopfloor testing 'first-offs', performing time-consuming destruction testing, examining questionable product, and attending to customer returns either from the factory or from warranty returns. The final layer in the quality hierarchy consisted of the operators who were responsible for the self-inspection of the parts they manufactured or assembled. Arguably the most important tool for the maintenance of quality by these people was Statistical Process Control (SPC).

The power of SPC lay in the immediacy of the reporting. The product was not just gauged to ensure that it either did or did not have a particular attribute (generally the attributes tested were determined by the Quality Assurance Department in consultation with the customer, although the Toolroom, Engineering or the Materials Department were also involved when appropriate). vIn addition, variable measures were taken to allow the operator to determine the performance of the production process. This allowed immediate feedback on the process rather than a measure of the result of the process. It meant that the capability of the process to produce product within specifications could be measured while the job was being run. If process problems were detected then adjustments could be made to realign process operations.

During a period of participant observation an instance was observed where the workers regarded a particular type of SPC charting to be worthless as it did not add to the knowledge about the quality of the component. After discussions with the Quality Inspectors, the Engineering Department and the Materials Manager it was agreed that the workers were right, and a meaningful measure that the workers suggested was introduced. SPC charting against the new measure was conducted with more enthusiasm, in providing workers with increased control over the quality of the components they were producing. It was expected that in the future, inspection of product would become the responsibility of shopfloor workers, with the assistance of specific expertise when required. The importance placed on quality by shopfloor workers is illustrated in the following extract:

> The leading hand showed me the job very carefully and told me what to look for should things go wrong. He was quite insistent about quality and told me that the parts should be perfect and to ask him if I had any questions. I asked him if people really were careful about quality and checking things He looked at me as if I was silly and simply said 'of course!'. He told me that these were safety components and they had to be just right. (Participant Observation Notes, July 1991)

A healthy attitude to quality existed on the factory floor, the people were well trained in quality inspection, and on-the-job training emphasised the need for quality. However, the author's experience was that all too often the capacity to produce quality parts was thwarted by poor tools and equipment. For example:

> Every hour I had to check the quality of the welds on the nuts with a torsion wrench. I had real trouble with this because the spanner head wouldn't fit the nut (too large). The correct spanner has never been supplied! (Participant Observation Notes, July 1991)

Workers were concerned about producing quality parts; as one said, 'there is no satisfaction in producing scrap' and they worked out means of ensuring quality was maintained. Curiously, the lack of appropriate testing tools may have been more a consequence of poor communication than lack of management interest in providing and maintaining appropriate equipment. The author's experience was that machinery was altered very quickly after a written complaint was received by management. She found some workers had no faith in the capacity of management to respond and, as a result, failed to put in written requests or even to complain about their difficulties to their supervisors. Whatever the true nature of the blockage it was clear that an almost tangible communication barrier existed at the plant. It was of concern to the management and shopfloor people alike and was one aspect of working life that both groups would like to have seen improved. In spite of this, the reality was that HASA's products met the specifications of their customers. Returns were very low and there was a high level of customer satisfaction.

The importance of maintaining healthy relations with customers and suppliers was also considered to impact greatly on quality. It was for this reason that effort was spent on incorporating both customers and suppliers into the HASA 'family'. HASA's approach to the development of good customer–supplier relations was creative and varied.

THE DEVELOPMENT OF EXTERNAL CUSTOMER–SUPPLIER RELATIONS

In the automotive industry each customer had their own demands and requirements about quality. Schemes like the Ford Q1 system were very complex to operate but were a necessary part of being a supplier to that customer. The need to operate a sophisticated and planned quality system was vital to the company in order to maintain its customer base. The quality assurance system had to comply with the needs of the customers. However, there were aspects of the various customer quality systems that were measured at HASA solely because the customer wanted those particular measurements; they had little internal value to HASA:

> There's been quality systems around for a long time and these are always subject to review. Whilst it's OK to have a system there in black and white per the Australian Standards, it doesn't necessarily work and doesn't necessarily reflect the changes that you have to make to keep pace. Things change very quickly. (Executive Interviews, 1991)

The demand for quality from HASA's customers required not only that HASA manufacture to stringent standards but also that HASA's suppliers provide the company with quality components or raw materials. To ensure that this happened, HASA monitored the performance of suppliers. The company maintained a benevolent attitude to suppliers and had worked at building a healthy relationship with them because suppliers were regarded as an extension of the company. Suppliers who had difficulty providing or maintaining consistent quality had been offered assistance in the first instance.

In 1988 HASA conducted a seminar for its suppliers to communicate to them their requirements for quality and to inform suppliers about recommended systems for quality assurance. Forty suppliers attended. Later HASA assisted some suppliers to establish their own quality systems. Those that were unable to respond to HASA's requirements were dropped from the supplier list. Since 1988 the number of suppliers has been halved. The second supplier seminar, held in late 1991, was attended by the twenty suppliers that Hendersons then used. The theme of the seminar was 'Achieving win–win solutions' and the message to suppliers was that they need to consider themselves an extension of HASA. As the use of Electronic Data Interchange (EDI) increased, the level of trust between supplier and customer needed to increase. The emerging technology of lean manufacturing that HASA was moving towards required a highly integrated customer–supplier relationship. HASA expected that the attitude its employees had towards quality would be mirrored in the employees of its suppliers.

Understanding what happened to the product when it reached the external customer was regarded as important. Each week a different small group of shopfloor employees, accompanied by a Quality Inspector, was taken to General Motors Holden Australia Limited or Mitsubishi to visit the production line where their product was used. These visits were instituted in mid-1988 when the quality programme was well under way. The workers are able to talk to the people who used their parts and in this way a working relationship had been built up with the external customers and some improvements in product and product handling was the result. For example, there was concern over the number of returns of a seat back from one of the customers. Workers from HASA saw their parts being handled roughly at the assembly plant and worked out, with the assembly plant workers, that the method of packing the parts made them lock together in transit and so made them difficult to unpack. Together they worked out a new packing method which not only prevented damage to the parts but also enabled more parts to be packed into each stillage. The less tangible benefits from the programme were a sense of ownership in the products that were manufactured at HASA and an improved understanding about why products were designed the way they were. It was anticipated that this programme would be enhanced in the future by the occasional inclusion of customer assembly line workers in the continuous improvement groups.

Interstate customers, Nissan and Ford, were visited fortnightly and Toyota was visited monthly by the Production Manager and a representative from the Quality Department. The purpose of these visits was to maintain a strong relationship with the customer both at shopfloor and management level and to emphasise the customer orientation of the company. Any problems that might be experienced by the customer were dealt with rapidly and at first hand.

KAIZEN, QUALITY GROUPS AND CONTINUOUS IMPROVEMENT GROUPS

HASA relied heavily on Kaizen and Quality Groups to provide a high level of innovation in production and design. Quality Groups tended to concentrate on one product and were department-based, whilst Kaizen groups had a broader range of topics and considered aspects of management seemingly unrelated to production. In both cases the membership of the groups was drawn from a cross-section of levels and Departments in the factory to maximise the variety of input to the process. The number of meetings of these groups fell during the recession as direct–indirect labour ratios became critical, however, the management recognised that this was detrimental to long-term performance and re-introduced them on a monthly basis in mid-1991.

The trend for the future was the amalgamation of Kaizen and Quality Groups into Continuous Improvement Groups (CIGs). Drawn from a vertical slice of the organisation, these groups were learning problem-seeking and problem-solving techniques from a consultant. The value of this training lay not only in the techniques learnt, but also in the visual manner that progress on projects was reported on the shopfloor. Large display boards outlining the problem and how it was being solved and by whom were located in the appropriate departments making the information available to anyone who cared to examine them. The overall plan was to formally capture the ideas from these groups, to ensure that they were used and to record the benefits that flowed from them. A 'Productivity Improvement Program' was instigated to collect information about costs and savings from each idea. It was anticipated that cost savings would eventually be used to contribute to productivity gains under Award Restructuring.

CONCLUSION: THE ROUTE TO RECOVERY AT HASA

Since 1986, Hendersons has undergone a number of significant changes, including: the use of shopfloor statistics and participative management techniques; a focus on health and safety; and the development of CIGs. For example, operators are now responsible for the quality of the material they produce and this is supported by a written Quality Policy Statement. There has also been extensive training in Statistical Process Control (SPC) with each operator being taught the fundamentals of the system. SPC is now used widely throughout the factory by shopfloor personnel to control processes and improve quality. In short, responsibility for quality has been devolved to shopfloor operators who are now expected to recognise and remedy faults as and when they arise.

The managerial objective of developing a highly specialised and flexible workforce which can be easily accommodated within rapidly adjusted production arrangements to meet changing market demands, is being achieved. Both the company and its employees valued the move towards multi-skilling and increased operator training, both in terms of meeting the company's quality and productivity objectives and in terms of employee's job satisfaction and employability. For example, the emphasis which Hendersons places on succession training and career planning is important to the company's long terms strategic goals which depend on a highly skilled, flexible workforce and the long term employment of individuals in whom training investment has been made.

The next step for Hendersons is a more concerted move towards lean manufacturing, in which skills can be developed within close-knit teams for career progression. The award of a grant of $420 000 from the Australian Best Practice Demonstration Programme (through the Department of Industrial Relations and the Australian Manufacturing Council) is being used by the company to accelerate these change objectives. It is anticipated that over the next two years consultative mechanisms will be enhanced to enable strategic plans to be devised co-operatively. Training programmes are also being developed to support individuals in redesigning their own jobs within the context of the company's strategic plan and finally, it is hoped that organisational redesign will follow from this iterative process.

QUESTIONS

1. Evaluate the importance of contextual issues (internal relations/external business market) in highlighting the 'need' and decision to introduce quality programmes.

2. What was the value of the early focus on Health and Safety at Hendersons?

3. Give an example of the increased customer consciousness.

4 What do you understand by the term Statistical Process Control (SPC) and how important is it to quality management?

5 'Quality management often forms part of a number of other changes and rarely occurs in isolation'. Discuss this statement in consideration of the experience of Hendersons Automotive.

CHAPTER 9

The Development of Process Improvement: Teams and the Measurement of Outcomes at Alcoa's Kwinana Refinery

Alan Brown

INTRODUCTION

This case study focuses on the Alcoa alumina refinery at Kwinana in Western Australia (WA). Originally established in 1962, it is the oldest of Alcoa's three alumina refineries in Western Australia, and is located on the heavy industry coastal strip just south of the Perth metropolitan area. It has an annual capacity of 1.7 million tonnes of alumina. Raw bauxite is mined at Jarrahdale, some 40 kilometres to the east and railed to the refinery.

In 1986, the management at Kwinana made a decision to introduce a quality initiative in order to improve the plant's efficiency. This case outlines the reasons for change, the development and functioning of quality teams, and the methods for measuring the organisational effects of quality programmes.

COMPANY BACKGROUND

Alcoa of Australia is an unlisted company which is 44 per cent owned by Western Mining Corporation, 51 per cent by the Aluminium Company of America, and the remainder by Australian institutional investors (Alcoa, Annual Report, 1991). The company was first established in 1961 when the exploration joint-venture partners of Western Mining Corporation, Broken Hill South Limited and North Broken Hill Limited negotiated with the Aluminium Company of America to form an Australian company to develop the local aluminium industry. Today its primary activities concern bauxite mining, alumina refining and aluminium smelting and rolling. It also has gold mining interests.

The Australian operation of Alcoa employs some 6 500 people and sales revenue for 1991 was $2500 million (Alcoa, Annual Report, 1991). In 1991 the company contributed 5 per cent of Australia's exports. During the late eighties demand for aluminium has generally been good with virtual full capacity utilisation rates of aluminium smelters worldwide (Annual Report, 1991). In 1990 all three Alcoa alumina refineries in Western Australia have operated at full capacity. However, the world aluminium market tends to be subject to the cyclical tendencies of world commodity prices which have fallen since 1988. Profits and sales revenue fell sharply in 1991 (Annual Report, 1991).

In Western Australia, Alcoa mines bauxite and refines alumina which is then shipped to Victorian and overseas aluminium smelters. Some 4000 people are employed at three mine sites, three alumina refineries and the administrative headquarters. Approximately 10 per cent of the alumina from Western Australia is exported to the Geelong and Portland smelters in Victoria, with most of the remainder going to the South East Asian market. Approximately 18 per cent of the world's alumina is supplied from the WA operations. The Kwinana plant is currently building up a diversified market of other consumers of alumina apart from the traditional aluminium industry. A growing portion is being used for other purposes such as ceramics, water treatment and fire retardants.

The Kwinana refinery has a workforce of approximately 1100 employees with some 850 involved in direct operations and maintenance activities. The employees of the plant are represented by five unions—the Australian Workers' Union (AWU), Australian Electrical, Electronics Foundry and Engineering Union (AEEFEU), Metals and Engineering Workers' Union (MEWU), Construction, Mining and Energy Workers Union (CMEU) and Federated Clerks Union (FCU)—with approximately half the workforce being members of the AWU. Alcoa has had a single-site award since 1972.

THE CONTEXT OF CHANGE

A combination of factors help explain the introduction of quality improvement at Alcoa, Kwinana. First, the viability of the plant was under question in 1986 with 25 per cent of the plant capacity shut down mainly due to a depressed worldwide aluminium market. From a peak in 1980, world aluminium prices had fallen significantly during the early 1980s. The search for operational efficiencies in Western Australia took the form of process improvement to improve product quality through enhancing employee skills and developing greater teamwork. Considerable capital investment had already been placed into two newer plants which were originally commissioned during the early eighties. They produced better quality alumina at lower prices than the Kwinana plant and had introduced teamwork, employee participation, multi-skilling and a flat management structure. Thus, process improvement was seen as a potential means of improving the efficiency of Kwinana without large capital expenditure.

Second, a 1986 industrial relations agreement between Alcoa and the AWU introduced concepts such as teamwork and multi-skilling into the workplace. These were designed to improve productivity as part of a trade-off for a pay increase and provided an opportunity to introduce quality improvement teams (over half the workforce belonged to the AWU). The plant viability issue also helped create a favourable climate for change since both management and employees were aware that if plant performance did not improve there was a possibility of a temporary or permanent shut down.

Third, both the appointment of a new Chairman of the Board in 1988, who supported the adoption of TQM in the American and Australian operations of the company, and the appointment of a Quality Manager for WA operations in 1987, played an important part in promoting quality management. Acting as internal consultants, they have endeavoured to increase the awareness and understanding of TQM amongst all of Alcoa's managers. For example, plant managers have been encouraged to adopt the principles of quality improvement through conference attendance, seminars, company visits and extensive reading. This third factor has been a significant part of the conception period of the change to TQM, although elements of TQM, such as teamwork, were already part of the Alcoa culture.

THE FORMATION OF PROCESS IMPROVEMENT TEAMS

Organisational change has been a part of Alcoa's culture for most of the early eighties and, as far back as 1986, the Kwinana Plant Manager organised an off-site seminar for management, supervisors, union officials and operators (a vertical slice of the company) on quality management. Nevertheless, despite a high degree of enthusiasm shown by participants, it was discovered that quality was easy to talk about but difficult to practice. No-one knew how or where to start. In 1987, Alcoa personnel were given exposure to quality initiatives at the Point Henry aluminium smelter in Victoria and a US consultant (Luftig) on Statistical Process Control as the search for the substance of TQM commenced.

In mid-1988 a further management seminar was organised with a view to creating cultural change conducive to quality management and the involvement of people. The creation of work teams was seen as crucial in order to obtain the involvement of employees and to develop quality improvement. Although very frustrated with the time it would take, the plant manager's view was that changes needed to be introduced in a subtle way in order to be accepted. Thus, in considering the establishment of TQM, a company-wide training and implementation programme was deliberately avoided even though resources would have been available. The AWU and MEWU officials were informed about management's intentions and had no objections, helping provide a positive political context for change.

To further develop the focus of change, in 1988 the company began examining what progressive companies were doing in the quality area and focused on BHP's approach. The Kwinana management group felt that a quality programme should be based on the standardisation of operating methods, identifying problems in processes and employee involvement. A Quality Facilitator was appointed in 1989 and began examining processes within the plant. Further direction for quality improvement throughout Alcoa's WA operations came early in 1989 with the establishment of a central Quality Development Department as a consulting/resource group plus a Quality Strategy Team with management representation from all WA sites to act as a steering group. Each location has its own activities which are led by part-time quality managers who are members of the Alcoa quality strategy team. At Kwinana, the maintenance manager was assigned this role.

All of these developments were somewhat piecemeal, reflecting the interconnectedness and dynamics of change. A combination of forces was pushing for TQM while the search for a focus and how to operationalise it were somewhat difficult and time consuming. Eventually, two teams were established as a pilot to demonstrate the potential benefits of TQM rather than make any grand announcements concerning a new programme. This signalled the start of quality and process improvement in an operational sense. These were known as Process Improvement Teams (PITs) and comprised a cross-section of people with relevant experience. Their composition was decided by management.

Two trouble spots within the plant (building numbers 36 and 46) were chosen for the pilot projects. These reduced plant efficiency and affected quality so they were seen as important test cases for TQM and process improvement. Successful outcomes from the PITs' efforts would hopefully be seen positively by other workers. The AWU and FCU were fully supportive of the plan at this point.

The newly formed PITs were given the task of using the methodology of process standardisation and improvement to improve operating processes. This still forms one of the guiding principles of quality improvement in Alcoa and involves identifying critical operational processes, determining if these are performing predicably and achieving their goal (in control and capable) and taking steps to improve the process if it is found to be unsatisfactory. Several quality co-ordinators would interview and discuss the relevant issues with a section of people involved in the process. The standardisation phase involves the work team developing a flow chart or standard operating procedure which maps out a particular organisational process. This serves as a guide for the team on how to operate the process. They are also responsible for collecting data on performance, and noting deviations from the procedure so that it can be evaluated over time. The second step is to identify areas of process improvement and to suggest possible actions. Team problem solving incorporates basic statistical, team problem identification and problem-solving tools including the Plan-Do-Check-Act (PDCA) cycle (see Chapter 2) which has been modified by Alcoa to incorporate eight steps.

The team from building 46 failed for several reasons, including: the lack of clearly defined goals, unrealistic team expectations, inadequate management support, lack of implementation strategy and limited training. It was resurrected in December 1989. A more structured problem-solving process was introduced and a local facilitator, rather than one from outside the area, was used. The other team reported significant improvements, with one supervisor indicating that whilst he was extremely sceptical at first, he is now a strong supporter of quality improvement teams. Overall, the outcome was positive enough and since that time a number of PITs have been established at Kwinana. They all work on projects identified by management with the focus on getting processes 'in control and capable'. The teams evaluate their own activities by defining measures of success or failure at the outset in a task statement and usually disband once this is completed. Team reports are then presented to a management quality committee consisting of senior managers from various areas of the refinery.

For the most part, teams are usually cross functional with a typical team comprising: an engineer, a team facilitator, a supervisor, a number of operators and several fitters. Team size may range from twelve to fifteen and meetings are usually held on days when members from different shifts can attend. Teams normally meet monthly for a period of three hours. Moreover, members of PITs receive four days of training, comprising two days of team processes and two days of the Alcoa eight-step quality improvement process. The training is conducted by the Quality Facilitators plus consultants from the central Quality Development Department or Quality Facilitators from other locations. On-the-job facilitation is done by any one of up to thirty-four facilitators.

Apart from the PITs, Kwinana has also introduced what it terms 'Natural Teams'. These consist of a supervisor and work crew who work in a common function and owe their origin to the industrial agreement of 1986 whereby teamwork would be implemented in order to raise productivity and efficiency. Their brief is to identify and resolve problems relating to their immediate work situation. Team members receive two days training in meetings procedures, group dynamics and individual differences in groups. Some also have a one-day course on the PDCA problem-solving and decision-making process. Where a team decides to embark on a quality improvement project, this is negotiated with area managers and solutions to problems are presented to supervisors or area managers.

The main problems encountered in establishing teams centred around the resistance of people to change, perception that it is just another passing fad, the view that problems can be solved without adopting such a long-winded process and foremen and supervisors finding it difficult to adjust their managerial styles. Some initial problems with teams arose where operators became involved in monitoring processes and recording statistics as performance and process problems. The initial fear was that this would enable supervisors and managers to monitor employee performance since people would be required to identify errors which they may be responsible for. Some saw it as a technique for increasing management surveillance of employee behaviour. One comment by a manager was that he felt that there was very little resistance from managers and supervisors, with some initial scepticism from foremen and workers. Union support has grown with time although the AWU and FCU have been particularly supportive from the outset.

In 1992 there were thirty PITs operating at Kwinana and around forty-five Natural Teams. This represents about half the workforce. Areas where supervisory and managerial resistance are likely have been left aside for the time being. Not having the full support of all unions has also limited expansion throughout the plant. This highlights the important consideration given to internal politics in introducing change. Management believe that the resisters will eventually become involved as they see the benefits of TQM. A team reward scheme was introduced in 1991 to encourage good teamwork and effective problem solving. Teams are evaluated on a number of criteria by Quality Facilitators and this permits members of teams to accumulate points which count for shopping vouchers.

The support structure for TQM consists of two main components: first, the support from group administration headquarters; and second, the location component. This enables each mine site and alumina refinery to have its own quality improvement activities which are based on specific requirements and allows for a degree of local autonomy. Overall support for TQM in Alcoa is provided by a combination of senior WA operations management, a WA Quality Strategy Team and the Quality Development Department. The Quality Strategy Team was dropped in 1991 and the WA management team took over this role.

INITIAL OPERATION: MEASURING THE OUTCOMES OF CHANGE

Advocates of TQM promise a number of qualitative and quantitative improvements including: less waste, fewer warranty jobs, reduced errors, improvements in morale, communication, teamwork and job satisfaction. In the case of Alcoa, there are two ways of measuring and evaluating quality improvements. Teams establish their own targets for individual projects which may be quantifiable savings resulting from successful team projects, safety improvements and so on. Furthermore, the number of teams in existence and the number of team projects successfully completed are important indicators in the initial stages of TQM. In the broader context, it was company policy to have all critical processes in control and capable by 1993 with a number of indicators being used to measure overall refinery performance. These include: production tonnages, safety, conversion efficiency, labour productivity and critical product characteristics. This second form of measurement provides all Alcoa sites with targets which can be monitored and also integrates TQM into strategic plans.

Whilst Alcoa has some measures of the impact of changes resulting from quality improvement, the research discovered that there was common agreement amongst those interviewed that significant positive outcomes had resulted in terms of teamwork and problem solving, which had also made work more interesting for employees. For example, a frequently expressed view was that where teams had developed solutions to problems or improvements to processes, then they would tend to display a high degree of commitment to the new procedures. In other words, the fact that employees now have an opportunity to make their work safer, easier and more interesting is bringing about a high degree of involvement in team activities.

Another benefit deriving from the quality programmes is improved communication. The project basis of PITs, in particular, enhances communication between people from differing backgrounds in the organisation, so helping to reduce departmental and divisional barriers. The team problem becomes the focal point and can break down the barriers between staff and wages employees, and reduce inter-union conflict where members of different unions work on a common problem. Another major benefit of the Quality Improvement Teams is finding solutions to problems based on measurement and statistical analysis rather than judgement based on past experience. This is particularly important in a high technology industry where guesswork can lead to extra expense and further problems. Thus, the cross-functional nature of PITs allows a diversity of perspectives to be aired and can result in significant process improvements.

A related benefit is the standardising and documenting of work processes and flows. The significance of this becomes apparent when there are up to five different shifts in the plant which operates twenty-four hours per day. If each operator on each shift does not have any standard documented procedures to guide them, then it can lead to different levels of performance and tolerance. In a process-type operation this can lead to considerable variation in performance including product quality. Whilst such operating procedures were previously present, they were usually passed on by word of mouth. Now they are being documented and flow charts constructed by the people who are doing the job.

In quantitative terms, the cost of introducing change has been measured against dollar savings, which over the first eighteen months amounted to several million dollars. Further measures of performance have been developed as part of an industrial relations agreement (Section 115 Agreement) between management and the AWU and FCU. Whilst reductions in accident rates are occurring, it would be inappropriate to attribute these entirely to TQM.

On the question of union involvement, improvement in communication was identified as an important contributing factor to the development of a more harmonious and open system of industrial relations. For example, whilst not all unions fully supported the adoption of TQM, individual union members have still been allowed to participate in team activities. Over time, those unions which were initially reluctant to get fully involved have become more interested as the employee benefits of TQM have become evident. There still remains considerable effort to increase commitment from all unions.

CONCLUSION

From the outset, management at the Kwinana refinery never adopted what could be termed a 'package' TQM programme, as offered by any number of the various TQM experts. Rather, a variety of approaches was tried. The process intent concept was foremost and was based to a large degree on its application at BHP. Moreover, the initial use of several pilot teams reduced the magnitude of change and helped to minimise potential resistance. Expanding the number of Quality Improvement Teams has taken place over a period of time and has not been introduced into areas of the plant where resistance may lead to failure. Thus a strategy of starting small scale and producing tangible outcomes to enhance wider acceptability was adopted. Hence, it is only relatively recently that quality improvement has been brought together in an integrated manner through company-produced booklets, and TQM is now being integrated with strategic plans and changes in the areas of industrial relations and human resource management in order to facilitate further cultural change. The company has found this approach necessary to reinforce progress to date and sustain motivation among employees and the process improvement teams. Senior management view the process of change as an on-going dynamic with no clear end point in the quest for a total quality organisation. This case supports the comment in Chapter 4, that the TQM change process is an odyssey.

QUESTIONS

1. Describe the operation of the Quality Improvement Team.
2. What was the difference between PITs and Natural Teams at Alcoa?
3. How can TQM outputs be measured?
4. What measurable outputs were found at Alcoa?

CHAPTER 10

Evaluating Change:
Senior Management Assessment of Service Quality at Laubman and Pank

Patrick Dawson

INTRODUCTION

Between 1989 and 1991 the Laubman and Pank Group set about establishing Total Quality Management (TQM) in the form of a Service Excellence Programme (SEP). The programme was introduced without the aid of consultants and by August 1991, the Adelaide Branch Manager was recommending that the programme be re-implemented through the use of external consultants with the aim of achieving service excellence and developing a 'sustainable competitive advantage that our competition will find difficult if not impossible to emulate'. This chapter set out to examine the evaluation phase associated with the process of establishing a total quality organisation. Attention is focused on senior management assessments of Laubman and Pank's quality initiative. A number of unforseen 'problems' in managing the process of change are also identified and the importance of training and supervision are highlighted.

COMPANY BACKGROUND

Founded in Adelaide, the Laubman and Pank Group has expanded considerably in recent years and now operates through sixty-three branches in six States and Territories of Australia (Bluntish, 1991:50). Their primary business is optometry and involves: eye examinations and prescriptions for individual customers, and the dispensing of vision aids (in contrast, an ophthalmologist is a medical practitioner specialising in the treatment of eye disease and eye surgery). Trained optometrists are employed to examine eyes and visual functions of clients and to prescribe glasses, contact lenses or other vision aids. In addition, an optometric assistant or 'Dispenser' will assist the optometrist in dispensing optometrist's spectacle prescriptions. Dispensers may also deal with prescriptions. The Laubman and Pank Group is also involved in the manufacture and supply of lenses, spectacle frames and contact lenses through its laboratories set up under the organisation Tescol Pty Ltd.

SENIOR MANAGEMENT ASSESSMENT OF SERVICE EXCELLENCE

Senior management were generally positive about the benefits of the Service Excellence Programme and did not view TQM as simply an operational technique for improving the organisation and control of work, but as a management system which comprised a series of methods for encouraging employees to identify with a common set of values and beliefs. Whilst in theory senior management recognised the broader strategic significance of TQM for developing high-trust relationships and improving customer service; there was also a tendency to focus on TQM (particularly within the laboratory setting) as a scientific methodology for identifying and establishing documented procedures and quantifiable indicators. To a certain extent this can be explained by the tendency for some senior managers to confuse quality assurance techniques with total quality management principles. Typically, however, senior management recognised and identified with the strategic significance of the cultural dimension:

> We changed such basic things as—we no longer refer to people now as 'patients'; they're 'clients'. The two hardest things we had to do was to get them to use the word 'client' and for the optometrists not to wear a white coat. The optometrists were equally as comfortable behind a white coat, and in some cases they confused those things with service excellence; whereas it wasn't. So if you didn't have a white coat to protect you, you had to be more professional with your client. The other thing was that to get the staff to believe that we really meant what we were about, we had to go over the top. We almost ran the risk of giving the shop away, because if there was a complaint, no matter what, we'd replace whatever was wrong. (Senior Management Interviews, 1991)

In changing the culture of the organisation and moving away from traditional conservatism towards a client-based culture, there have been a number of other symbolic changes. These changes have been primarily associated with dress codes and language—for example, first names are now used throughout the organisation in an attempt to break down some of the communication barriers between senior management and other employees. Employee commitment and involvement was identified as the keystone to TQM. Service excellence was viewed as a vehicle for changing the culture of an organisation and developing new work practices based on the knowledge and understanding of the people directly involved in daily operations. Senior management maintained that it is only after attitudes have been changed that you can begin to replace traditional methods with new working practices. Thus it was stressed that attitudinal change should precede major system changes:

> It's a people thing: you've got to get attitudes changed. Then the system starts to flow and you'll see new work practices; you'll see new ways of doing things; you'll see paper-work cut out; you'll see all those things happening that streamline the operation. And you'll see people saying, 'Shit! That is not good enough, because I know the expectation of this section, of my boss, is that those glasses are not good enough.' (Senior Management Interviews, 1991)

Interestingly, whilst senior managers tended to agree that service quality was also about managing cultural change, they tended to downplay other senior managers' perceptions of the importance of managing people and changing attitudes and beliefs. In part this can be explained by the history of the company, and the legacy of conservatism and tradition, which is still perceived as the major shaper of senior management attitudes. In other words, whilst there is a certain public agreement about the need for a shift in the culture of the organisation, there is also a belief that conservatism still dominates senior management decision-making. As the Chairman of the Board indicated:

> We've got to reduce that level of conservatism without going overboard, so we'll be seen as more modern, more aggressive, more commercially orientated and more up-front generally. (Senior Management Interviews, 1991)

Following the introduction of service excellence, greater authority has been devolved to front-line staff in dealing with customer concerns and complaints. For example, if a customer returns to a Laubman and Pank retail outlet with a damaged frame, then staff are now able to deal directly with the customer and have the authority to make up a new frame. Previously, these types of decisions would have had to be referred to the manager of that branch or the person responsible for the area of operation under question. As a senior manager commented:

> It was about giving the people right up-front the authority to make decisions that were going to cost us money, but if they perceived it to be to the benefit of the client that was okay. That was really, I guess, short-circuiting or bypassing a lot of the systems that we'd put in place. And really, to try and get through the concept that the extra effort was necessary to give the service that we were aiming to give. (Senior Management Interviews, 1991)

However, this change did present some problems, in that some staff were engaging in actions which went beyond the normal expectations of clients and resulted in additional costs for the company. A classic example was given of an incidence where a customer had returned a pair of spectacles for minor repairs and was due to go on holiday to Cairns. The person then went on holiday and indicated that they would be happy to pick up their glasses on their return. However, a branch employee sent a special courier up to the resort in Queensland, which cost the company $56 to deliver for the $8 repair job. In this case, it was argued that the employee had over-stepped the bounds of reasonable service and was making decisions which were creating additional and unnecessary costs. Nevertheless, in recounting this story the senior manager stressed that whenever these situations arose it was important not to be overly critical of the 'offending' employee but rather, 'counsel' them about appropriate actions and behaviours in working towards service excellence.

In terms of professional staff, there have been some problems in convincing optometrists to fully embrace the new client-based culture. For example, in discussing the question of getting optometrists to accept change, one senior manager commented that:

> This is a pretty cynical view, but most of them come out of university and they can't wait to put the white coat on and [be] seen as a doctor, and wander around sort of making noises like, 'Mmmm, mmmm', and jotting down little notes that can't be read. When we took their white coats off them and when we told them that diagrams of dissections of the eye had to come off the wall and that they actually had to communicate with the client, they thought this was dreadful. There was such a reaction. (Senior Management Interviews, 1991)

Another branch level 'problem' arose in cases where staff began using the service excellence programme to hide the real causes for refunds:

Quite often the reason for the refund that they might write down is 'service excellence'—nothing more, nothing less, just 'service excellence.' And that's a real problem, because (a) you don't know whether or not it really is service excellence or someone just covering their backside; and (b) it hides the real cause. It shows the symptoms but it doesn't show what the cause is, and unless you know what the cause is you can't do anything about it. (Senior Management Interviews, 1991)

In short, the introduction of service excellence to the retail outlets has taken a number of years and is still defined as being in its early stages of adoption. Senior management identified the need to maintain senior management support over a long period of time, and the need to invest adequate funds to ensure that the new service philosophy is further developed and refined. The senior management group also indicated that the focus on customer–supplier relations and the greater emphasis being placed on the supply of quality products had created some conflict between manufacturing and retail personnel:

You had a set of people who were saying, 'These people are not supporting us in our desire to provide this better service and service excellence to the front line.' So it creates a lot of internal stress and you've then got to look at your whole system, because inevitably they're wanting, and a lot of ours were and still are, although we keep working at them, in being able to provide the back-up. (Senior Management Interviews, 1991)

Another 'obstacle' which has emerged has been middle managerial and supervisory resistance to change. In the view of one senior manager, this was consequent of the traditional emphasis placed on technical knowledge as the authority base for supervisors. As a result, laboratory supervisors were well placed for dealing with contingencies and directing staff in the day-to-day control of service operations. However, by placing greater emphasis on the knowledge of operative staff in correcting and adapting process operations, the traditional authority base of the supervisor has been undermined. Although attempts are now being made to redefine the function of middle management, not enough attention has been given to this problem and supervisory resistance has resulted:

We've had a philosophy of our managers still retaining a large chunk of technical work, and when they've got a bit of free time from that, managing the staff. Very, very slowly we're wearing that away, saying that we want professional managers. We want a laboratory manager who needs to know a bit about lenses and the technical side but, above all else, his major skills have to be in people management: to be able to motivate leading hands and so forth. (Senior Management Interviews, 1991)

Consequently, there is a need to redefine supervision and make the expectations of the position clear not only to supervisors, but also, to operative staff and the senior management group.

Training was identified as a key ingredient to the successful introduction of a Service Excellence Programme and it was suggested that this is often an area which can be overlooked. On this issue, the Chief Executive Officer indicated a requirement for customised training packages which would fulfil the needs of different groups (geographically, demographically and occupationally):

Different people in different regions and different degrees of sophisticated markets: different age groups, demographics, income levels, require subtle differences in the way that they're approached. That means that the staff residing and working in those places need to have that bias built into their training. So it's not just a matter of 12 disciples rushing out into the scrub to give the word. So I guess they're the things that I've found to be interesting challenges because they're difficult to measure whether you're doing it right or whether you're doing it wrong.(Senior Management Interviews, 1991)

Supervision and training were therefore seen as major factors which could facilitate or inhibit the successful management of TQM. As the Chairman of the Board indicated:

Unless it works at the level immediately above the operator level it isn't going to work at all; it doesn't matter what senior management do. I think that's a lesson well learned. (Senior Management Interviews, 1991)

In evaluating how successful the introduction of the Service Excellence Programme has been in Laubman and Pank, the senior management group argued that the programme had proven more successful in some areas than others, and that the programme was still in its 'infancy'. One senior manager, in assessing the arguments for and against TQM, argued that:

The positive side is that we have given people better signposts, and they can see themselves moving in the right direction. A number of them get a fairly big kick out of it. The down side is really the other

> side of the coin: frustration if something isn't done right; disappointment, wondering whether you're the only one who's really trying to do things right or whether you're not, whether anybody really cares, or whether anybody really notices you. (Senior Management Interviews, 1991)

Finally, in evaluating how close the organisation is to fully embracing a new service quality culture, the Managing Director of Laubman and Pank responded:

> I reckon half-way. Certainly, we've got significant improvements: there's no doubt about that—big improvements. But I think I'd be kidding myself if I said we were there. I know we're not there, because I'm out and around the branches and with our people all the time, and I constantly see areas where…we're falling well short of what we want to be doing. But I do think we're a lot better than we were two years ago. So we've taken a quantum leap forward, and I reckon we're probably half-way there. (Senior Management Interviews, 1991)

CONCLUSION: AN ASSESSMENT OF TQM IN THE LAUBMAN AND PANK GROUP

In the views of senior management, the Laubman and Pank Group have commenced an important journey which requires planning, evaluation and revision to meet the changing conditions associated with operating in a rapidly changing business market environment. They firmly believe that the language and culture of an organisation is closely aligned with the attitudes and behaviour of staff. Consequently, in managing the transition towards a client-based culture, the 'medical' white coat has been replaced and it is now company policy to refer to customers as 'clients' rather than 'patients' (although in practice the word 'patient' was still extensively used, highlighting how expected shifts in attitudes have not been as extensive as originally envisaged).

On the question of the extent to which Laubman and Pank have established a total quality organisation, senior management assessments varied. Whilst there was general agreement that TQM programmes—which set out to achieve a transformational change in attitudes, behaviours and working practices—will take a number of years, some claimed they were close to achieving these objectives whilst others felt that they were still in the early stages of change. These different assessments of change also reflect the different management attitudes towards the effects of business development and growth on the traditional belief and value systems rooted in Laubman and Pank as a 'family business'. For example, whilst some senior managers felt 'threatened' by the relinquishing of traditional values which could no longer keep pace with the exigencies of competitive business market developments, others believed that TQM provided an opportunity for reuniting an increasingly disparate organisation (as a result of rapid expansion) into a more integrated business exhibiting a common set of beliefs and values. Moreover, the development of a culture based on employee involvement and company identification was seen to support the continuation (and re-emergence) of belief systems associated with the historically smaller optometric operation of Laubman and Pank pre-1980. In other words, the collaborative 'family business' atmosphere could be created and maintained within a larger and more geographically dispersed optometric business of the 1990s. Unlike previous quality schemes, this change programme centred on the development of a culture which would act to unify and integrate employees throughout the Laubman and Pank Group. As such, considerable attention has been given to evaluating the programme and deciding on the next phase in the process of establishing a total quality organisation.

In terms of the processual framework for understanding TQM, developed in Chapter 4, evaluation and appraisal is an important process in the 'successful' management of change. In the case of TQM, the route to change is rarely straightforward and often reflects the complex and unforeseen nature of large-scale change programmes (the case which follows illustrates this through presenting an overview of the process of managing change, from the conception of the need to change to evaluation and re-implementation). In Laubman and Pank, a considerable amount of time and money has been given to transforming belief systems within the organisation from those based on traditional conservatism towards a more client-based organisational culture.

QUESTIONS

1 Why is change resisted? What reasons are given to explain the resistance to TQM changes in this case?

2 Discuss whether, and the degree to which, different employee assessments of change reflect different attitudes towards the traditional belief and value system of Laubman and Pank?

3 Examine the TQM decision-making process and evaluate its strengths and weaknesses.

4 To what extent do the experiences of TQM at Laubman and Pank (service and manufacturing company) compare and contrast with those of the State Bank (service company) and Tecpak Industries (manufacturing company)?

5 What is cultural change? Explain the role of symbols in cultural consciousness.

CHAPTER 11

The Process and Politics of Change at Vicbank

Cameron Allan

INTRODUCTION

The implementation of TQM at Vicbank (a pseudonym is used in this case) involved three distinct periods and provides a clear illustration of the political nature and non-linearity of organisational change. Vicbank recognised that in a highly competitive market context, they would have to constantly strive to improve their internal efficiency if they were to sustain their competitive advantage. Vicbank identified that the type of change required was a system of continual improvement. This remained the overriding objective over the entire change period which can be divided into three periods.

To achieve their objective in the first period, Vicbank selected TQM as an on-going method of process improvement and brought in outside consultants to set them on the path to organisational change. But the implementation of TQM was never straightforward. Although adopted successfully in some areas of the organisation, the TQM programme had minimal impact in other areas. The central difficulty stemmed from the character and politics of middle management resistance. In the second period, senior managers revised their implementation strategy and developed their own novel solutions to gain management commitment through cultural change. These experiments also failed to secure total management commitment to the change process. In the third period, Vicbank brought in outside expertise to help them develop a clear sense of direction and provide them with a step-by-step improvement methodology.

COMPANY BACKGROUND

Vicbank was originally a building society established in 1959 as the Renown Building Society (RBS—another pseudonym used to hide the identity of the company). Like other building societies, RBS offered only a narrow range of financial products, such as home loans and small personal loans, but did not compete with banks for credit and commercial services. Through the 1960s and early 1970s the organisation grew slowly, having just 200 staff in 1974. But in the late 1970s and early 1980s the organisation actively sought to expand its market share through media advertising and the expansion of its branch network. By 1986 the organisation had assets of $1 billion and had developed an excellent reputation in what had become a highly competitive market.

Associated with the growth of the organisation was an increase in the firm's percentage of operating expenses. This was predominantly due to the wide geographic dispersion of the organisation's branch network in the Victorian country areas. As a result, the company was aware of the need to improve its effectiveness and competitiveness by reducing costs where ever possible. Although there was a clear understanding of the need for change at the senior level, the issue to be resolved was how to make the necessary changes.

THE CONCEPTION OF A NEED FOR TQM

Traditionally, the organisation sought to control overhead costs through an annual cost reduction exercise. But some managers were unhappy with this approach and felt that there had to be 'a better way, than every year going through a cost cutting exercise'. It was thought that there would have to be a more systematic and structured approach to cost control. In 1986 the organisation became aware of the systematic TQM approach to cost reduction being applied in Australia. TQM, or Total Quality Control (TQC) as it was then called, was promoted by an Australian TQM consulting group which advocated the adoption of quality improvement teams using statistical tools to identify and rectify inefficient work systems.

To evaluate TQM, a pilot TQM project was established. Two managers attended an external TQM training course and put together a TQM team to examine a known inefficient accounting process: monthly reporting. This project proved highly successful by reducing the production of monthly reports from thirteen days to five days. With the success of this project, it was thought the TQM methodology might profitably be introduced into other areas of the organisation.

At the same time in 1986, the organisation also decided to enlist the services of a large accounting group to examine the internal efficiency of the firm's operation to identify possible areas of improvement. The accounting group spent several weeks examining the firm's operation and used their 'overhead cost management' approach to identify and quantify the potential cost and benefits of achieving cost reductions. The final report, in October 1986, suggested that large savings could be made in key problem areas in the building society.

PERIOD I: THE PROCESS OF ESTABLISHING TQM

In late 1986 it was decided to introduce TQM throughout the entire organisation. TQM was attractive because it offered the building society the opportunity to use their own staff in the TQM methodology of continuous improvement. The overhead cost management study, though, had proved extremely useful because it had identified a number of areas were improvements could be made. This provided the company with a number of clearly identified problem areas that could be tackled through the TQM methodology. As a senior executive said:

> What appeals to me about the quality process…was that it was a way for cost saving by getting people involved to fix the process up…so if you get the process right you are going to start to save money. (Executive Interview, 1991)

As part of the implementation strategy, a consultant was contracted to train and acquaint all levels of management with the tools and philosophy of TQM in early 1987. These managers in turn were expected to support their staff to participate in TQM improvement teams to rectify the organisational inefficiencies identified in the overhead cost management report. In addition, one full-time person was appointed to be responsible for overseeing and supporting TQM implementation. This person was given the title of Manager, Organisational Development and was expected to provide training and guidance to the TQM teams. It was hoped that once staff had been equipped with the tools and philosophy of TQM, they would be able to use them to identify, analyse and correct inefficient work systems on an on-going basis.

In the implementation stage, the outside TQM consultants ran a series of small workshops for managers, commencing with the most senior team and then progressively moving through to the lower levels of management. These sessions normally took half a day and provided managers with an overview of Deming's version of TQM. Managers were introduced to the origins of the TQM concepts, the major TQM tools and how they might be applied, as well as examples of how they had been successfully used in other companies. The Manager, Organisational Development, read widely on TQM and actively promoted the use of TQM throughout the organisation.

The initial reception of TQM was mixed. A small number of managers, mostly in administrative areas, readily adopted the ideas and actively encouraged their staff to establish TQM improvement teams and to improve inefficient work systems. Many successful projects were run, some producing some quite considerable savings. In most other areas, TQM was either half-heartedly adopted or not implemented at all. At one level, the resistance to TQM expressed the deeply held view of many that this type of change was not necessary as the organisation had been preforming reasonably well. At another level though, a lot of resistance was directed towards the concept of TQM itself. Many managers were not impressed with the TQM training sessions and formed the view that TQM was superficial and of no relevance to their own functional areas. Part of the difficulty lay with the consultant's method of presentation, which was very blunt and forthright and based on extensive manufacturing rather than service-oriented examples. Additional problems arose because many managers felt that their departments were already overworked and simply did not have the time to do TQM projects. This was further hampered by the short deadlines many departments had to work to, which meant that even though managers and staff were willing to adopt TQM methodology, short-term business needs dictated otherwise.

The Routine Operation of TQM

Only in a very limited number of areas in the organisation could it be said that the implementation of TQM had become a routine operation. Even in these areas, the TQM methodology was used progressively less often. This was due to the practice of general staff undertaking TQM activities in addition to their normal duties. Time spent on TQM projects had to be made up later, normally as overtime. The enthusiasm of general staff soon waned, with the exception of few dedicated personnel who continued to partake in TQM improvement projects up until the end of 1991.

In an effort to bolster the implementation of TQM, more staff were allocated to the Manager, Organisational Development, in early 1988 in the form of one full-time and four part-time support officers. With the addition of these staff the Organisation Development Unit was renamed the Quality Support

Centre. These additional staff, it was hoped, would be able to encourage and promote the diffusion of TQM in the organisation. Despite these efforts, though, the TQM initiative was being overtaken by other developments.

A REAPPRAISAL OF TQM

In the mid-1980s, the Federal government de-regulated the banking industry, allowing limited numbers of overseas banks to compete in Australia and making it easier for building societies to become banks. RBS welcomed the opportunity to change to bank status and become incorporated as 'Vicbank' in July 1988. Transition to bank status was high on the corporate agenda and TQM tended to get lost in the multitude of other organisational changes happening at this time.

From mid-1988 to mid-1989, there was a gradual re-evaluation of the successes and failures of the TQM change process. It was recognised that despite the good progress that had been made in a few areas of the organisation, overall the TQM change programme had not been implemented in the way it was hoped for. It was recognised that many managers felt that they had neither the time nor inclination to pursue the TQM initiative. This was clearly demonstrated in June 1988 when a survey of managers was conducted to ascertain their views on TQM. Only 50 per cent responded and, of those that did, there was a clear lack of commitment to TQM.

The organisation, at this stage, began to realise that many other organisations were experiencing similar difficulties in implementing TQM through their contact with other TQM organisations. Vicbank staff attended TQM conferences, seminars and discussion groups, and began to realise that management resistance to TQM was commonplace. Re-appraising their progress to date, Vicbank concluded that they had focused too heavily on statistical process improvement and not placed enough emphasis on cultural change to gain management commitment. Having reached the conclusion that the organisation needed to introduce some form of cultural change it was not at all clear how this might be done.

PERIOD II: ORGANISATIONAL CULTURE AS THE PATHWAY TO SUCCESSFUL TQM

Vicbank wished to institute some form of cultural change but were unaware of any clear models or options to adopt. As a result they experimented with some of their own ideas, which were first outlined in a report given to the Corporate Planning Conference in late 1989 by the manager of the Quality Support Centre. The report suggested that the failure to implement TQM successfully was due to a lack of management commitment to a culture of quality improvement. Part of the difficult lay with the Quality Support Centre which had taken too strong a role in implementing TQM, such that many managers felt little ownership for TQM. To rectify this problem, the report proposed a plan to implement a new form of TQM based on cultural change. This plan suggested that TQM, or Service Quality as it was termed, be made the single overriding corporate mission. This would, it was hoped, give TQM a higher organisational profile and demonstrate to everyone in the organisation that senior managers were committed to the concept. Following this, it was proposed that the concept of Service Quality needed to be defined in a way that people could readily understand. The definition offered in the report contained the following dimensions of Service Quality: tangibles, reliability, responsibility, assurance and empathy. These dimensions, it was argued, break down the corporate strategy of Service Quality into something that was meaningful to all and to communicate these dimensions was to communicate the corporate strategy. The next proposal was to cascade this message throughout the organisation so that everyone was aware of the corporate mission and the importance it held for senior managers.

In addition to communicating the new corporate strategy, though, the report made the novel suggestion of recommending that the HRM system be used to monitor and ensure that Service Quality was being adopted. To ensure compliance with this new cultural dimension of Service Quality, the report suggested, it would be necessary to develop some basic 'quality standards' which would be included in job description and monitored as part of the firm's existing performance evaluation system. In this way it would be possible to ensure that individuals were actively pursuing Service Quality by monitoring performance and adjusting the reward system accordingly. To co-ordinate the overall implementation of this revised TQM strategy, it was recommended that a Service Quality Council be formed.

The senior management team agreed with the report's overall assessment but elected to proceed with only some of the recommendations. The corporate plan was altered to make the pursuit of Service Quality the single corporate mission. It was also accepted that cultural and attitudinal change were essential and needed to be linked to the performance evaluation system. This is illustrated in the Managing Director's own words:

> If you keep doing one-off projects you are not going to get the culture going right through. It has got to be a total push all the way through the whole organisation to get the feeling and philosophy right through. A special project gets done and then gets

dropped...They [staff] see it as finished then and not ongoing...It really gets back to the attitude of the people involved; we have got to convince them that it is the way to go; that it will impact on their own performance in their own areas, and it will be of benefit of them in their performance appraisals.

But the senior executive team did not agree, though, that it was necessary to form a Service Quality Council to implement the new TQM strategy. It was felt that the responsibility should lie with individual managers and not with an external 'policing' body. Instead, the executive team agreed to establish a short-term steering committee which would develop a strategy to communicate the new corporate mission and develop the basic 'quality standards' to be included into job descriptions.

The steering committee, made up of a group of senior and middle managers, was set up in late 1989 and developed a series of basic 'quality standards' to be included in all job descriptions. There was some difficulty attempting to define standards that would be relevant to all staff, so the committee chose a series of the most basic standards, such as answering the phone within three rings, and left the development of more pertinent individual standards to each manager in consultation with their own staff. The committee also developed a glossy brochure containing the new Service Quality corporate mission statement and a message about the new quality standards. Following this, the committee disbanded.

At the same time, considerable discussion was taking place about the role of the Quality Support Centre in this new period. Given that it was felt that the Centre had taken too much of the responsibility away from individual managers to implement TQM on the first occasion, it was decided that the Centre should be disbanded with its staff allocated to specific areas in the bank to directly assist managers and staff with their TQM activities. The role of the Quality Support Officers would be to not just assist in TQM improvement projects but to impart the philosophy of SQ and to assist areas in formulating relevant quality standards to be built into job descriptions. In effect, though, all but one of the Quality Support Centre staff members found other jobs elsewhere in the organisation.

The responsibility for implementing the new policy of incorporating quality standards into job description lay with a senior executive who wrote to the senior managers in early 1990 instructing them to relay the policy decision 'down-the-line'. Whilst senior managers were clearly aware of the policy, in practice, little was achieved. Few areas attempted to implement these changes. Similarly, there was no formal implementation strategy for the Service Quality brochure. Though produced, the brochure was never distributed.

However, some areas did attempt to incorporate the quality standards into job descriptions. This occurred mainly in areas where Quality Support

Centre staff had been providing assistance. This new initiative at no point reached the stage of routine operation. Whilst the objective of the new TQM strategy was to gain management commitment to a culture of Service Quality, this had not been achieved. So in September 1990, senior managers sought to revitalise the Service Quality strategy by enlisting the services of outside TQM consultants.

PERIOD III: THE USE OF CONSULTANTS IN THE RE-ESTABLISHMENT OF TQM

In this third period, the organisation persisted with TQM because it felt that TQM offered a viable mechanism to improve organisational efficiency. The main difficulty confronted was finding a satisfactory method of implementing it. In their search for a suitable implementation strategy, the organisation began to rely increasingly on the advice of external consultants. The first of these consultants was from a local university.

The objective of the seminar with the TQM university consultants was to refocus the TQM effort and to enlist the support of managers to the change process. The seminar was held in September 1990 with all senior managers and addressed some of the basis concepts of TQM and the importance of management commitment to the process of cultural change. A questionnaire was completed by all those who attended the seminar which indicated that although it was agreed that TQM was important to the success of the organisation, senior management were not actively involved in improvement activities nor publicly demonstrating their commitment to TQM. Moreover it was felt that TQM had not been properly resourced, managed or co-ordinated. The seminar concluded with managers giving their commitment to the concept of TQM and the following objectives being set: first, to have Vicbank Service Quality Standards communicated in a manner to give common understanding to all levels, interpreted at all levels and reflected and quantified in job descriptions and personal action plans and performance review process; and second, to establish a process to ensure maintenance of Vicbank Service Quality Standards.

To assist the implementation of these objectives, the steering committee was re-convened to develop a strategy and a timetable to co-ordinate further implementation of TQM and acceptance of appropriate standards. One of the central issues debated by the steering committee was whether the Service Quality brochure should be communicated to staff through a series of workshops or through a cascading process. The cascading process tended to be favoured (each level of management demonstrating their commitment to the level below), but it was suggested that if the organisation was going to go to the expense of communicating the Service Quality message, then it would be wise to employ a communication expert to advise them of the best method of doing so. A communication consultant was contracted for the job.

The communication consultant met with the steering committee several times in early 1991. Over the course of these discussions a number of issues emerged as potential problems for an effective communication strategy: Was the organisation committed to Service Quality? Did lower levels of management possess the facilitation and leadership skills to effectively communicate and cascade the Service Quality brochure? How would the quality standards be set, monitored and built into the performance appraisal and action planning system? Were staff likely to be receptive to Service Quality? In effect, the steering committee was questioning the organisation's ability and commitment to effectively implement the Service Quality change programme.

The outcome of these discussions was a decision to survey the views of staff members before proceeding any further with the dissemination of Service Quality. A TQM staff survey, it was thought, would give management a clear view of how extensively TQM ideas had been accepted in the organisation as well as highlighting any problem areas that would need to be addressed.

The communication consultant was given the task of locating, assessing and recommending a TQM survey to the company. The consultant recommended that a pre-prepared survey offered by an American TQM company be used. Vicbank accepted this recommendation and the survey was administered to all staff March 1991. The completed surveys were then sent to the USA and the results were returned to Vicbank in May.

The results of the survey were presented to the entire management team by the communication expert in May. The main findings indicated that Vicbank's performance was similar to other American banks. No better or no worse. Staff were well aware of TQM but did not rate the bank's performance on TQM highly. Unfortunately, the TQM survey also contained an enormous amount of detail, which after several hours of discussion began to confuse the managers:

> We all ended up totally confused, because there was a lot of data, a **lot** of data. And as people got to the end of the day and got a bit tired a bit of rationalising went on. 'maybe they didn't really answer it the right way'…'maybe they answered the way we wanted to hear it'…'maybe that's not what they really meant'…'we probably really haven't got a problem after all'…that sort of stuff…The key outcome was that we were confused. (Executive Interview, 1991)

Given the complexity and ambiguity of the survey and the confusion the results created, it was decided that the American TQM consultant who had designed the survey be brought out to help the organisation interpret or 'get inside' the survey results. There was a strong feeling among the steering committee that the management team really need to 'get their collective heads together' before they could proceed any further. Also, it was decided that in addition to interpreting the survey results the American TQM consultant would also be able to assist the organisation to translate that information into a Strategic Quality Plan.

Immediately following the May 1991 presentation of the survey results, the senior management team elected to appoint a senior executive to the position of Executive Manager of Quality/Special Projects. The Quality Support Centre was then reformed with several of the previous staff returning to the Centre. This was a clear indication that more resources were being put into the revitalised TQM effort.

At the same time the senior executives also elected to bring in a large accounting firm to review the effectiveness of the company's internal operation. As was the case in 1986, the organisation's ratio of operating costs was still in excess of their major competitors and of concern to senior executives. Similar to the overhead cost management study undertaken in 1986, the organisation had elected to have an external consulting group analyse the firm's operations and make recommendations as to how competitiveness could be improved. The accounting review team spent several weeks with the organisation and submitted a report to Vicbank just prior to the arrival of the American TQM consultant. The report highlighted several areas where the firm could make improvements.

In October, the American TQM consultant spent a week with all levels of the management team, interpreting the survey results and providing the organisation with an overall quality strategic plan and implementation process. The consultant's interpretation of the survey results indicated that the organisation was reasonably effective but no more or less than other firms. To implement TQM, the consultant recommended the following strategic plan be adopted to address the improvement possibilities identified in the recently completed internal review.

First, the consultant recommended the formation of a Quality Council, including all senior executives, to oversee the implementation and strategic direction of TQM in the organisation. Second, the formation of Process Action Teams (PATs) was recommended. The PATs were permanent fixtures with a role to continually review and develop strategic TQM activities as directed by the Quality Council. Each PAT was chaired by a senior executive who selected their own teams, allocated functions to each participant, set objectives, timelines, and allocated resources. The methodology to be used by these teams to identify improvement opportunities was called the Quality

Improvement Process (QIP). QIP was a management tool which consisted of a series of workbooks which took the user through a systematic methodology to identify problems and opportunities for improvement. Essentially, the role of these PAT teams was to identify the problems to be solved by lower level problem solving teams.

Third, it was recommended that below the PATs two types of lower level problem-solving teams be formed: cross-functional Corrective Action Teams (CATs) and intra-functional Problem Solving Teams (PSTs). These teams would be set up at the behest of managers, PATs or the Quality Council to solve small work problems. In most cases though, it was anticipated that these teams would be used to address sub-projects identified by PATs. CATs and PSTs would be managed: participants would be nominated, objectives, guidelines, timelines, training, resources would be specified in advance by managers or PATs. The methodology to be used by PATs and PSTs was called Quality Basics which consisted of a series of workbooks which took the users through the main TQM statistical tools for problem solving.

In late 1991, Vicbank adopted these recommendations and put in place a formal TQM strategic plan which had a clearly defined structure, levels of responsibility and a methodology for improvement. The advantage of this newly adopted approach was that managers had a central role to play in the improvement process with each one of them making a personal commitment to support TQM (although, at the time of writing, the effectiveness of this new approach is not known).

CONCLUSION: THE POLITICS AND PROCESS OF MANAGING CHANGE

This case demonstrates how the introduction of TQM can become a complex political process marked by a series of critical junctures at which important decisions that shape the pace and pattern of change are made. Vicbank recognised the need to change, identified TQM as the appropriate mechanism for change, but struggled with the implementation. When the implementation process failed, the organisation attempted to identify the weaknesses and to build strategies to overcome them. A central element of this revised strategy was a recognition of the importance of cultural change to secure managerial commitment to the change process. Despite the recognition of the need to bring about cultural change, the organisation was unaware of an effective manner in which to achieve it. As a result, they were constantly evaluating and re-appraising their implementation strategy to achieve their objective of continual improvement. The outstanding feature of this case is the determination of Vicbank managers to persist in the face of opposition and to continually adapt the implementation strategy in the light of emerging contingencies.

The case also illustrates that organisational change is dynamic and non-linear. The organisation recognised the need for change and proceeded with implementation in what appeared as the most fruitful manner available at the time. As successive difficulties arose, the organisation evaluated and re-appraised the progress to date, assessed new options and implemented new strategies to overcome resistance and bring about organisational change. This cycle of experimentation and revision demonstrates that the pathway to organisational change cannot be represented by a straight line or Roman road but rather, is a complex, temporal and iterative process. The outcomes of and the barriers to change are never fully known at the outset. The change process will always involve the unanticipated. Only in the act of attempting change do these problems and their potential solutions become manifest.

QUESTIONS

1. Describe the history of the central staff group responsible for TQM. Why did their activities change?

2. Why is implementation of change strategy not straightforward?

3. What techniques were used at Vicbank to assess progress? Suggest new strategies for TQM.

4. Evaluate the utility of a processual approach for examining the management of organisational transitions.

CHAPTER 12

The Context and Substance of Change: the Different Experience of TQM at Two Plants Within Pirelli Cables Australia Limited

Patrick Dawson

INTRODUCTION

The preceding case studies have examined a range of issues and themes surrounding TQM at different timeframes during the process of establishing a total quality organisation, with the case of Vicbank illustrating the utility of a processual approach for analysing change. In the case reported here, it is shown how a similar approach to TQM and its implementation may lead to very different employee experiences of change within physically adjacent plants located on the same manufacturing site. The importance of local contextual factors is highlighted and it is argued that the substance of TQM, or its philosophy and principles, may not be able to accommodate cultural diversity on the shopfloor. In the case of Pirelli, for example, factors such as gender, ethnicity and language are all shown to be important elements which have not been adequately taken into account in consultant packages or descriptive guidelines on the successful introduction of TQM. The case concludes with a critical discussion of the comparative lessons to be learnt from the Pirelli experience.

COMPANY BACKGROUND

In March 1989, Pirelli embarked on the process of establishing a TQM programme in their Australian operations. A steering committee was formed from Pirelli Cables Australia Limited (PCAL) senior executives, who were trained by Blakemore Consulting in the principles and philosophy of TQM. The Managing Director acted as the Chairman of the Steering Committee, and other key personnel were trained as facilitators in preparation for project team formation. One of the major strategic objectives of TQM was to bring about a 'culture of change' and initiate a shift in employee attitudes towards greater involvement and the development of high-trust relationships.

PCAL consists of three manufacturing sites and eleven sales branches (including one in New Zealand). The Minto site, the newest plant, is located in an outer southern suburb of Sydney and specialises in power and building wire cables. The oldest plant is at Dee Why, a northern Sydney suburb, where production operations centre on the manufacture of telephone cables. Two plants are located in South Australia at the Adelaide manufacturing site at Camden Park, this operation produces plug and cord sets for the automotive and white goods market (approximately 15 per cent of the plug and cord sets are exported—mostly to Asia—fitted to electrical appliances and then imported back into Australia (Adams, 1990:29)).

In the case study reported here, shopfloor responses to change have been drawn from interview material collected from two distinct and physically separate plants in Adelaide. There are considerable differences between the personnel, equipment and production processes used at the cable manufacturing plant and those employed at the cable processing plant.

The Cable Manufacturing Plant (CMP) comprises comparatively complex equipment for the manufacture of single and multi-core flexible cables. The extrusion equipment is old and therefore requires routine maintenance, the operators are predominantly male (46 of the 47 employees) and the equipment is operated on a three-shift basis.

In contrast, the Cable Processing Plant (CPP) is predominantly female (90 of the 106 employees) and is based largely around labour-intensive, repetitive manual processing operations. This plant processes cable manufactured by the cable plant in order to service customer requirements (for example, in the type of plug and length of cable). However, Pirelli Cables has little worldwide expertise in the area of processing (cable manufacturing predominates) and, consequently, the cable processing plant is largely isolated from the other Australian manufacturing operations.

THE SHOPFLOOR EXPERIENCE OF TQM IN CABLE PROCESSING

The introduction of TQM in the Cable Processing Plant (CPP) was met with a certain degree of scepticism by employees. They were uncertain as to the nature of the programme, concerned about the potential effects on the work process, and doubtful about claims for greater employee involvement. Local management advocated that TQM would enable shopfloor personnel to get involved in operational decision-making through group problem-solving meetings. The intention was to get employees with detailed knowledge of shopfloor operations to contribute to, and be part of, employee teams which would tackle shopfloor problems in order to improve the work process and increase the efficiency of shopfloor production. In the words of a line supervisor:

> When they first introduced us to it, like in many places, you don't want change, so you don't want it and everyone was very negative. Then we went to the meetings and brainstorming sessions. It does work. I am on a TQM committee and we do the ARTOS (cutting and stripping machine). We do not get the breakdowns now that we used to have. It has helped people, because they know that they can go to management and ask for anything to do with their jobs. Almost always they get it. If it costs a lot of money, not so much so, but the management do try. (Supervisor, 1991)

Operatives also indicated that whilst they were initially doubtful about the purpose of TQM, they now saw TQM as a positive development:

> I was asked to go on a committee, which I wasn't too keen on at first. I couldn't see why I should go and my supervisor didn't have to, to be quite honest. I thought he was off-loading something on to me. That is the truth. (Shopfloor Interviews, 1991)

Employees who had been involved in TQM activities claimed that TQM was of benefit both to shopfloor personnel and to the company as a whole. The benefits to employees were in the possibility of improving working conditions and reducing some of the stress and frustration associated with rework caused by minor problems; the potential advantage for the company was in increased efficiency rates and reduced scrap. TQM was also seen to have facilitated greater communication between shopfloor personnel through improving employee understanding of the processes involved in manufacturing. For example, there is now a greater willingness among operators to help each other out if there are problems in particular areas. The view that there has been a movement towards teamwork was supported by the union representative in the cable processing plant, who, in describing the work process noted that:

> You start off at the moulding process and then it comes to our line. Because it goes through stages, everyone has to do their bit before it

comes to the end. It is a team that works on the line. If something isn't right, someone will come and say that it is a little bit too long, and ask for it to be shortened. (Shop Steward, 1991)

In part, the acceptance of TQM in CPP can be explained by the success of the original TQM team, which looked at the problem of downtime with the cable cutting and stripping machines (known as the ARTOS TQM). In the view of those interviewed, the ARTOS TQM was instrumental in winning over shopfloor employees to the benefits of TQM. For example, a piece of internal correspondence from the production manager to all TQM teams in December 1990 highlighted the success of the ARTOS TQM. The document outlined the paid efficiencies for the last eighteen weeks (which averaged out at 103 per cent compared with 65 per cent for the first ten weeks of TQM) and then set about thanking individual team members for the various contributions, concluding with a: 'Thanks to all the team, your efforts and ideas is what TQM is all about'. This support and attention from management has further served to boost the morale in CPP and, in particular, the benefits of TQM to the team members. These individuals in turn influence the views of other operators on the shopfloor:

People communicate. Before, they didn't say what was going wrong and you would look at their sheets and ask them what happened, and they wouldn't really say what was wrong. They thought it would reflect on them if they had a problem, rather than complain or say anything, they would put up with it. Everything is a lot more open than it was before. (Shopfloor Interviews, 1991)

Although teamwork remains largely a function of the group-problem solving activities associated with TQM (work is still organised largely on a one-operator-per-machine basis and there is a set rate for each machine which operators are expected to meet), interviewees argued that improved inter-personal communication on the shopfloor and the greater collaboration between employees in helping each other out, does signify the movement away from individual-based machine-oriented work regimes, to a work process based on more open communication and greater group effort.

In evaluating the effects of TQM on shopfloor operations, one operator commented that:

Before TQM started we didn't have things like the machines running through our lunch break and things like that. Now we keep the machines running right through. They are making more plugs now...[Our supervisor] looks after us a lot too. She sticks by us. If we have problems, she will be there to help us out...It is a combination of things. Before they would let things slide. Now people have got to do things right the first time. Now we can explain and give them [management] our views on what the problems are. Now they listen and involve us and the staff on the floor know what is going on. Before they [management] didn't do that. (Shopfloor Interviews, 1991)

On being asked to describe the union view on TQM the shop steward of the National Union of Workers (NUW) indicated that there had been no union involvement and that there had been no involvement by the various shop stewards other than being members on some of the TQM teams. In short, the evaluation of TQM by supervisors, operators and union representatives were all favourable and supportive of the more general move towards greater teamwork and collaboration on the shopfloor.

THE SHOPFLOOR EXPERIENCE OF TQM IN CABLE MANUFACTURING

The experience of TQM in the Cable Manufacturing Plant (CMP) contrasts in a number of significant ways with that of the Cable Processing Plant (CPP). First, whilst there was general support for the philosophy of TQM, criticisms were levelled at the way in which it was being used and 'abused' within CMP. Second, there was a greater discrepancy between line supervisor's views of change and the attitudes and perceptions of machine operators. Third, sectional and inter-personal conflicts were identified as major obstacles to collaborative teamwork and the development of less adversarial systems of operation. Finally, the local management team and line supervisors were viewed as a major problem impeding the successful introduction of TQM. As one operative commented:

TQM here will never take off unless management changes their attitude. They have to listen to the people on the floor. When we ask for something to be done, it has to be done. We had a problem out there [shopfloor] on 90% of the machines and management didn't want to know about it. It actually took an electrician 5 minutes to fix all the machines and for 2 years we were asking for it to be fixed. The company somehow finally got the message and it was fixed (Shopfloor Interviews, 1991)

The problems of poor management were also highlighted by operators in the areas of the setting up and running of TQM groups and in the general management of the plant. Whilst there were a number of responses which indicated considerable dissatisfaction with the way operations and employees were being managed, all respondents showed a clear understanding of the general philosophy of TQM and provided positive evaluations of the potential value of these techniques in allowing employees to help identify ways to improve efficiencies on the shopfloor:

> TQM is a fantastic idea if it is managed properly. If we had TQM managed properly, within six months we could double our production easily. (Shopfloor Interviews, 1991)

During the time of the shopfloor interviews the industry was experiencing a major recession and a number of employees had recently been retrenched at the Adelaide site. Consequently, there was considerable shopfloor support for changes which could potentially improve the efficiency of operations, make the company more competitive and secure future job opportunities. In some cases, the increasing pressures associated with working under 'poor management' combined with the threat of unemployment had led to very negative attitudes to work.

There was a general feeling among shopfloor employees that action should be taken to make Pirelli Adelaide more profitable so that customers could be retained and the further retrenchment of staff would not be necessary. On this count, the operators described the frustration which they felt through working within a system (with TQM) which had improved the communication between management and the shopfloor, but which had not changed management's willingness to act upon the recommendations made by operators. TQM was seen to have created more work for operators and yet had failed to deliver on the promise of employee involvement in management decision-making. Whilst it was recognised that TQM had facilitated greater liaison between various occupational groups and hierarchical levels within the plant, it was claimed that management action remained the preserve of 'management'. In practice this meant that if a TQM team suggestion was made by a manager or supervisor, then there was a good chance that it would be acted upon immediately; whereas, if a suggestion was made by operators, it would take a considerable time before any action was taken, and only then if continual support for the suggestion had been made by employees and the recommendation had been restated over a number of months. In short, the communication channels had been opened with TQM, but the monopoly on ideas for decision-making had remained in the hands of management. This 'split' between management and the workers was also seen to be reflected in the management of the TQM teams, which were largely structured on a hierarchical basis. As one operator recalled:

At the TQM meetings, I will say as much as I want to say, but I have to work here still. We had a meeting last Tuesday. They asked us to try things different ways, and we do, but the moment we ask them to do something, they say no, we can't do that. They expect us to give, but they won't do anything for us. (Shopfloor Interviews, 1991)

In evaluating the effects of TQM on shopfloor operations, interviewees claimed that many of the problems experienced on the shopfloor were the result of management incompetence and their failure to ensure that trained operators are working reliable machines. They claimed that poorly trained ill-equipped operators will produce scrap no matter how many TQM teams management initiate. From a shopfloor perspective, training was therefore identified as a major issue which wasn't being tackled adequately by management. The common view on the shopfloor was that employees should have comprehensive training provided for the machines which they were expected to operate. In addition, interviewees argued that the machines provided should be able to operate at the set standards. In practice, operating equipment at the prescribed pace often resulted in an increase in the level of scrap produced. On this point one operator complained that managers themselves were sometimes the cause of scrap through insisting that a machine runs at a certain prescribed pace:

He asks why you can't produce more on your machine. I tell him that I am producing at the best pace for quality and quantity. Then he speeds the machine up. 'The book says that this is right so that is what you should be doing'. What the book says goes according to him. If he does that to me again, his number is going on the ticket—so his name goes on the scrap. (Shopfloor Interviews, 1991)

Thus, from a shopfloor viewpoint, the problem of plant inefficiencies and high levels of scrap were seen to be the consequence of bad management, poor equipment and inadequate training. As one operator indicated:

I have been on the machine for two weeks now and I have only had one full day of instruction. I have taught myself. People on other machines who have seen me struggling have come over and helped me a bit, but I haven't been allocated any training...It takes about 9 months to a year to learn the machines properly. (Shopfloor Interviews, 1991)

From an operator perspective, working conditions had deteriorated, morale had plummeted and the solution to the problem, whilst obvious, was overlooked by management and the blame was laid to rest on the workers. Thus, one of the biggest failings of local management was seen to stem from their inability to relate to shopfloor workers:

> I try to keep on the right side of them, that is only sensible. But there doesn't seem to be any empathy between the management and the workers. They treat us like machines. (Shopfloor Interviews, 1991)

In contrast, line supervisors were far more supportive of local management and argued that there was now far greater communication and integration between different areas within the site, and that the local management group had successfully achieved some significant changes in the organisation and control of work which had brought about substantial improvements in operating efficiencies. Finally, in terms of the future of TQM within the plant there was again a difference of opinion between the line supervisors and machines operators. In evaluating the future of TQM one supervisor argued that:

> There is a long future for TQM. It has given people the freedom to say what they feel. It has brought out the fact that the people on machines know what is going on out there. The bosses don't really know what makes them tick. (Supervisor, 1991)

In contrast a shopfloor operative claimed that there was no future for TQM in the plant:

> The way it is right now? Nowhere. We have a TQM meeting, but nothing is ever done about it. They are irrelevant. They don't mean anything to us. (Operator, 1991)

CONCLUSION: QUESTIONS OF CULTURE AND COMMUNICATION

The shopfloor experience of TQM in the CPP contrasts with that of the CMP. In the former, TQM was generally seen as a positive development which had improved the work environment of supervisors and shopfloor employees. In the latter, TQM was criticised heavily by shopfloor staff whilst being supported by line supervisors. Apart from the differences between the two plants, there were also a number of similarities. In particular, on the question of English language fluency and ethnic origin as a factor facilitating and inhibiting employee involvement in TQM, and the problems of inter-personal conflict and poor communication between the different shift operators:

> We have problems with nationalities. We have got Portuguese, Yugoslavs, Maltese, Australians, English—that causes problems. There is not much trust in our section between the three different shifts. If you think someone has done you a dirty, it is very easy to get them back. But you may be only imagining it. We have two operators who haven't spoken in the last three years. They don't even acknowledge each other. Personality clashes…It is pathetic and I don't believe it is as bad as some of the operators think it is, but there are definite problems. (Shopfloor Interviews, 1991)

Within both plants, it was claimed that the majority of staff who were not involved (apart from the nightshift) were Asians and did not understand English that well. As one interviewee commented:

> Sometimes the language barrier is too much of a problem. We can't explain everything that is going on that clearly in the meetings. I think it is also their culture that they don't bring up trouble. They just do their job and then they go home. (Shopfloor Interviews, 1991)

There are a number of people employed at PCAL who are not fluent in the English language. This raises the problem of communication both between employees—who are now expected to work together as a team rather than as individual machine operators—and within the TQM teams themselves. For the most part, there has been a general reluctance for those who speak English as a foreign language to get involved in the TQM groups. However, attempts to integrate these employees into TQM initiative have been made. For example, English classes for non-English speaking employees are provided by the company. These classes are scheduled twice a week for two hours (one hour company time and one hour private time). Although this programme is serving to improve the situation, the capacity for TQM to involve non-English speaking personnel remains severely constrained by the language difficulties these people encounter. Furthermore, the attitudinal differences expressed within the dominant Anglo-Australian culture compared with the other ethnic groups also serves to impede multi-cultural integration within the workplace. As a shopfloor supervisor commented:

> When they (the different ethnic groups) first come they stayed together a lot of the time. Some of them just didn't speak because

they have been used to not being able to. Some will always put their eyes down and not look at you when they speak, not because they are afraid, but because that is the way they have been bought up. But lately I have noticed that the Australian girls have been sitting with the others. It is a lot better than it used to be. They seem happy, which is good. (Supervisor, 1991)

From the experience of introducing TQM at PCAL, language and ethnicity have been key factors which have constrained the degree of employee involvement among non-English speaking employees. This finding has implications for another common issues across the two plants, namely, the movement from machine-based to team-based work arrangements. Although in practice the shopfloor is organised so that an individual employee will operate a particular machine, there is a movement towards more teamwork on the shopfloor in the sense that:

They (shopfloor operators) talk about their machines. If something goes wrong, the people on TQM know what is going on, so they transfer jobs to the other fellows. It makes people work together better. Whereas before one would come off a machine and another would go on and that was it. If I am not around, they pass work on, whereas before they would go off and the other fellows would stand their waiting…People are not afraid now to come up and say that something is wrong with their machines. In times gone past, you didn't say that anything is wrong with your machine until it collapsed in a heap in front of you. These days it is not like that at all. (Shopfloor Interviews, 1991)

The use of TQM to encourage shopfloor personnel, to work together as a team, again raises the question of ethnicity and language as factors influencing an employee's reluctance to be involved with TQM. The general assumption is that the option is there for any who wish to take it, as one operator commented in criticising people who didn't want to be involved in TQM:

Well, they still have to change as they go. If they don't like the changes, bad luck, they are introduced anyway. They have to accept the fact that the changes are happening. If they are not involved, then they are stuck with the fact they are changing. I don't see why anyone wouldn't want to be in on it. (Shopfloor Interviews, 1991)

This also raises the question of the voluntary nature of TQM. On the one hand, it is argued that people do not have to get involved in TQM, and on the other hand, it is argued that those who do not wish to be involved must nevertheless accept and live by the decisions of the TQM group. In this sense, TQM is not freely open to all employees (in not being able to adequately accommodate non-English speaking employees), nor is it a non-threatening voluntary activity (in that decisions made within TQM groups could have significant consequences for the re-organisation of work of those not involved). In short, TQM is a philosophy of change based upon open communication and employee involvement in the organisation and control of work. The main thrust of these changes is towards collaborative teamwork, multi-skilling and cultural commitment. In practice however, there are a number of factors which can influence the speed, direction and shape of change, and these have been illustrated in discussing the different shopfloor experiences of the Cable Processing and Cable Manufacturing plants at Pirelli Cables Adelaide.

QUESTIONS

1 Explain the different environments for the introduction of TQM at the CMP and CPP plants.

2 Describe the different outcomes at the 2 plants.

3 What reasons would you suggest explain the differences?

4 Describe the cultural problems that are demonstrated by the case.

PART *III*

Quality Management in Perspective

CHAPTER 13

TQM, the Case Studies and Management Theory

INTRODUCTION

The case studies in Part II of the book raise a number of issues that can be related back to our earlier discussion on management theory and TQM. In Chapter 3 we explored TQM's roots in earlier management theories. We noted that the development of new ideas of best practice in management needs to be explained in terms of changing contexts, because there is no inevitable rationality in the spread of managerial ideas. Chapter 3 also argued that management is a highly complex social process and that multiple frames of reference are helpful if we wish to unravel that complexity. Bureaucratic, political and cultural frames of reference provide three lenses through which we can view the intricacies of managerial process. This chapter looks at the case study companies to see what can be learnt about the context for the introduction of quality management. In order to analyse the content of the TQM prescriptions introduced, the chapter also studies the experience of these firms through the three perspectives on management. We explore what can be learnt about the bureaucratic, political and cultural aspects of TQM.

Why do managers adopt new managerial methods? Is it because of the inevitable spread of superior ideas, or because particular ideas appear to be relevant for certain contexts and circumstances? Are new methods adopted simply because they represent the latest trend, and their adoption brings with it a fashionable image of up-to-date sophistication?

The case studies do not provide a detailed guide to the context in which their managements chose to adopt the prescriptions of TQM. Nevertheless several cases noted that commercial pressure lay behind the search for improved managerial practices. Some companies faced direct pressure from customers. Accom first introduced quality assurance in response to the demands of significant clients, and Hendersons faced similar pressure from it's major customer, Ford. At Alcoa, managers were stimulated to consider TQM by the threat of plant closure, while Tecpak saw the need for a flexible and quality-oriented approach to small production runs as their major competitive edge, and quality management methods seemed to fit this need.

At the State Bank of South Australia, the introduction of quality management was linked to the Federal government's policy of increased competition in banking, and the arrival of a new Managing Director, eager to exploit the new opportunities and find methods to support radical changes in organisational direction.

Whatever the commercial stimulus to look for new methods of management, the managers within the case study companies were concerned to revise their managerial processes, and found external consultants, training courses and topical managerial publicity all guiding them in the direction of the current interest in quality management ideas.

Although all companies were investigating or implementing some form of quality management, the detailed orientation of each company varied. The case studies suggest that quality management is a term used to cover a complex range of different practices and procedures. In order to sort out some of the complexities involved, we discuss the case study findings in terms of the three perspectives on managerial processes outlined in Chapter 3. We review the bureaucratic, political and cultural aspects of the quality management initiatives.

THE BUREAUCRATIC ELEMENTS OF TQM

All managerial prescriptions rely to some extent on systematic, formal administrative rules and regulations. The theory of bureaucracy explores and explains why bureaucratic administration is important to management, and in Chapter 3 we reviewed the bureaucratic theories on administrative controls. In that chapter we raised the question of whether TQM represents a new form of bureaucratic organisational control, or whether it should be seen instead as the antithesis of bureaucracy. Does quality management help cement and reinforce centralised, formal, organisational control, or does it replace bureaucratic structures of centralised control with something more fluid, flexible and decentralised?

Is TQM market-oriented and anti-bureaucratic?

Free markets can be seen as the antithesis of bureaucracy because markets regulate behaviour through the terms of negotiated contracts, rather than through administered, organisational rules and regulations. Tuckman (1994b) put the argument that TQM could be seen as anti-bureaucratic, because it seeks to replace bureaucratic metaphors with market-oriented ones. TQM prescriptions de-emphasise an organisation's reliance on hierarchies of authority and instead encourage the idea that people should relate as members of networks of contractual relationships, both within the organisation and with external suppliers and customers.

One of our case studies provides a powerful image of the market-orientation of TQM. At Laubman and Pank, a feature of the TQM programme was to make the optometrists give up their white coats and symbols of medical expertise and call their 'patients', 'clients'. It is interesting that this switch from relationships of hierarchical, medical status to market-oriented, service-based relationships was not welcomed by the optometrists:

> When we took their white coats off them and when we told them that diagrams of dissections of the eye had to come off the wall and that they actually had to communicate with the client, they thought this was dreadful. There was such a reaction.

Clearly the optometrists associated their symbols of professional status with a personal power that they did not wish to relinquish. In this example, professional status was replaced by more market-related relationships. Laubman and Pank also tried to de-emphasise organisation-based hierarchical status by the use of first names between all members of the organisation.

The case studies therefore give examples of some attempts to introduce more market-oriented relationships into organisational structures that had previously relied on hierarchies of authority and administered, centralised controls. TQM may be used to introduce market-based relationships into organisations and it is possible to find some examples of a shift from bureaucratic hierarchies to more market-oriented relationships inside the case study companies. However there is plenty of evidence to suggest that TQM also uses managerial processes that are firmly placed within the traditional, bureaucratic traditions of organisational control.

The case studies provide examples of times when TQM was used to introduce more administrative order into what were once market relationships. For example, Tecpak used its quality management initiative to construct more stable networks of regular customers and suppliers. Under their TQM policy they replaced short-term contractual relationships with their

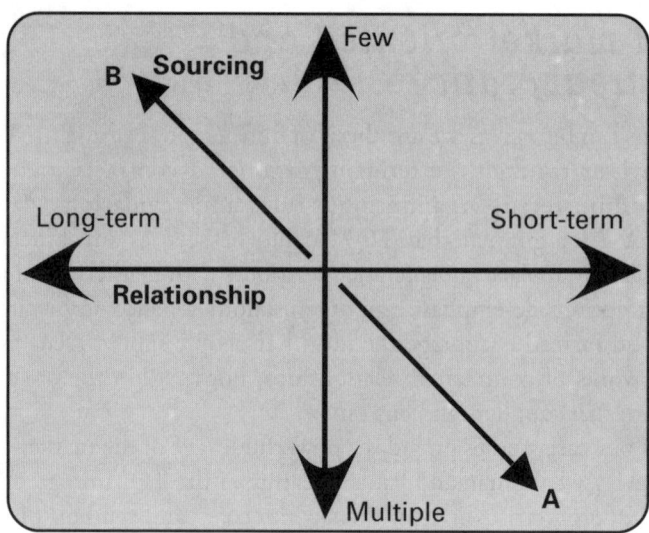

Figure 13.1 Relationship with suppliers

suppliers, with longer-term, more administered relationships. They sought to build a framework of understandings based on trust, with formal administrative structures for the reciprocal exchange of information. Hendersons gave their suppliers training in their quality techniques and requirements, and those suppliers chosen for a long-term relationship were networked into an electronic data information system. Both companies therefore sought to replace limited, strictly contractual, market relationships with their suppliers, and develop relationships based on more pervasive administration and trust. This change in the relationship which many TQM companies now have with their suppliers is shown in Figure 13.1. Increasingly, companies are looking to reduce their number of suppliers and develop longer-term relationships as part of a closely knit network of organisations. In the case of external customers, it is not unusual to develop inter-organisational TQM teams which may tackle common problems between the two organisations. In our case studies, the suppliers did not become part of Tekpac's or Hendersons' formal organisation. However by creating collaborative networks among their suppliers, both companies were introducing bureaucratically structured administered procedures for issues like information exchange and staff development.

TQM and bureaucratic task controls

The increased formalisation of operational processes or 'bureaucratisation of task control' is mentioned throughout the studies. More precise, standardised, and documented rules and regulations are mentioned in several contexts and are a standard part of TQM. These managerial techniques are introduced to increase task controls. Laubman and Pank used TQM as a scientific methodology to establish documented procedures and quantifiable indicators for measuring performance in their laboratories. At Alcoa, standard practices had previously been passed by word of mouth. TQM introduced quantified flow charts and the formal documentation of all operating procedures in order to enhance control of the twenty-four hour, five-shift system. At Vicbank one of the few outcomes to emerge from an attempt to define 'quality standards' was classically bureaucratic—that the 'phone be picked up within three rings'. Hendersons used the full rigour of a Ford's new Statistical Process Control (SPC) policy to back the Defect Prevention Policy that was in place. Tecpak used weekend seminars to train key employees in TQM's statistical processes, and managers were concerned to improve the use of statistical recording in order to show the benefits of improved practices.

TQM prescribes bureaucratic rules and regulations to improve the efficient running of standardised operational processes. It uses measurement and formalisation techniques that date back to the management theories of Scientific Management. However, even if we recognise these bureaucratic aspects of TQM, it is still important to ask whether the purpose of TQM's bureaucratisation is new. Weberian bureaucracy was analysed as a set of techniques that were used to turn organisations into powerfully efficient tools in the hands of their owners and controllers. Scientific Management is often presented as a classic set of bureaucratic methods concerned to foster the centralisation of organisational control. Does TQM have a different approach to the use of these administrative processes? Are the quality standards of TQM used in a different way? Are they used, for example, in a way that empowers employees, or builds devolved authority and decentralisation into organisational structures?

To explore this area, we need to review the impact of TQM on the management of employees. We start by exploring the extent to which TQM is associated with bureaucratic personnel or human resource management policies.

TQM and bureaucratic personnel policies

In Chapter 3 we noted that the classic bureaucratic ideal type proposed by the German sociologist, Max Weber, could be divided into two sets. One set of standardised organisational controls was associated with task performance, hierarchies of authority and specific, specialised job definitions, all designed to allocate work in a rationally planned and systematic way. (This set is clearly involved in the Scientific Management prescriptions.) The other set of standardised managerial controls was associated with equitable and meritocratic personnel procedures.

Bureaucratic personnel policies prescribed standard procedures for open and meritocratic recruitment to the organisation. They prescribed written, formal, equitable policies for performance appraisal, job allocation, regrading, promotion, grievance handling, and rewarding and disciplining employees. Bureaucratic personnel policies were designed to create employment structures based on merit or expertise rather than patronage, and to encourage loyalty to rational organisational objectives as a protection against the corruption that occurs when people exploit organisational resources for other ends.

Bureaucratic personnel policies are associated with traditional public sector employment, and are used by large Japanese corporations for their regular or core workforce of permanent employees (Gospel and Palmer, 1993:47–53). The career-employment policies of the major Australian banks have traditionally had many features that are similar to those found in the administrative sections of the public service.

It is therefore interesting to note that the introduction of TQM into the State Bank of South Australia was associated with policies that were designed to alter their traditional, bureaucratic personnel policies. At the bank, TQM was introduced at the same time that significant changes were taking place in personnel policies. The bank's policies had once supported a traditional banking career structure, based on school-leaver recruitment and progression up a career ladder of positions, with promotion heavily dependent on seniority. These policies were challenged by new selection, appraisal and promotion systems.

At the State Bank, competition for employment from the external labour market had once been restricted to the entry grades of the career ladder. Progress in the bank thereafter was based on the operation of administered systems of internal transfer and promotion. The new Human Resource Management policies introduced at the same time as TQM were designed to bring more competition into staffing decisions. Open competition and merit rather than seniority were to be the new criteria for recruitment to higher positions. However, the case study notes that the new personnel policies caused resentment, and that this affected employee reactions to TQM, associating it with suspicion and fear.

In this case, although the change was away from the traditional 'closed bureaucracy' model of human resource management, the changes in personnel procedures were not all anti-bureaucratic. Instead, they retained the formal, clearly specified and equitable procedures associated with bureaucratic personnel administration, but introduced new criteria for assessing merit. Accumulated organisational experience and knowledge of the bank's operating procedures were downgraded as criteria for promotion. Merit was to be based not on organisational knowledge and seniority, but on measures of performance that could be recognised in external markets for skill.

Tecpak provides another case in which TQM was used to influence personnel policy. In this case it would appear that new policies were designed to reshape the general structure of the workforce, as an alternative to introducing formalised rules, and to handle selection, promotion, performance appraisal etc. Tecpak used TQM to formalise their task and operating procedures. They introduced bureaucratic job definitions, and they identified and recorded tasks at all levels of the organisation. As a result, work levels intensified and employees' skill requirements increased. It was hoped that employees at the bottom of the status hierarchy would have more autonomy from close supervision, and more responsibly for tasks that had once involved the supervisors. Tecpak provided training for their employees to help cope with their clearly defined, expanded work roles, however they did not introduce formalised personnel procedures. Indeed, the formalisation of human resource management policies was not even considered until New Zealand's new Employment Contracts Act required thought to be given to enterprise agreements. Throughout the introduction of TQM, the company continued its traditional, informal approach to selection, recruitment and general staffing policies.

At Tecpak, TQM was not used to introduce formalised personnel procedures, but it was used to reshape the workforce. A skilled technician who refused to fit the TQM culture and display the appropriate, co-operative attitudes was dismissed two months into the TQM initiative. The company's wide use of casual labour was reviewed and management sought to introduce a system of trained, more permanent casuals surrounding a core workforce. These changes can be seen as a move to the core–periphery model of employment that has been noted as a part of the Japanese method for helping to build both loyalty and flexibility into a workforce. However, the Tecpak case does not provide evidence on the success of this policy. In summary, TQM was not used to bureaucratise employment policies, but it was associated with personnel changes that are best discussed in the context of 'strategic HRM'.

TQM and Strategic HRM

Strategic Human Resource Management has been used to describe a number of new approaches to personnel management (Gardner and Palmer, 1992:204–213). However, the definitions of both Human Resource Management and Strategic Human Resource Management cause confusion and disagreement. One definition of HRM sees it as a specified set of best practices. Under this definition, managerial responsibilities for personnel decisions and staff development should be integrated into line management, and up-to-date policies should be developed and implemented by the most senior managerial levels rather than relying on separate, specialist professionals (Torrington, 1989). Another definition of HRM suggests that best practice should vary in line with different economic constraints. HRM developed at a time when comparative research was demonstrating some stark contrasts, for example between Japanese and Western employment policies. This has given rise to the idea that strategic HRM might require personnel policies to vary with different business strategies. The Japanese use bureaucratised, secure employment relationships for the regular or core employees in large companies. However the privileged job status and security of these core workers is bolstered by a dual labour market. The secure, 'primary' jobs are surrounded by a 'secondary' labour force in less secure, less formalised employment relationships. The 'best' policies and conditions are not available for the whole workforce.

The success of the Japanese economy has stimulated much thought on the way that the best personnel policies may vary in different economic contexts. A number of typologies have been produced to suggest the ways personnel policies might logically be expected to vary in different situations. Schuler and associates use Porter's (1985 and 1987) distinctions between innovative, quality enhancement and cost-reducing management strategies and hypothesise the links with different personnel policies (Schuler and Jackson, 1988; Dowling and Schuler, 1990). Collins (198) uses Miller's (1986) categories of innovative, differentiator and low-cost production strategies to suggest that advanced, formal HRM policies would be appropriate for innovative differentiators, while more restricted and mechanistic personnel policies would be appropriate for low-cost producers. The Dunphy-Stace model relates different human resource strategies to business strategy, with the mediating variable of different management styles of organisational change (Dunphy and Stace, 1990:129; Stace and Dunphy, 1991:281). Four different strategies for organisational development are identified and related to the two variables of the style of change management and the scale of change required. The Stace and Dunphy model was based on an empirical study of thirteen organisations in the Australian service industry. Other empirical studies are now following, and suggest that reality is highly complex. Simple models may not capture the complexities of choice in terms of HRM policies, or the constraints that managers face if they attempt to introduce or change policies in any particular direction (see Gardner and Palmer, 1992:213–218).

Strategic HRM has become associated with a complex array of different types of personnel policy, with considerable debate about their causes and effects. Are any particular personnel policies associated with TQM? Or does TQM pick up the latest strategic human resource management ideas and suggest that personnel policies will vary according to economic variables, or the nature of the business strategy, or management's style of change management?

The emergence of TQM has obvious implications for personnel policies, but the theoretical attempts that have been made so far to relate TQM to particular human resource management policies do not give a clear picture of what might be expected to emerge (Hill, 1992; Wilkinson, 1993). A survey of 4000 managers in the British Institute of Management found that quality management often failed because it focused on formalised standards and processes and neglected staffing issues (Wilkinson, Redman and Snape, 1993). One area of obvious confusion in the TQM literature on staffing issues is that modern personnel policy gives heavy weight to individual performance monitoring and appraisal. The American literature links this to individual rewards. However the prescriptions of TQM emphasise collective, not individual, responsibility for performance (Palmer and Saunders, 1992; Wilkinson, Marchington, Goodman and Ackers, 1992; Daley, 1992). Although there has been much discussion of the importance of links between HRM and TQM, the notions of how these links should be made is still confused. The evidence from our case studies is that it is not easy to decipher a clear relationship between TQM and particular HRM policies.

At Tecpak, TQM was associated with changes in the labour force which permitted the development of new commercial strategies. Higher levels of toolmaking skills were developed in the maintenance department. This enabled the company to make tools that were previously sub-contracted out and what was once supplied by the external market became an organisational function. However, this was not part of an articulated set of new personnel policies for TQM.

Vicbank was the only case company to attempt to develop a highly formalised policy linking TQM with particular policies for HRM. The Manager of the Quality Support Centre produced a report for a Corporate Planning Conference in 1989 which outlined ways to match human resource policies to new TQM quality standards for work processes. The report argued that job descriptions should incorporate the new TQM-based work standards. The performance monitoring of these standards would then be done in a way that enabled information on performance to be used as part of the staff appraisal system. The report therefore recommended a direct link between TQM work standards and individual performance appraisal. Deming's (1986) insistence on collective or system-based performance evaluation and his attack on individualising performance monitoring had no place in these recommendations. The British survey noted above also found 40 per cent of respondents using quality indicators in the appraisal of individual performance, with 29 per cent linking this to performance-related pay or bonuses (Wilkinson, Redman and Snape, 1993:25). At Vicbank, the Quality Support Centre recommendations on personnel policy were not derived from the TQM literature as far as the use of individual monitoring systems was concerned, but the ideas were linked to other personnel recommendations commonly associated with TQM (see Blackburn and Rosen, 1993).

At Vicbank, the recommendations of the report were not fully implemented. The Quality Council which the report advocated to oversee the implementation of the recommendations was never established. Instead a steering committee was set up to attempt to develop the standards which would be written into job descriptions. This steering committee of senior executives found great difficulty identifying standards that would be specific enough for use in job descriptions. The task was therefore devolved to lower levels of the organisation. In the end, only a few management areas even attempted to implement the strategy of linking quality standards with job descriptions. The initiative did not reach the stage of routine operation. Despite the many attempts to implement TQM at Vicbank from 1988 to late 1991, the attempt to link HRM policies to TQM standards does not appear to have been successful.

It may often be easier to standardise and bureaucratise work processes than employment relationships. Whereas it may not be too difficult to find a common rationality about the best methods for producing a product, or agreeing the best use of material resources, reaching agreement on rational employment relationships may be more difficult. Employees have objectives which are not necessarily shared with their employers. People have the ability and right to express and promote those separate interests and within management there may be many perspectives on appropriate ways to manage employees. This is the area where the bureaucratic assumption that managerial action will be perceived as rational and legitimate is most likely to be challenged. It is appropriate at this stage to see what light a political frame of reference throws on the impact of TQM on managerial processes.

THE POLITICAL ELEMENTS OF TQM

Chapter 3 explained how the political perspective on management focuses on the use of power in organisations. The bureaucratic perspective recognises and explains some uses of power, but bureaucratic theory sees power in terms of the formalised, legitimated authority allocated to organisational positions, and to rationally determined objectives and rules. This view of power is significant, for formalised organisational authority can be a most powerful organisational resource. However, organisational power can also be based on such things as expertise or personal charisma. Power may be associated with politically dominant ethnic, class, caste or gender groups, and may be strengthened by alliances that stretch beyond the organisation's boundaries. These other power bases may work to challenge bureaucratic hierarchies and rational-legal procedures, and when this occurs bureaucratic models and theories do not provide good explanations of the conflicts that emerge. A bureaucratic perspective can therefore misinterpret much of the political behaviour found within organisations.

If a political perspective is brought to bear on TQM, new issues are thrown into focus. Instead of discussing the most rational structures and policies, a political perspective addresses the impact of TQM on power relationships at work. Power relationships will be affected by TQM's changes in formal job specifications and organisational authority, but we need to consider whether or not TQM affects the distribution of power in other ways.

TQM and employee empowerment through job redesign and teamwork

The prescriptions of TQM claim to 'empower' employees. Two proposals in particular have this intent. The first concerns changes in bureaucratic job definitions, so that responsibility and authority for quality control is taken from supervisors or quality controllers and devolved down through all jobs within the workforce. The second 'empowering' proposal uses teams to enable employees to discuss and contribute to decision-making directed towards the continuous improvement of operating system performance. Figure 13.2 illustrates these proposals. The next chapter notes that the formal shift in responsibility from supervisors to supervised can generate resentment from middle managers as they see a loss in power. In this section we review the use of teams within the case study firms, before we go on to discuss the impact that other TQM prescriptions may have on the distribution of power.

Several of our cases demonstrate the importance of teams in TQM, and

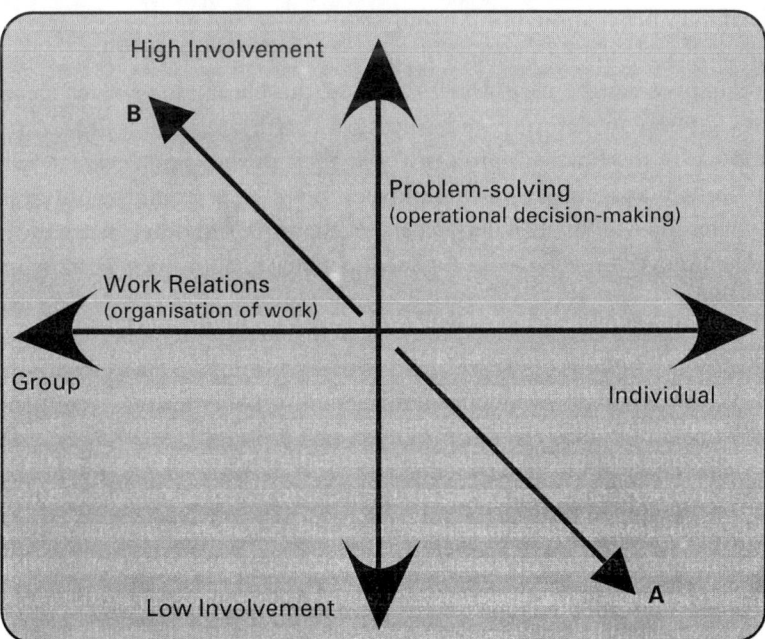

Figure 13.2 Employee empowerment strategies

their use as mechanisms to involve employees in managerial decisions. At Hendersons, employee involvement was used to help solve a major problem that had arisen with lost time, injuries and high workers' compensation costs. In 1985 an average of 218 hours per month were lost to injuries in the Hendersons Automotive South Australia factory. From 1986 the company therefore focused on the need to improve their health and safety practices. In 1986 management appointed an employee from the shopfloor to act as a health and safety representative. This cautious start was seen to bring the advantage of some employee participation in the solution of health and safety problems. Therefore the number of employee health and safety representatives was increased to four, and they were elected by their shopfloor colleagues, rather than appointed by management. An occupational health and safety committee was established, consisting of these four plus a management representative, and was given the job of preparing an occupational health and safety policy. When the new policy was implemented, the employee representatives were used to communicate the policy to employees in 'Five Minute Safety Talks'. This communication and training function developed into a regular half-hour session each fortnight. Hendersons therefore provides a good example of the use of employee involvement in the solution of managerial problems. Elected safety representatives developed managerial responsibilities, and the ability of employees to elect these representatives increased the formal, constitutional power of employees. As a result of these policies Hendersons gained the National Safety Council's five-star award for three years and gained exempt status from the South Australian WorkCover system on the basis of their occupational health and safety management.

Health and safety is one area where common interests between employer and employee can be clearly identified. In the Hendersons' case, management's interest in defining and solving a health and safety problem was prompted by the financial problems that their previous policies had generated. Both management and employees saw a clear common interest in improving the health and safety record of the firm. On other issues the success of employees' involvement for solving managerial problems can be more problematic.

Hendersons teams appeared to work well in areas other than safety. Hendersons relied heavily on Kaizen and Quality Groups to encourage a high level of innovation in production and design. Quality groups were department based and tended to concentrate on one product, while Kaizen groups were deliberately multi-departmental and were given broad-ranging briefs. In both cases membership of the groups was drawn from a cross-section of status levels to encourage the flow of new ideas and, over time, the groups were merged into Continuous Improvement Groups.

Hendersons adopted the system of sending a different small group of shopfloor employees each week, accompanied by a quality inspector, to one of the locally based clients where their product was used. This enabled employees to develop some relationships with external customers and use their ideas and initiative to solve mutual problems. Some notable improvements arose from these visits. One group discovered that seat backs were difficult to unpack at the customer's location because the packaging was being damaged in transit. Improved packaging was designed. Employees were less likely to be sent on the quality inspection visits to interstate customers, but the involvement that did occur was clearly related to joint interests in improving performance in the market.

In other cases, employee empowerment through teamwork was not so successful. The Pirelli and Alcoa Kwinana refinery cases suggest that the success of employee involvement through quality teams may vary in different contexts. At the Pirelli Cable Processing Plant, employees and management both told the case study researcher that improved communications and greater collaboration had resulted from the work of the teams, and that this had improved the efficiency of production. However in the Cable Manufacturing Plant the same policies were seen to have generated frustration and disappointment. Here employees complained that management had proved to be unwilling or unable to respond to the their suggestions and proposals for improvements. At the Alcoa plant, some teams were regarded as successes, others as failures.

In many of the companies studied, a range of initiatives was introduced to encourage greater employee involvement in workplace issues. The movement was away from individual-based work practices with low employee involvement towards group work and higher levels of involvement in operational decision-making. TQM encourages this shift through the use of group problem-solving TQM teams. In practice, however, the areas in which the TQM teams sought solutions were determined largely by management, who also decided whether or not the proposed solutions should be implemented. In this sense, the involvement of employees remained limited and controlled by management. Furthermore, whilst TQM facilitated group work, in companies where employees were assigned to individual machines or specified areas of operation, they only experienced group work if they were part of a TQM team. However, in one case TQM did facilitate a change in machine set-up procedures, and this now encourages group involvement.

A study of human resource management practices in the companies that won the Baldridge Awards (Blackburn and Benson, 1993) concluded that, although many companies made some use of teams, advanced forms of self-managing or autonomous teams were not found. It would seem that TQM is not leading to major new uses for teams, nor universally applied teamwork concepts. A bureaucratic approach to management tends to assume that all parties should share the same interests, values and attitudes to change at work. Teamwork under a unitary perspective can only improve communication and ease the speed of rational, agreed decision-making. How could it fail? A political approach assumes that organisations consist of a plurality of conflicts of interests and values. People may not all share the same goals, nor agree on the best means to common goals. Under these assumptions teamwork may prove as difficult to manage as more conventional methods for controlling and co-ordinating staff.

Several of the cases show that the prescriptions of TQM were not universally accepted by employees or managers. There were times when people did not feel empowered by the changes that were being introduced, and therefore reacted against them.

TQM and the power of knowledge and information

If all organisational members are not automatically empowered by TQM, then we need more detailed discussion of the political impact of quality management prescriptions. What power resources are involved when TQM teams are operating? There would appear to be two different sources of power provided by team participation, both voice and knowledge. The teams give their members the right to a voice on operations and process improvement issues. This right to be heard is not backed by constitutional powers, for example that the majority vote wins. Instead it is a right to be heard, but with managerial prerogative still having the ultimate say. As the Pirelli cable makers found, management did not always listen to the voice of the team. However, for many people involved, the right to be heard, if not to decide, did represent an improvement in their power position. The second source of power relates to the power of knowledge and information. Employees will be 'empowered' because they are given access to new information. The new techniques of statistical performance review and the open availability of statistical measurements to team members will give employees new access to the information which they may be able to use to increase their ability to influence managerial decisions.

The claim that TQM decentralises power down the organisation by giving employees access to more performance-related information is often contrasted with Scientific Management's centralisation of power. Braverman (1974) first put the argument that Taylorism drew power away from employees by using their knowledge of production to increase the power held by managers at the top of the organisation. Braverman's argument was that before the advent of Taylorism, employee experience provided the knowledge base which was used to improve task performance. Scientific Management introduced work study and scientific measurement and these gave management direct access to the information needed to design improved work processes. Through work study, the industrial engineers could reduce the value of the skills of tradesmen because their knowledge of work methods and skilled processes no longer had scarcity value. The knowledge gained by work study enabled management to centralise planning for production and operations management, and thereby gain greater control over the labour process.

It could be suggested that TQM centralises power in organisations because, like Scientific Management before it, it greatly increases the information on process performance available to top management. As noted in Chapter 3, Sewell discussed the increased surveillance of employee performance permitted by electronic monitoring and the information that this element of TQM makes available to management. The use of computerised information technology to provide constant up-to-date statistics on performance and the achievement of quality standards can be seen as a technique, like the earlier work study, to reduce employee freedom and increase the control of management at work. It ensures that employee performance is constantly under managerial review. However Sewell notes that in the case he describes, the increased surveillance was not resented by employees. He suggests that it was seen as legitimate because it was universal and socially imposed. If increased surveillance involves peer pressure and peer review, then employees may not feel a decrease in control. They may feel that the increase in information about performance, and the increased visibility of achievements and failures bring an enhanced control over the work process for the benefit of everyone, both employers and employees. In Sewell's case study the increased disciplinary gaze was accepted in the context of job enlargement and improved, more consultative, personnel practices. If this finding is common in TQM companies, then the employee involvement in the evaluation of process performance recommended by quality management is serving to increase a sense of mutual control, it is not seen as top management gaining greater control at the expense of their staff.

In one of the cases described in this book there were initial fears expressed about the increased surveillance brought about by TQM, but these fears later appeared to have been overcome. At the Kwinana refinery of Alcoa, management introduced the detailed monitoring of processes and used advanced methods for statistically recording operational process performance. At first this increased surveillance generated fear and suspicion, because employees were concerned that their supervisors would be able to use the new sophistication to pinpoint and allocate blame. However the system gained union support and the extensive use of teams was seen to have contributed to the acceptance of TQM's tighter methods of monitoring and process control.

TQM is designed to ease the flow of productivity-relevant information around the organisation. Both management and employees should become more informed. Do they all therefore gain power, or is the increased knowledge of some parties used to the detriment of others? The cases give no evidence that employees used their increased involvement in decisions to management's disadvantage, nor that sectional interests were able to make use of the increased information flows to further their own sectional interests against those of others.

TQM teams and the politics of organisational flexibility

Teams may also alter the power relationships within an organisation by encouraging the development of new alliances and perspectives. If teams are formed to cut across traditional departmental structures, they bring together people from different functions and skills. They create opportunities for new alliances to be formed and this may affect the balance of power at work. Old loyalties to the traditional sub-units in the organisation can be weakened, and new political alliances formed in support of organisational change (Dawson and Webb, 1989). Teams provide opportunities for junior staff to bring themselves to the attention of more senior managers, and juniors who support the new management policies may gain preference for better jobs. Teams, especially those with cross-functional membership, therefore provide new opportunities for political action from organisational members. This can be used to build new alliances within the organisation that undermine support for the status quo and bolster support for change.

At Alcoa, two Process Improvement Teams (PITs) were initially established in 1989 to demonstrate the possible improvements that could come from TQM. The PIT members were chosen by management from a cross section of people with relevant experience. One of these teams was seen as successful and the other was reformed with a local, rather than an external facilitator. In 1992, thirty PITs were operating with from twelve to fifteen members chosen to represent different functions. The team members would, for example, consist of an engineer, a team facilitator from the Central Quality Development Department, a supervisor, a number of operators and several fitters. They would meet once a month for three hours and were briefed to establish their own targets. There were also about forty-five 'Natural Teams' formed as a result of an industrial agreement. These comprised supervisors and work crews and were created to find methods of raising productivity. As a result of these two initiatives, half the workforce was involved in teams. A team reward scheme was introduced in 1991 in which teams were evaluated on a number of criteria by Quality Facilitators and points could be accumulated towards prizes of shopping vouchers. The Alcoa study suggests that the major benefit of this team activity was the employee commitment to improved operations that team involvement can bring.

At the State Bank of South Australia after the 'religious' conversion of the general manager to TQM, and a weekend retreat in which the senior executive committed themselves to the new policies, a complex net of quality-related teams were set up throughout the bank. Management established cross-functional Quality Improvement Teams, assisted by Quality Improvement Leaders and Quality Facilitators. In addition voluntary Quality Teams were set up for specific problems to enable staff to use their own experience, knowledge and imagination to improve service to customers. The main purpose behind the establishment of these teams appears to have been the creation of a culture which would support flexibility and change.

CULTURAL ELEMENTS OF TQM

We first discussed the impact of TQM in terms of bureaucracy, and the creation of administrative systems. We then considered the politics of TQM teams and employee involvement. The political perspective analyses political accommodation. Our remaining perspective on management focuses on culture. This cultural perspective explores the establishment of moral order, and ideas of legitimacy, value and meaning.

Chapter 3 raised several issues associated with the cultural perspective on management. For example, is TQM's search for a common culture of support and commitment realistic? Is it possible for TQM to establish integrated cultures, and can a 'paradigm shift' in values lead to organisational cultures that support flexibility and continuous change? Is the cultural impact of TQM itself dependent on culture, or can it only occur under certain cultural conditions? Finally, is TQM itself simply a passing but popular fad? Are quality management techniques introduced more as a symbol of modernity and fashion than because of concrete, material benefits?

TQM and integrated, supportive culture

The concept of culture relates to the ideas and assumptions which are developed by people in any social group, and which have a major impact on group behaviour and judgements. A quality culture has been defined as 'a culture that nurtures high trust social relationships and respect for individuals, a shared sense of membership of the organisation, and a belief that continuous improvement is for the common good' (Hill, 1991a).

Cultural change to create a quality culture is seen as an essential part of TQM in the popular literature, and yet cultural change is problematic. 'Despite the growing awareness of cultural issues, comparatively little attention has been paid to the practical, day to day processes involved in creating, managing and changing organisational culture' (Williams, Dobson and Walters, 1991). All the literature on TQM indicates that to be successful, TQM requires a cultural change, but that's usually where the literature stops (Wilkinson, 1993).

The case study companies used various techniques in an attempt to improve their organisational cultures. In pursuit of cultural change, managers invested in training, team building and energising social and cultural events. For example, one of the objectives behind the formation of Tecpak's 'Roadshow Meetings' on Saturday mornings was to generate mutual trust and commitment to change. When these meetings became a forum for expressing fears and doubts, communication skills sessions were organised in order to ensure that differences of view could be negotiated through. The State Bank of South Australia saw its training and leadership strategies as an attempt to change the organisation's culture away from prioritising bank rules and towards giving greater value to customer satisfaction, performance and profit.

Although attempts were made to change cultures, it is difficult to quantify success. Tecpak's difficulties in communication were matched at Pirelli's Cable Manufacturing Plant. At Accom the General Manager was thought not to trust or respect his staff, and this was seen as a barrier to cultural improvement. Vicpak first made statistical process improvement the centre of their TQM initiatives. Later they realised that they had not placed enough emphasis on gaining managerial commitment and developing a culture to support their desired changes. A survey of Vicbank managers in 1988 sought views on TQM and a desultory, 50 per cent response rate produced answers that showed a clear lack of commitment to TQM. The company decided to work on culture, but having decided that cultural change was necessary, they found that it was not clear how that change would be implemented.

TQM and unitary cultures

The cultural ideal assumed by TQM is difficult to define with precision. The advocates of cultural change seek more open, flexible, less segmental cultures in which people can appreciate the value of different contributions and skills in the achievement of common, overarching goals (Kanter, 1986). Few would disagree with the argument that major barriers to good decision-making arise from narrowly focused and biased assumptions. If an organisation suffers from rampant segmentalism, such that separate units spend their energies undermining each other's credibility rather than co-operating to common ends, it is not difficult to agree that a poor culture has developed. Similarly a culture that places great value on the current organisation and distribution of power is going to resist both major changes and continuous improvement. However, we need to get beyond a superficial analysis of culture as excellent, positive and supportive.

As a strategy of control, TQM attempts to manage values and beliefs in the development of a cohesive and unitary organisational culture. This cultural control strategy overlays existing structural control mechanisms (for example, rules and procedures, hierarchical reporting and command structures) and tries to engage employees with company values through the development of high-trust relationships. Quality cultures emphasise the need for unifying values that highlight the common bond of membership rather than the significance of separate units, and they also emphasise an optimistic attitude to change. In both areas the desirable culture requires certain types of trust. For a unifying culture, people need to trust that their interests are better served through the wider group than through their more local, smaller associations. For an optimistic approach to change, people need to trust that their interests will be better served by change than by resistance to it. If employees do not believe that the new policies will serve their interests better, then attempts to impose a new value system can become fairly transparent and, rather than improving relations, can serve to exacerbate existing divisions within the workplace.

TQM has been heavily influenced by the managerial practices of Japan, and by Western management's desire to emulate the culture of employee commitment to organisational goals, seen to result from Japanese management. However the context in which Japanese organisational cultures have developed is very different from those in the West. Japanese management arose in the context of an extraordinarily homogeneous society. Japan was deliberately protected from external influences for the centuries before the Meiji Restoration in 1868. Cultural norms support homogeneity, not cultural pluralism. After the Meiji Restoration, the political economy of Japan was built to create a hierarchy of economic organisations; it was not based on notions of individual rights, entrepreneurial and economic freedom or the value of competition between competing interests. The social controls that developed in this context assume the need to administer group activities towards common goals, and they emphasise structures of co-ordination and hierarchical control. In contrast the managerial controls of Western cultures have developed more techniques to build alliances between stakeholders who have different allegiances. Western employment relationships tend to be based on an open market for labour, and on individualistic rewards and sanctions. In contrast, Japanese companies are characterised by: lifetime employment for core workers; collective decision-making through exhaustive consultation; paternalistic authority relationships; and strong family-type loyalties to employing organisations (Burnes, 1992:83). Loyalty to and identification with the company are heavily reinforced by these major structural differences. The Japanese system provides many sanctions to support cultural homogeneity and company loyalty. In contrast, both Australian culture and Australian-based companies are far more culturally diverse. Once again, this highlights one of the major weaknesses of existing TQM programmes, namely, the assumption that unitary cultures do (or should) exist within organisations. There is a tendency to sidestep the problems of cultural diversity in an uncritical acceptance of TQM principles to Western workplace cultures.

Our case studies raise the question of the cultural relativity of the prescriptions of TQM. At Pirelli it was clear that TQM was not well suited to building employee commitment in all contexts. In that case, major problems were associated with lack of English language skills, which hampered the use of employee involvement to shape attitudes. Problems also arose because of the conflicting loyalties and lack of trust shown by the workforce in the Cable Manufacturing Plant. If this proves a common problem, then the culturally mixed environment of Australian business needs to be given far more consideration before TQM can be adapted for our use.

Is TQM itself a cultural fad?

Is TQM a cultural 'fad' whose introduction has little or no relationship to measurable productivity gains (see Zeitz and Mittal, 1993)? The case studies give some indication of the cultural legitimacy of TQM. At Hendersons, TQM was introduced after a new management team with a new brief for recovery was brought into the company in 1986. Its legitimacy was strongly reinforced through the values of their major customer, Ford. The State Bank of South Australia adopted TQM when a new Managing Director announced that he wished the bank to be a catalyst for change and looked to American business practice as the source of legitimate solutions. He returned from a tour of the United States 'with religion…' and organised a weekend retreat in which the executive made a commitment to TQM. A substantial budget was allocated to the initiative and attempts to assess best management practices were made, although these were not formally measured or appraised. In order to overcome the 'cultural barrier' of employee resistance to change, the bank adopted a cascade process in which small group sessions were held down four levels of the organisation. For the final level of 2500 staff, a 'One-Day Event' was held to bring every employee in Australia to a fanfare presentation at the convention centre to discuss missions, goals and values in an atmosphere of gaiety and entertainment.

From the case studies, there is evidence that TQM was adopted in some cases because it was seen as the latest culturally approved, exciting way to manage. If this is part of the attraction, then we can assume that fashions will change. The next managerial techniques will be called something else, as a culture of novelty promotes new versions of the old, traditional ideas.

CONCLUSION

The case studies serve to illustrate the old truth that management is a complex process. TQM is the latest movement for reform in a long history of developments in management thought. The quality management movement advocates many prescriptions that have roots in earlier Scientific Management and Human Resource Management theories, but there are distinctive ideas within TQM that create a new package of proposals. However, the content of the quality management package is not totally coherent or precise, and the case study companies show that different ideas were adopted and developed in different ways in different contexts. This evidence of the diversity of managerial responses to the TQM package should not be a cause for surprise or concern. The managerial processes is complex and needs to adapt to many unpredictable constraints. The needs of different companies are unlikely to be totally caught within any single schema for reform. TQM provides a range of ideas that might be useful in the current situation and it is clear that companies selected different elements from the package of ideas, and adopted them in different ways. All companies in the case studies adopted some of the quality management ideas, but none of them illustrates the total adoption of a precise, coherent package of TQM reforms. This finding is important, for it suggests that the introduction of new managerial ideas gives rise to complex issues that need to be explored.

We found it useful to unpack ideas in the quality management movement by using three different analytical perspectives. In this chapter we used the case study evidence to discuss the implementation of bureaucratic, political and cultural elements of TQM.

Bureaucratic or administrative prescriptions—for example that decision-making should be based on systematic, statistical data about the performance of operating systems—have been present for many years. TQM uses advanced statistical techniques combined with the power of computers to provide more sophisticated data, which could be used by the workers involved in production. This element of the TQM package was important in many of the case study companies, and some companies used them not only to improve managerial control of the operating process within the company, but to introduce a network of administered relationships between their customers and suppliers. In management theory it is not clear whether TQM is attempting to increase or reduce the use of bureaucratic, administered controls at work. We concluded from the case study companies that TQM represented new forms of improved administered control, but that this increased control was generally accepted by the workforce because it occurred in the context of some employee involvement and was generally seen to increase efficiency. The rational-legal legitimacy of bureaucratic theory supported the increased monitoring and use of statistical data. Improved administration occurred in a way that did increase organisational control, but the devolution of improved information made the old exercise of hierarchical authority seem less oppressive. The more sophisticated, administered controls could even be used to build more reliability into relationships that were outside the boundaries of the organisational hierarchy. In a few of the case study companies, new information technology was used to link suppliers and customers into collaborative networks of administered controls.

The evidence on the use of new administrative procedures for personnel, rather than operational issues, was less clear-cut. Most of the case study companies did not associate their quality management techniques with the latest prescriptions for human resource management. Only in the areas of training and teamwork was there a clear link between TQM and particular policies for personnel. The use of new quality teams was an important feature of the TQM initiatives which were designed to empower employees to enable them to take part in the management process. To study the impact of teams, we shifted from the bureaucratic to the political-analytical lens.

Viewed through a political perspective, the managerial prescriptions of TQM relate to the distribution of power over managerial decisions. The case studies enabled us to discuss the use of quality teams and the meaning of employee involvement under quality management practices. Teamwork was a common and important aspect of the package of changes introduced under TQM but the case studies found examples of success and failure in the use of quality teams. If the creation of a network of teams is expected to generate a paradigmatic shift in employee perceptions about management, then the evidence is disappointing. However it was clear that in some cases the ability of team members to express a voice was seen as empowerment. In other cases the right to a voice did not overcome the problems that arose from management's decision to disregard that voice. The teams probably achieved a limited impact in the difficult area of employee empowerment. However they had an important role in building flexibility into organisational structures. Team members were usually chosen to represent different functions, departments or status levels. This created new units within the organisation, responsible for studying and promoting organisational change. The teams acted to remove people from the influence of their old organisational units, and give them new social relationships in which there was an incentive to generate change. This was seen to weaken the attitudes resisting change and give opportunities for advancement to people prepared to sponsor continuous improvement.

The importance of attitudes for the acceptance of (or resistance to) change highlights the cultural elements of management. One of the factors that distinguishes TQM from earlier managerial theories is the recognition that organisational culture is significant, and might be amenable to managerial manipulation. All the case study companies made attempts to improve the organisational cultures that they had, using training, teamwork, the cascading of information from top management and various cultural events to bring people together in a spirit of understanding and positive thinking. However these techniques could not revolutionise organisational culture in the timeframe of the case study research. A major finding from our case studies is that the proposed mechanisms and directions of cultural change under TQM are not sufficiently clear. As cultural management is a relatively new element in managerial prescriptions, this is not surprising. TQM tends to reflect a preference for the unified culture believed to exist in large Japanese companies. However, the value of this type of culture and its relevance in other settings still needs to be explored. From the case studies it was clear that multiculturalism in Australia creates a different context that needs to be considered in any further study into the impact that TQM can have on organisational culture.

CHAPTER 14

TQM and Management Practice: the Process Of Change Reappraised

INTRODUCTION

Managing change for competitive advantage has been the focus of an increasing number of books published in the management area (see for example, Twiss and Goodridge, 1989; Waterman, 1987). Many commentators suggest that companies are now actively seeking out and implementing programmes which hold the potential for making their organisations more competitive (Vessey, 1991:23–33). Inflexible work practices, poor employee relations and traditional hierarchical reporting and command structures are deemed inappropriate to emerging future organisations. For example, Kanter, Stein and Jick (1992:247) claim that: 'Because of the volatility experienced by many organisations in today's emerging global economy, the new model of a flexible, lean organisation emphasising networks rather than hierarchies and decentralisation rather than top-laden bureaucracy, makes increasing sense'.

The search for the ingredients of competitive success has been the focus of a number of studies since the early 1980s when Peters and Waterman (1982) identified eight major determinants of organisational excellence. They claimed that:

- organisations should have a bias for action through encouraging innovation and through active response to problem situations,
- they should develop closer relationships with their customers,

- they should foster and support the entrepreneurial spirit among their staff and aim to increase the level of responsible autonomy among their employees,
- employees should be treated with respect and dignity in order to ensure productivity through people,
- all employees should be driven by the values of the organisation,
- companies should do what they know best and should restrict diversification,
- flat organisation structures and slimmed-down bureaucracies enable greater flexibility and provide for more rapid communication,
- simultaneous loose–tight properties should be established through high levels of self-supervision and the development of a common cohesive organisational culture.

As Peters and Waterman conclude:

> We find that autonomy is a product of discipline. The discipline (a few shared values) provides the framework. It gives people confidence (to experiment, for instance) stemming from stable expectations about what really counts (1982:322).

This work, in putting forward a simple recipe for achieving organisational excellence, has proven to be very influential. In a similar vein to TQM prescriptions, high-trust cultures, productivity through people, and closer relationships with customers were all identified as key ingredients to competitive advantage. Little attention was given to the potential diversity of organisational forms and there was an assumption that blueprints for success can be identified, implemented and sustained to ensure company survival in turbulent and competitive business environments. In practice, however, these simple management recipes have not stood the test of time and have been criticised for trying to present simple prescriptions of a 'one best way' for modern organisations to follow (Burnes, 1992: 72). This inability to deliver practical long-term solutions highlights the problem of management books which identify and codify supposedly best practice strategies for achieving organisational effectiveness based on common sense interpretations of organisational life. (see for example, Goldsmith and Clutterbuck, 1984; Schonberger, 1986). As Kriegler and his colleagues have pointed out: 'the vast body of research on organisational effectiveness has adopted a narrow quantitative focus which usually fails to respect the profoundly complex and interdependent nature of what is essentially a dynamic social system capable of infinite variation' (Kriegler et al., 1988:6).

For all the criticisms levelled at past prescriptions, manuals which provide simple solutions to complex problems remain an attractive management commodity. Consequently, many of the pitfalls and failures associated with implementing pre-planned packages for organisational success reassert themselves with amazing regularity only under different titles and names. For some commentators, the continual push for newly labelled change packages and techniques has resulted in a proliferation of management fads (Mitroff and Mohrman, 1987:69) and an increased tendency for companies to imitate other organisations (DiMaggio and Powell, 1983). Furthermore, whilst Eric Abrahamson has argued that 'fads and fashions may constitute vital processes that animate random variations from which increasingly efficient innovation can evolve' (Abrahamson, 1991:609), some of the simple recipes associated with TQM packages may contribute more to the wealth of consultants than to the performance of organisations.

In the 1990s, codified blueprints for implementing particular techniques, such as World Class Manufacturing, TQM, and Best Practice Management, have largely replaced the broader 'excellence recipes' of the 1980s. But once again, the complexities of managing large-scale transitions which incorporate cultural as well as structural change are largely downplayed. It would seem that the lessons of the past are forgotten under the dazzling banners of new methods and techniques for organisational success. The view taken here is that organisational change should be understood as a process and that unitary notions of culture do not accurately reflect the realities of organisational life in Australian and New Zealand companies. Furthermore, organisational politics is a major determinant on the process and outcomes of change and yet, are often absent from recent theories on managing change (see for example, Dunphy and Stace, 1990). What is required therefore, is a processual approach for understanding change which is sensitive to the political, contextual and substantive dimensions to managing ongoing transitions. As Dawson (1994:182) has indicated elsewhere:

> No longer is it appropriate to talk of long term stability followed by change followed by long term stability but, rather, organisational transition should be viewed as an ongoing process which may develop from partial incremental commitments as well as by the formulation of corporate strategies for the wholescale introduction of new organisational arrangements. For these reasons, caution should be given to studies which present linear models in an attempt to construct commandments of change or to prescribe the best way to manage organisational transition. In short, change needs to be man-

aged as an ongoing and dynamic process and not as a single reaction to adverse contingent circumstance.

In the sections which follow, the main elements of a processual approach to managing change, and particularly TQM, are outlined. Although no attempt is made to provide a simple blueprint for managing the introduction of TQM, a set of general lessons are developed, based on the processual analysis of the empirical material presented in Part II. The chapter also examines the extent to which the seven main elements of TQM developed and discussed in Chapter 2 were in evidence within the case organisations. It is shown how TQM is never as clearly defined as many of the prescriptive manuals would have us believe. The chapter concludes by emphasising that there are no simple solutions to the complex problem of managing large-scale change.

UNDERSTANDING TQM: A PROCESSUAL APPROACH

The transition towards a total quality organisation takes time. In the companies that we studied the introduction of TQM was viewed as an on-going process which required continual management effort. It wasn't simply a case of unfreezing an organisation, changing and then refreezing new behaviours but, rather, involved managing a series of organisational transitions in which unforseen critical events during the process of change could serve to impede, hasten or redirect the route to change. The pathway towards the adoption of TQM was never clearly defined, nor did it follow a logical linear path. The politics of organisational decision-making and the conflicts associated with major change all played their part in shaping the nature, direction and content of the various TQM programmes. However, whilst it is not possible to construct a sequential model of stages in the adoption of TQM, there was a temporal history to all of the change programmes.

As indicated in Chapter 4, time was used as a major frame of reference in our empirical case studies of the introduction of TQM in Australian and New Zealand companies. The three general timeframes on which our processual framework was based comprised: conception of a need for a quality initiative; process of establishing total quality management; and operation and on-going change. Moreover, whilst we wanted to avoid any implication of a rational linear path for the adoption process, we did feel that it was important for analytical reasons to construct data categories around the various activities and tasks associated with the management of change. These comprised: evaluation and appraisal, identification of type of change, implementation, initial operation, preparation and planning, search and assessment of options, and system selection. It was shown how activities within these categories often stop and start at different time periods throughout the change process. For example, in the case of Tecpak, senior management became aware of the possibility of introducing TQM in 1987, they made several attempts to implement Deming's fourteen principles and they hired the use of a communications consultant on more than one occasion. Whilst we can trace the history of TQM from initial conception through to present day activities, there has not been a logical sequence or series of pre-defined stages associated with the programme of change. As organisational researchers, we can examine the temporal history of change programmes in terms of their beginning, middle periods and conclusion (although in practice, it is often impossible to identify actual start and end points of change), and we can also examine different activities and tasks associated with change. For example, in analysing implementation strategies, we may find (as in the case of Tecpak and Vicbank) that they change over time, and stop and start, and that, in consequence, there is rarely one simple phase which we can call 'implementation'. In analysing the Vicbank case, the process of establishing TQM was further subdivided into three distinct historical periods (their TQM project commenced in 1986 and continues today). This was done in order to clarify the complex, temporal and iterative nature of their change programme and make the analysis accessible to readers. In short, the processual framework which has been used in this book has allowed us to identify certain tasks and activities and then to locate them within a temporal history of change.

The processual approach has also been useful in explaining transition management. The three major determinants of change we identified consisted of the context, substance and politics of change. The context of change was taken to refer to factors within the external environment and those internal to the organisation, such as: administrative structures, technology, human resources, history and culture, and the product or service of an organisation. The substance of change referred to the defining characteristics and content of change. Finally, the politics of change, refers to the process by which certain well-placed individuals, groups or powerful coalitions can influence decision-making and the setting of agendas at critical junctures during the process of organisational change. Through combining these three dimensions with the three general timeframes on the process of organisational change a processual framework for understanding TQM was developed and employed in the analysis of the case study material presented in Part II (see also, Figure 4.1.). Our findings from a processual analysis of the case material can also be used to compare the principles of TQM outlined in Chapter 2 with management practice, and to identify a number of general lessons on the process of establishing TQM, and this is the intention of the sections which follow.

COMMON FEATURES OF TQM PROGRAMMES IN PRACTICE

The seven common features of TQM programmes identified in Chapter 2 comprise: a management philosophy of change; an emphasis on continuous improvement; application of appropriate quality control techniques; group problem-solving of process operations; a focus on 'internal' and 'external' customer–supplier relations; a commitment to employee involvement; and a climate of trust, co-operation, and a non-adversarial system of industrial relations.

From a processual analysis of the empirical case studies the importance of contextual factors in colouring the nature of the TQM experience is highlighted. For example, not all companies embraced TQM as a total management approach to quality improvement. Although there was general support for an ideology of participation and collaboration through involving employees in managerial decision-making, the level of senior management commitment varied across the case organisations. For example, Accom Industries was a small company which had only just begun to think about the benefits of adopting a TQM programme. Although they were committed to quality assurance and accreditation, the conflicting views between the managing director and the general manager on the benefits and problems of employee involvement programmes put into question the level of management commitment behind the 'possible journey towards TQM'. In other words, whilst they can be identified as an organisation committed to quality management, Accom management were not united in their commitment to employee involvement. In practice, the absence of strong and active support among the senior executive severely limited the potential for TQM to become a mainstream management philosophy of change. In these cases, TQM came to be treated in a similar vein as other piecemeal initiatives like quality circles, and suffered the same types of setbacks and problems.

On the question of continuous improvement, the case studies illustrate how TQM group-based activity is by its very nature temporary. The notion of continual TQM improvement is a misnomer in so far as the activities are typically project based and oriented to solving discrete problems within a pre-defined timeframe. The formation of Process Improvement Teams (PITs) at Alcoa's Kwinana plant highlights how teams are formed to solve discrete problems. In this case, two initial PITs were formed to act as test cases for TQM and process improvement. The Kwinana case is also interesting because the company introduced what they termed 'Natural Teams' comprising employees with common concerns who work together to improve productivity and levels of workplace efficiency. In short, whilst the cases illustrate a general trend towards teamwork on the shopfloor, TQM teams were typically cross-functional teams set up to tackle particular problem(s) over an expected timeframe. In many cases, the initial TQM teams were established to tackle the major company problems which had already been identified by management. Consequently, whilst initial projects may solve major problems and save the company large sums of money, in the longer term, the benefits of TQM may become less evident as achievements are restricted to minor system changes. However, this may also detract attention from one of the major aims of TQM, which is about gaining greater organisational flexibility. To have a system which supports the need for continuous change is central to achieving the acceptance of employees to the need to adapt to revisions and changes in company strategies. In this sense, TQM is about increasing human resource adaptability to meet the demands of operating within rapidly changing business market environments (see also, Dawson, 1994a).

In evaluating the applications and use of appropriate quality control techniques, the emphasis has to be on the word 'appropriate'. What was deemed important at the outset changed considerably during the process of introducing TQM. Whilst all the companies identified some benefits from establishing benchmarks from which improvements could be gauged, these were often far simpler measures than those promoted during the initial periods of change. For example, on the question of the shopfloor use of statistical techniques, the empirical evidence suggests that these methods tended to be overemphasised in the training programmes provided by consultant groups. For example, in the case of Pirelli, statistics formed a central part of the Blakemore Consulting training programme and yet, in practice, it was found that employees did not always understand or use the range of statistical techniques available but, rather, relied on one or two individuals to provide visual graphs to monitor the group's achievements (Dawson, 1994:76–7). In the case of Tecpak, training in statistical process control was identified as a need later in the change process and was provided by an external quality manager. This external consultant spent a weekend training five key staff members in the use of simple statistical techniques, such as Pareto charts, fishbone diagrams and machine process control charts. Like Pirelli, a small number of staff became responsible (or the 'experts') in the visual presentation of shopfloor data. In short, the statistical side of TQM tends to be emphasised in prescriptive material, consultant packages and training programmes and yet, little use was made of these methods by employees as a whole.

With regard to the group problem-solving of process operations, the techniques which tended to dominate within the TQM groups were not so much statistical as group-oriented approaches—such as brainstorming, which was often used in initial meetings. Measurements were taken of processes which were being considered for improvement, and these proved to be particularly useful when a discrete area had first been identified. In Pirelli, for example, measuring the scrap rate of a particular machine, brainstorming the problem, then implementing one or a range of possible solutions, then measuring any changes in the scrap rate, is a simple and classic example of how basic measures are often used as indicators of success or failure of TQM team solutions. In such cases, the key activities centred around group problem-solving. Within these groups, key ingredients to the process of problem-solving were: easy communication, good internal relations, an open-minded approach, a willingness to listen to different views (acceptance of conflict in perspective) and a good facilitator or group co-ordinator. This highlights how many TQM training programmes should be redesigned to reduce the emphasis on statistics and increase the focus on interpersonal skills and the nature of group dynamics. In the case of Tecpak Industries, an early emphasis was placed on 'talk skills' for use in meetings. A communications consultant was hired who provided staff training in personal and interpersonal communication. However, in organisations such as Pirelli, whose employees comprise a multi-cultural workforce, employee participation in group problem-solving was found to be limited to those fluent in the English language. In this sense, TQM was not well suited to building employee commitment within a workforce that was culturally diverse. This demonstrates how much TQM has been influenced by the managerial practices associated with the extraordinarily homogeneous society of Japan.

The focus on internal and external customer–supplier relations was a common feature of TQM programmes in practice. Many companies were looking to improve external relations and to break down some of the internal barriers between departments and units. For example, Hendersons developed a new company strategy based on the need to be 'customer-driven'. The initial focus was on improving internal customer–supplier relations and facilitating more open communication within the company. Once they had improved internal relations they then set about developing their external customer–supplier relations. For example, in 1988 forty suppliers attended a seminar conducted by Hendersons to communicate their requirements for quality and to inform suppliers about recommended systems for quality assurance. On the customer side, regular weekly visits are made by a small group of shopfloor employees and a quality inspector to their major customers in South Australia (interstate customers, such as Ford and Nissan, are visited fortnightly). In this way, TQM was not only seen as a new management approach to improving external relations, but also as a vehicle for achieving greater communication and establishing new networks over existing structural arrangements. In some companies, however, the principle of internal customers and suppliers has only been partially achieved. One of the major practical issues which the TQM literature does not adequately address is how to accommodate multiple intra-organisational relationships. For example, in cases where an individual or group may have to service multiple customers (such as the next stage in the process, as well as opposite numbers on alternate shifts) then a conflict of interest may result and offset the benefits associated with a system based on simple linear customer–supplier progression. In practice therefore, the assumption that by operating a system of internal customer–supplier relations more co-operative work environments will be created and sustained is a myth rather than the organisational reality of operating under TQM.

The commitment to employee involvement varied across the companies studied. As illustrated in the Accom case, conflicting managerial views about employee involvement is likely to influence a company's commitment to such schemes. In the case of Laubman and Pank, although senior management recognised the potential for TQM to develop high-trust relationships and encourage employee involvement, there was a tendency to focus on TQM (particularly within the laboratory setting) as a scientific methodology for identifying and establishing documented procedures and quantifiable indicators. Moreover, whilst there is a certain public agreement about the need for a shift in the culture of the organisation and a movement towards greater employee involvement, there was also a general belief that conservatism still dominated senior management decision-making and that there would be some resistance to embracing programmes of change which sought to radically transform existing cultures and operating philosophies. Hence, whilst it is not uncommon for management to verbalise a commitment to employee involvement, such involvement was, in practice, often restricted. There were a number of reasons for this. First, some companies did not involve all their employees in training programmes or assign them to TQM problem-solving groups. Second, in order to understand TQM and communicate within the groups, employees need to have a certain level of English language fluency. For those employees within the multicultural workplace where English was their first, second or even third language, problems of communication posed as a major barrier to their involvement in TQM teams (see also, Dawson 1994b). Third, existing organisational arrangements sometimes prevented staff involvement, for example, as in the case of permanent night shift employees (see Dawson, 1994a).

The final common feature of TQM programmes centres on developing a climate of trust, co-operation, and a non-adversarial system of industrial relations. In practice, there were considerable differences not only between companies but also between plants located on the same site of a single company. Contextual dimensions and the politics of change were important determinants shaping the outcomes of change on employee relationships and the system of industrial relations. For example, the case of Vicbank illustrates the non-linear political processes often associated with the transition towards a new form of operating culture, whilst Pirelli highlights the two very different experiences of adjacent plants operating on the same manufacturing site. The Pirelli example also demonstrates how companies who are downsizing may find it particularly difficult (if not impossible) to build trust in a context where job security is threatened. Whilst TQM offers the potential to develop network relations and better communication channels within an organisation, TQM will not by itself solve the problem of poor employee relations. In some cases, the introduction of a programme which talks of a brave new culture of trust and co-operation may simply exacerbate intra-organisational conflict. Once again, it is important to stress that organisations comprise a range of different sub-cultures and that, whilst TQM may represent espoused values and change the surface levels of culture, deeper levels of culture are far less open to rapid change. In short, TQM is not a panacea for management–union conflict nor for poor relations with staff, but it can be used as a means of improving communication and employee relations at work. It is not TQM which determines outcomes, but how TQM is developed, managed and used in different organisational contexts.

GENERAL LESSONS ON THE PROCESS OF ESTABLISHING TQM

In this section the findings from the case material are used to draw out eight general lessons on the implementation of TQM. Perhaps the main lesson which can be drawn from a processual analysis of TQM is that there is no one best way to establishing TQM. Transition management must be sensitive to the character of change, the context in which change is taking place, and the views and reactions of employee groups and key political players. Successful strategies for establishing TQM in one company may be entirely inappropriate for another comparable company. If we look across the case organisations we can see both comparisons and contrasts in the type of change strategies adopted. For example, the State Bank of South Australia formed a cross-functional implementation team and adopted a top-to-bottom approach whereby employees at lower levels in the bank's organisation structure were progressively introduced to the philosophy and practice of service delivery. This cascade method centred on progressively training and educating each 'level of staff about the values, the mission, the strategy, and the management principles of the new service quality philosophy. Four levels were included in the cascade training process. The top twenty members of the executive team comprised level one. The second level involved some 200 members of the senior management group. Level three comprised some 700 managers and supervisors and level four comprised the remaining 2500 staff members employed by the bank. This final level in the training programme was preceded by a large-scale staff function known as the 'One-Day Event'

This change strategy proved very successful and compares with the approach adopted by Vicbank. As part of Vicbank's implementation strategy, a consultant group was contracted to train and acquaint all levels of management with the tools and philosophy of TQM. These consultants ran a series of small workshops for managers, commencing with the most senior team and then progressively moving through to the lower levels of management. These sessions normally took half a day and provided managers with an overview of the origins of TQM concepts, the major TQM tools and how they might be applied. A full-time person was appointed to be responsible for overseeing and supporting TQM implementation and was given the title of Manager, Organisational Development. However, in contrast to the State Bank's initiative there was no high profile 'One-Day Event', nor was there a general acceptance of the commercial benefits of TQM. Some employees viewed TQM as simply unnecessary whilst others criticised the TQM training sessions and formed the view that TQM was superficial and of no relevance to their own functional areas. They were particularly scathing of the consultant's method of presentation which was seen to be too blunt and forthright and based on extensive manufacturing rather than service-oriented examples. Unlike the State Bank, Vicbank had not fully taken on the responsibility for implementing TQM but, rather, had largely left the programme of change in the control of outside consultants. In contrast, the State Bank spent considerable time and effort planning and preparing a comprehensive training programme which was tailored to the needs of a financial services organisation. Furthermore, the initial implementation of TQM at Vicbank was not marked by serious management commitment nor was there any real ownership of the programme by the company's managers. Moreover, in the case of Vicbank, the message of TQM was not effectively communicated to staff. However, it should be noted that during a later period, Vicbank did identify methods of communication as an issue and employed the services of a communication consultant to help them effectively implement a service quality change programme. Thus, whilst there are similarities between the implementation strategies of these two banking organisations, there are also some noticeable differences. Finally, as the Vicbank case illustrates, organisations are themselves changing and therefore what may be an appropriate implementation strategy in 1994 may not prove effective in six months time. In short, there are no simple prescriptions to the problems of managing change towards the establishment of a total quality organisation.

A second and related lesson is that change is a non-linear dynamic process, the outcomes of which cannot be assured even with the best made plans of experienced and professional change agents. Large-scale operational change generally unfolds over time and consists of management omissions and revisions as well as unforeseen employee responses, technical problems and contingencies. Once again, Vicbank provides a good illustration of this point, where the initial introduction of TQM was met with significant middle management resistance. Consequently, senior managers have to revise their implementation strategy and develop their own novel solutions to gain management commitment through cultural change. Similarly, in the case of Tecpak, initial attempts to implement TQM proved unsuccessful and senior management set about revising their strategies and using an external communications consultant to communicate the philosophy of TQM to their staff. In short, the organisational adoption of TQM is a large task which will take a number of years, require considerable planning, involve numerous revisions and modifications to planned changes, and is unlikely to be marked by a line of continual improvement from beginning to end.

This last point leads on to an experience common to the case organisations and is one we describe as the TQM blues. Many of the companies passed through a number of different 'states of mind'. At the outset there was awareness, followed by action and the implementation of plans which brought about a state of excitement and expectant enthusiasm. However, after the honeymoon of TQM the realities of managing large-scale change hit home: enthusiasm wanes, the high profile of change agents is replaced by the pressures of meeting output targets and deadlines, and there is the possible awareness that only a few teams have actually succeeded in meeting or exceeding their objectives. The TQM blues can result in the simple rejection of TQM or it may lead to critical appraisal and revision of existing strategies. For example, in both Pirelli and Alcoa alumina refinery at Kwinana, there are some downsides and failures associated with the adoption of TQM. One of the most common frustrations stemmed from the failure of TQM teams. In the case of Pirelli, the acceptance of TQM in the cable processing plant can be partly explained by the success of the original TQM team, in contrast to the experience of the cable manufacturing plant. Similarly at Kwinana, one of the initial teams failed whilst the other reported significant improvements and changed the view of one supervisor from being highly sceptical to being strongly supportive of TQM. Conversely, failure brought with it some disillusionment and can initiate less positive feelings or what we term the TQM blues. Our studies indicate that a recognition of failure is important and that organisations should not discount failed teams, but learn from the experience and see it as part of the process of change. In the case of Kwinana, the team from building 46 failed for several reasons including: the lack of clearly defined goals, unrealistic team expectations, inadequate management support, lack of implementation strategy and limited training. We would suggest that, in many instances, organisations can learn more from their failures than from successful implementation strategies (which are generally praised rather than critically evaluated). In our studies, it was only those organisations who could manage the downside of change who have successfully developed and refined their TQM programme.

In examining the *substance* of change, the cases highlight variations in the characteristics of TQM programmes across companies. The main features of these programmes tended to reflect the assumptions and views of the major change agents. For example, in cases where consultants were used, the packages were generally predefined and laid out in a very structured series of steps on how to implement TQM. The content of the programmes was generally an adaptation of material derived from popular exponents of quality management, such as Deming, Juran and Crosby. There was also a tendency to overplay the importance of statistics—perhaps because this is an area in which expertise can easily be justified and one in which the relevance of training programmes can be supported. The statistical focus of many of the consultant packages also added 'scientific' credibility to their proposed schemes. Nevertheless, measurement mania was a problem encountered by some companies during the early experience with TQM. For example, Henderson Automotive recognised some of the benefits of measurement at an early phase during their quality change programme. Statistical process control was seen to provide 'as-it-happens' information which would allow process problems to be detected and adjustments made to realign process operations. However, in their enthusiasm for measurement there was also a tendency to measure first and then question the reason for the measure later. On this point, Verna Blewett notes that, during a period of participant observation, an instance was observed where the workers regarded a particular type of SPC charting to be worthless as it did not add to the knowledge about the quality of the component. After discussions with the Quality Inspectors, the Engineering Department and the Materials Manager it was agreed that the workers were right and a meaningful measure that the workers suggested was introduced. In short, it was often common for organisations to try to measure too much too soon without regard for the practical value of such measurements.

A related problem identified by many of the companies studied was the tendency to try to do everything at once. This could be seen, for example, in the creation of too many teams without due care and attention being given to what those teams would be able to do. It was assumed that the more TQM teams you had the closer you were to becoming a total quality organisation. Companies just beginning to implement TQM also had a tendency to overemphasise the importance of gaining some immediate returns which could be balanced against the cost of quality. Both of these issues were raised in the Pirelli case and have been discussed on an SBS educational programme on quality management (SBS, 1993). At the outset of change there was a tendency for companies to underestimate timescales and to focus on achieving immediate quantifiable results which could serve as indicators of success. It was only in retrospect that senior management reflected on the long-term nature of trying to establish a total quality organisation. In reflecting on these timescales, senior management emphasised the importance of communication both prior to implementation and throughout the change process. For example, in the cases of Tecpak and the State Bank, communication was identified early on as a central element to change management. Tecpak introduced 'Roadshow Meetings' where staff were encouraged to discuss company operations, make observations and express any concerns, whilst the State Bank organised their 'One-Day Event' which aimed to communicate senior management's intentions in an atmosphere of 'gaiety and entertainment'. For some organisations, such as Vicbank, it was often only after problems of implementation had arisen that senior management became aware of the importance of communication to the process of managing transitions. From the experiences of our case organisations, a lesson learnt would be to try not to do everything at once and be sure to communicate your intentions to employees throughout the change process.

Training was another issue which was raised by the substance of TQM programmes. There were two main weaknesses identified with the training programmes we studied. First, there was a tendency to train as many people as possible even if they were not going to be involved in TQM teams. In some cases, training and the formation of teams were misaligned. In contrast, we would argue that training should be carried out just-in-time and be organised on a needs basis. Second, courses tended to focus on statistical methods and techniques rather than on the important area of working in teams and developing interpersonal skills. For example, the senior management of Laubman and Pank identified training as a key ingredient to the successful introduction of a service excellence programme and it was suggested that this is often an area which can be overlooked. They stressed the importance of customised training packages which would fulfil the needs of different groups within the organisation. In contrast, the experience of Vicbank illustrated the problems caused through the use of inappropriate training materials, which in this case emphasised statistical measurement for manufacturing industries. In Tecpak, training was an on-going issue with the problem of poor communication and interpersonal skills being identified as a major barrier to the adoption of TQM. In all the cases reported in this book, training was an essential element to the management of TQM.

During the process of implementation, the substance of the change programmes were often modified by both internal change agents and employees who formed the initial problem-solving teams. In the cases reported, it was common for an organisation to modify their TQM scheme (to enhance some elements, revise others, and downplay or reject others, which formed part of the initial programme) and develop their own versions over time. A common characteristic of companies who had successfully developed and implemented strategies for the adoption of TQM centred on the adaptability and flexibility of their planned programme for change. On this count, the State Bank—which in the late 1980s and early 1990s was also making important strategic decisions which in retrospect have proven to be financially disastrous both for the company and the South Australian economy—did develop a particularly effective TQM change programme which was modified to meet its own organisational needs. The experience of the State Bank also provides a clear example that 'organisational success' depends on a range of factors and that company executives should not view quality management as a safety net to poor strategic management of their business activities and loose financial decision-making. A company who has successfully incorporated its quality management initiatives into its broader range of change programmes is Hendersons Automotive. This company has adapted a whole range of quality techniques to fit their requirements and continues to revise and modify existing policies to meet the managerial objective of developing a highly specialised and flexible workforce which can be easily accommodated within rapidly adjusted production arrangements to meet changing market demands. The next step for Hendersons is a more concerted move towards lean manufacturing (as part of the Australian Best Practice Demonstration Programme), in which skills can be developed within close-knit teams for career progression. Thus, companies such as Hendersons Automotive continually evaluate and modify their programmes and highlight the need for company TQM programmes to change over time.

The *context* of change raises a number of important considerations. The external context has been very influential in promoting the uptake of TQM. As indicated in Chapter 2, there have been a number of government-supported agencies which have publicised TQM and offered incentives for companies to take on accredited consultants to help them introduce TQM. Internally, one of the major obstacles to change, which was generally side-stepped or simply ignored, relates to organisational culture and the existence of subcultures. In Pirelli, for example, the contextual differences between two adjacent plants operating on the same site resulted in very different employee experiences of change. In this case, factors such as gender, ethnicity and language were all shown to be important elements which were not adequately taken into account in consultant packages or descriptive guidelines on the successful introduction of TQM. As Dawson (1994b) has indicated elsewhere, unitary notions of organisational culture are misplaced and fail to account for the cultural pluralism of many Australian companies which may also have to accommodate professional affiliations (see also, Bloor and Dawson, 1994).

With respect to the *politics* of change, the simple lesson is that the greater the support for change by all employees of the company, the higher the likelihood of success. In particular, it is important to try to obtain the support of senior management, local management, supervisors, trade unions and workplace employees. Senior management commitment and support is central to the transition towards a total quality organisation; without it, TQM can only ever be partial and is unlikely to form an integral part of management strategy. In terms of barriers to change, the absence of supervisory involvement was one of the most common mentioned obstacles to the introduction of TQM. For example, in both Laubman and Pank and Vicbank, middle management resistance was identified as a major obstacle to change. TQM, in placing greater emphasis on the knowledge of operative staff in correcting and adapting day-to-day operations, undermines the traditional authority base of the supervisor. Both cases highlight the need to redefine supervision and make the expectations of the position clear not only to supervisors, but also to operative staff and the senior management group. In conjunction with this redefinition, there is also a need to ensure that appropriate TQM training is provided at the supervisory level. It is perhaps ironic that supervisors are key players in programmes of change and yet, they often remain the forgotten men and women of industry and commerce (see also, Dawson, 1991a and 1991b). Interestingly, gaining trade union support was not an issue faced by the companies we studied. In Australia, unlike the UK, TQM was not a major trade union concern. At the time of the interviews many of the Australian unions were actively and deeply involved in award restructuring and elements of enterprise bargaining. In the case of Tecpak, unionisation has been actively discouraged and since 1984 there has only been one trade union member on staff. In this largely non-union firm there have been few problems and staff have not looked to outside representation for support. In short, whilst unions were informed of TQM programmes, there were no major industrial relations disputes.

These then are the main lessons which can be drawn from a processual analysis of introducing TQM into Australian and New Zealand companies. They can be summarised as follows:

1. *There is no one best way.* Be wary of simple prescriptions for the successful management of TQM.

2. *Accept the TQM blues.* Change will have its downside and be composed of omissions and unforseen events. This highlights the need for flexible and reviewable implementation strategies.

3. *Question measurement mania.* Do not measure for measurement's sake but consider the practical value of what you do.

4. *Don't try to do everything at once.* Successful large-scale operational change takes time.

5. *Train employees just-in-time.* Organise training on a needs basis and include more material on working in teams and interpersonal skills.

6. *Tailor your TQM programme.* Modify your TQM programme to suit your organisational needs. The content of TQM needs to be revised over time and should be evaluated and appraised on a regular basis.

7 *Be contextually aware.* Take account of external and internal contextual issues and do not underplay the importance of the multicultural workplace in Australian society.

8 *Seek support from all quarters.* Politics and conflict are often key determinants on the outcomes of change. For example, supervisors are often overlooked in change programmes and they can act as a major barrier or catalyst to change.

CONCLUSION

The implementation of TQM in Australian and New Zealand companies can teach us about both the process of organisational change and the complexity of the managerial process. In this book we have presented eight case studies on the recent experience of Australian and New Zealand companies who were considering or implementing TQM. In our analysis of the companies, we have discussed two theoretical areas to give more insight into the nature of the change process, and the nature of the management process.

On the issue of organisational change, the studies show that change does not take place in a simple linear fashion. Instead the process is one of stops and starts, of hesitancy, confusion and retreat as well as apparent progress. Neither the direction nor the rate of change are certain. The processual approach we have used in this book attempts to tackle the complex and turbulent waters of modern day change programmes (see also Dawson, 1994). We suggest that every change has a temporal history and that over this period there will be a number of tasks, activities, and decisions. The management of these transitional tasks may stop and start and interpenetrate and overlap with other tasks and activities. The three main groups of determinants which shape this process comprise the substance of change, the context in which change takes place, and the politics of change. What the processual approach allows us to do is to examine these factors temporally within the complex dynamics of organisational change.

On the issue of management theory and process, TQM can be seen as the latest in a number of movements for managerial reform in the twentieth century. It contains many elements from earlier movements, like the systematic measurement of Scientific Management or the teamwork of Socio-technical Systems Theory. However the cases suggest that the total package of TQM is not a clearly delineated, coherent whole. Different elements are introduced in a variety of ways, apparently with mixed results. People with high expectations of the changes were often disappointed. This is not surprising and serves to demonstrate the complexity of management. To unravel some of this complexity, we used ideas of reframing in order to view this complex data through a number of different perspectives. We chose the perspectives of bureaucracy (or administrative theory), politics (focusing on the use and distribution of power), and culture (focusing on ideals and legitimacy). These perspectives can be used to show why the bureaucratic elements of TQM can represent a powerful increase in managerial control and that employee involvement can increase the acceptability and legitimacy of these controls. However TQM's attempts to create a unified culture appear to be misguided or doomed.

The introduction of TQM into Australian and New Zealand companies is occurring within the context of other on-going changes. Organisational change can no longer be viewed as a one-off event which occurs every five to ten years. Lewin's three-stage model of unfreezing, changing, and refreezing, belies the reality of managing organisational transitions. Organisations are dynamic entities which do not change in the direction suggested by neat linear stage models of planned change. Whilst there may be certain activities and tasks associated with managing change, these would generally overlap and interpenetrate throughout the change process. In the case of TQM, where change is deliberate, it 'is a matter of grabbing hold of some aspect of the motion and steering it in a particular direction that will be perceived by key players as a new method of operating' (Kanter, Stein and Jick, 1992:10) . Steering a company towards the establishment of a total quality organisation is an on-going journey with no clear endpoint. Change continues ad infinitum and, as such, is best explained and understood from a processual perspective.

Our case studies have highlighted variations in the scale and nature of changes being introduced into Australian and New Zealand companies under the TQM banner. Whilst the simple scientific approach to TQM is likely to remain an attractive and saleable package to companies seeking quick-fix solutions, our empirical studies show this to be a TQM myth which needs discarding and replacing with longer-term and more culturally sensitive strategies of change. In short, TQM neither is nor should be a rigid set of principles nor can it provide a panacea to all organisational ills. These and the other lessons outlined in this book, underline the problems associated with importing managerial ideas from overseas and the importance of adopting a critical scepticism of proposals for simple solutions to complex problems.

APPENDIX *I*

A Guide for Interviewers

KEY CENTRE IN STRATEGIC MANAGEMENT, QUT* QUALITY MANAGEMENT CASE STUDY PROGRAMME

Objectives

The Key Centre in Strategic Management Total Quality Management (TQM) case study programme is designed to ascertain the ways in which TQM techniques have been introduced into Australian firms. The main objective of the programme is to assess the introduction, the implementation and the effects of TQM in Australia. TQM will therefore be analysed as it affects management, workers and their organisations, suppliers and customers and the organisation of work.

TQM is difficult to define and is understood to mean different things to different groups. This programme will employ case studies to explore the use of TQM in a range of firms and TQM will be taken to be those practices that the firms themselves regard as TQM.

The Project will be undertaken by a Key Centre in Strategic Management research team. Professor Gill Palmer of the University of Wollongong (with Research Assistant, Cameron Allan) will work in collaboration with Dr Patrick Dawson (with Research Associate, Verna Blewett) of the University of Adelaide. Other case study workers in Sydney, Perth and Queensland are

---

* Queensland University of Technology

being organised and will come under the direction of either Gill Palmer or Patrick Dawson.

Outcomes from the project will be a series of journal articles and a book based on the research findings.

Research themes

The study will relate to the literature in TQM, the emergence of managerial movements, Industrial Relations and Award Restructuring, HRM and Organisational Behaviour.

This research aims to determine if, in multi-plant firms, TQM is being implemented in different ways in different plants. Further, it is hoped to determine to what extent the practice matches the rhetoric.

A The spread of TQM—The mobilisation of a movement and the influence of change agents:

    1 The role of consultants in the transmission of quality management practices.

    2 The role of government (eg. NIES program) in the transmission of quality management practices.

    3 Ideologies/fashions of managerial reform movements.

B Customer/Supplier relations—This research will study the effect of TQM on the networks of customers and suppliers around the firm and with the firm.

    1 Changes in perceptions and processes for external and internal customers.

C TQM and HRM—The nature of the changes generated and their impact on the flexible use of labour.

    1 The use of labour, changes in the structure of training, skill formation, recruitment, promotion and reward systems.

    2 Changing communication and influence systems. Changes in the nature of the psychological contract between employer and employee. The creation of a new culture. Contrasts between administered and market relations.

D TQM and IR

    1 Quality initiatives and structural efficiency/award restructuring.

E Process of change

1 Continuous improvements vs freezing/unfreezing: Organisational Behaviour literature.
2 Competing histories of the change process from different perspectives.
3 Key symbolic events.

Methodology

Interviews will be conducted with the following personnel.

Key players

- senior level management and TU officials
- management, especially those instrumental to the introduction of TQM
- consultants

Other participants

- a subset in a part of the company where TQM was implemented: managers, supervisors, shop delegates and workers.

Questions/Areas to be covered

1 Background information about the firm

- company size
- number of employees
- industry sector/s
- recent history re: growth/decline in market share/profits/workforce/competition for last 5–10 years
- perception of change—the competing histories
- patterns of HRM/IR (look for changes due to TQM)
    - adverbial vs co-operation IRs?
    - relations with unions?
    - what type of appraisal/evaluation/reward systems?
    - any career routes?

- what kind of security, recruitment, dismissal, grievance procedures?
- what use of subcontractors, casual labour?
• any other attempts to reorganise work or change management labour relations in the recent past?
- collective employee representation, traditional role of union delegates, previous experience of joint involvement in managerial issues.

2   The decision to change

• what were the circumstances in which the decision to try TQM was made?
• why was it thought necessary to introduce TQM? was it a statutory requirement? was it a directive from head office? was it related to company performance, product or labour market conditions, etc.?
• who made the decision?
• what were the justifications?
• what were the expectations?
• why use a TQM approach over others?
• to what extent did union representatives feel involved in the decision to change?
• were there other mechanisms for involving employees in the early decision-making process?

3   Planning the change

• was there any planning?
• was there any type of consultative committee set-up to discuss the issues objectives of introducing a TQM package?
• who was involved: management, trade unions, eee, consultants?
• what were the objectives; eg, to reduce stock, to increase worker involvement, etc.?
• timeframe
• costing justification
• expectations

Packages

- what package/s were introduced?
- what techniques were they comprised of: statistical techniques?
- what did it cost?

Consultants

- who and why were these particular consultants chosen?
- what was their brief?
- what processes die they use and how influential were they in the implementation?
- was NIES support a important factor? were they subsidies?
- was there any worker involvement in the decision to *introduce* a package?
- what role for the unions?

4 Implementation of change (TQM)

- what were key stages in the process?
- timeframe?
- what problems encountered?
- what levels of management were involved in the implementation of TQM and what was their role?
- in what ways have workers been involved in the introduction of the TQM?
- were the unions involved?
- what involvement did the consultants have in the introduction and implementation of the TQM package/s?

5 Effects of change (TQM)—evaluated by the participants

Union perspective and views

- any change in unions attitude
- views of shop delegates

Management perspectives

- any changes to the role and responsibility of specialist and line managers at the top, mid and lower levels? their views and reactions?

Supervisors perspectives

- any change in the supervisors role?
- any change in the nature of subordinate–superordinate relations?
- supervisors evaluation?

Effects on the technical and social organisation of work

- has there been any change to the technical organisation of work—that is, a change to the way work is the physically organised?
- any change to the social organisation of work, which may include:
    - Quality Circles
    - Quality Improvement Teams
    - Other
- any change to demarcations, task structures, flexibility of labour usage?
- JIT effects

Effects on workers

- has worked intensified?
- any change in staff levels?
- what have been the effects on the quality of work experience for employees and their prospects eg. skill formation pathways?

6 Measurement of operational change
Qualitative and Quantitative Effects

- is there any meaningful measure in terms of productivity, profitability, or any other performance measure terms of morale, employee commitment?
- impact on suppliers/customers?
- changes in the patterns of HRM/IR
    - adversarial vs co-operative IR?

- relations with unions?
- what type of appraisal/evaluation/reward systems?
- any career routes?
- what kind of security, recruitment, dismissal, grievance procedures?
- what use of subcontractors, casual labour?

7 Future expectations

- where to next?

8 Assessment of change—evaluated by the case study worker

- do the implementation and effects of TQM accord with the stated/desired intention?
- is it possible to say that the effects are attributable to the implementation of TQM package?
- how do we assess the role of the state (if any)?
- how significant has the award restructuring process?
- how can we account for the HRM/IR changes?

APPENDIX II

Deming's Fourteen Points, Juran's Ten Steps and Crosby's Fourteen Stages to Quality Improvement

DEMING'S FOURTEEN POINTS

1. *Create constancy of purpose.* Continuous improvement through the elimination of all waste of materials, capital, and human resources has to become a way of life.

2. *Adopt the new philosophy.* When all waste is eliminated, quality improves, productivity increases, costs decline and competitive position improves. Companies unwilling to adopt this philosophy will be unable to compete with those companies that do.

3. *Cease dependence on mass inspection.* Use statistical tools to monitor the systems and to ensure that quality is built in, thereby eliminating the need for mass inspection.

4. *End the practice of awarding business on the basis of price tag.* Supplier price alone does not account for the expenses associated with the waste produced by delivery of poor quality material. Instead, depend on meaningful measures of quality along with price.

5. *Improve constantly the system of production and service.* It is management's job to work continually on the system and to seek continual improvements.

6. *Institute training on the job.* Human resources cannot be appropriately utilised if employees are not properly trained.

7 *Institute modern methods of supervision.* The responsibility of supervisors must be changed from sheer numbers to quality, and management must be prepared to take immediate action on reports from supervisors concerning barriers such as inherited defects, machines not maintained, poor tools, and fuzzy operational definitions.

8 *Drive out fear.* Co-operation and communication among all employees is necessary to detect waste, determine the causes and institute remedies. Management must work on those sub-systems that affect the climate to enable open, non-punitive discussions about problems.

9 *Break down barriers between departments.* People in research, design, sales, and production must work as a team to foresee problems of production that may be encountered with various materials and specifications. Effective system change will require joint inter-departmental teams to find proper solutions.

10 *Eliminate numerical goals, posters, and slogans for the work force.* Goal and slogans do not provide the vehicle for achieving quality improvements.

11 *Eliminate work standards that prescribe numerical quotas.* If a numerical quota is given, emphasis will be placed on production rate, rather than quality.

12 *Remove barriers that stand between employees and their pride in their work.* If management does not change the system that produces defective incoming material, or if the work process must be conducted with poor tooling and equipment, then quality work is not possible. Management must therefore eliminate any barriers built in to the system.

13 *Institute a vigorous programme of education and training.* Methods and tools for detecting and eliminating waste must be learned by all employees.

14 *Put everyone in the company to work to accomplish the transformation.*

JURAN'S TEN STEPS TO QUALITY IMPROVEMENT

1 Build awareness of the need and opportunity for improvement.

2 Set goals for improvement.

3 Organise to reach the goals (establish a quality council, identify problems, select projects, appoint teams, designate facilitators).

4   Provide training.

5   Carry out project to solve problems.

6   Report progress.

7   Give recognition.

8   Communicate results.

9   Keep score.

10 Maintain momentum by making annual improvement part of the regular systems and processes of the company.

CROSBY'S FOURTEEN STEPS TO QUALITY IMPROVEMENT

1   *Management commitment.* To make it clear where management stands on quality.

2   *Quality improvement team.* To run the quality improvement process.

3   *Quality measurement.* To provide a display of current and potential nonconformance problems in a manner that permits objective evaluation and corrective action.

4   *Cost of quality evaluation.* To define the ingredients of the Cost of Quality (COQ) and explain its use as a management tool.

5   *Quality awareness.* To provide a method of raising the personal concern felt by all employees toward the conformance of the product or service and the quality reputation of the company.

6   *Corrective action.* To provide a systematic method of resolving forever the problems that are identified through the previous action steps.

7   *Establish an ad hoc committee for the zero defects programme.* To examine the various activities that must be conducted in preparation for formally launching the zero defects programme.

8   *Supervisor training.* To define the type of training that supervisors need in order to actively carry out their part of the quality improvement programme.

9   *Zero defects day.* To create an event that will let all employees realise, through a personal experience, that there has been a change.

10. *Goal setting.* To turn pledges and commitments into action by encouraging individuals to establish improvement goals for themselves and their groups.

11. *Error cause removal.* To give the individual employee a method of communicating to management the situations that make it difficult for the employee to meet the pledge to improve.

12. *Recognition.* To appreciate those who participate.

13. *Quality councils.* To bring together the appropriate people to share quality management information on a regular basis.

14. *Do it over again.* To emphasise that the quality improvement process is continuous.

Bibliography

Abegglen, J. (1974) *The Japanese Factory*. Glencoe, IL: Free Press.

Abegglen, J. and Stalk, G. (1985) *The Japanese Corporation*. New York: Basic Books.

Abrahamson, E. (1991) 'Managerial Fads and Fashions: The Diffusion and Rejection of Innovations', *Academy Management Review*, 16(3): 586–612.

Adams, G. (1990) 'Redefining the Role of the Supervisor', unpublished MBA thesis, Adelaide: University of Adelaide.

Aguayo, R. (1991) *Dr Deming: The American Who Taught the Japanese about Quality*. New York: Fireside.

Albrecht, K. and Zemke, R. (1985) *Service America!: Doing Business in the New Economy*. Homewood: Dow Jones-Irwin.

Albrecht, K. (1992) *The Only Thing That Matters: Bringing the Power of the Customer into the Centre of your Business*. New York: HarperBusiness.

Alcoa of Australia, (1991), *Annual Report*, Alcoa.

Allan, C. (1991) 'The Role of Diffusion Agents in the Transfer of Quality Management in Australia', unpublished honours thesis, Brisbane: University of Griffith.

Barker, T.B. (1990) *Engineering Quality by Design: Interpreting the Taguchi Approach*. New York: Marcel Dekker.

Barnett, N.S. (1991) 'Management and Statistical Issues Affecting Quality Improvement in Australia', *International Journal of Quality & Reliability Management*, 8(5): 9–13.

Bemoski, K. (1991) 'The International Quality Study' *Quality Progress*, 24(3): 33–37.

Berry, L.L. and Parasuraman, A. (1992) 'Prescriptions for a Service Quality Revolution in America', *Organizational Dynamics*, Spring: 5–15.

Berry, T.H. (1991) *Managing the Total Quality Transformation*. New York: McGraw-Hill.

Berry, L.L. and Parasuraman, A. (1991) *Marketing Services. Competing Through Quality*. New York: Free Press.

Blackburn, R and Rosen, B. (1993) 'Total quality and human resource management: lessons learned from Baldridge Award-Winning companies'. *Academy of Managment Executive*. 7.3: 49–66.

Blakemore, J. (1989) *The Quality Solution*. Parramatta: MASC Publishing.

Bloor, G. and Dawson, P. (1994) 'Understanding Professional Culture in Organizational Context', *Organization Studies*, 15(2):275–95.

Bluntish, I. (1991) 'The Management of a Service Excellence Programme' unpublished MBA thesis, Adelaide: University of Adelaide.

Board, R. de (1978) *The Psychoanlysis of Organistions. A Psychoanlytic Approach to Behaviour in Groups and Organisations*. London: Tavistock.

Bolman, L. and Deal, T. (1984) *Modern Approaches to Understanding and Managing Organisation*. San Fransisco: Jossey-Bass.

Bolman, L. and Deal, T. (1991) *Reframing Organisations: Artistry, Choice and Leadership*. San Fransisco: Jossey-Bass.

Bowen, D.E. and Lawler, E.E. (1992) 'Total Quality-Oriented Human Resources Management', *Organizational Dynamics*, Spring: 29–41.

Braverman, H. (1974) *Labour and Monopoly Capital*. New York: Monthly Review Press.

Brocka, B. and Brocka M. (1992) *Quality Management: Implementing the Best Ideas of the Masters*. Illinois: Business One Irwin.

Brown, M.G. (1989) 'Commitment…It's not the Whether, It's the "How To"', *Journal of Quality and Participation*, December: 38-42.

Brown, R. (1992) *Understanding Organisations*. London: Routledge.

Burnes, B. (1992) *Managing Change*. London: Pitman.

Burns, T. and Stalker, G. (1961) *The Management of Innovation*. London: Tavistock.

Campbell, B. and Davies, L. (1992) 'Total Quality in Australia: A Resource Guide', Sydney: Australian Institute of Management.

Clark, J., McLoughlin, I., Rose H. and King, R. (1988) *The Process of Technological Change: New Technology and Social Choice in the Workplace*. Cambridge: Cambridge University Press.

Clegg, S. (1993) 'Accounting (In)action: Of Values and Occasional Irony: Max Weber in the Context of the Sociology Organisations' paper presented to *Wollongong Doctoral Consortium*.

Clegg, S. (1988) 'Radical Revisions: Power, Discipline and Organisations', *Organisation Studies*, 10: 97–116.

Crosby, P. (1980) *Quality is Free: The Art of Making Quality Certain*. New York: Mentor

Crosby, P. (1984) *Quality without Tears*. New York: McGraw-Hill.

Crosby, P. (1988) *The Eternally Successful Organization*. New York: McGraw-Hill.

Daley, D. (1992) 'Pay for Performance, Performance Appraisal, and Total Quality Management', *Public Productivity and Management Review*, 16,1: 39-51, Jossey-Bass.

Danjin, D. and Gershenfeld, C. (1992) 'Here We Go Again…Will TQM Go the Way of QWL?', *Journal of Quality and Participation*, 15(4): 94–97.

Dawson, P. (1991) 'The Historical Emergence and Changing Role of the Industrial Supervisor', *Asia Pacific HRM*, 29(2): 36–50.

Dawson, P. (1991a) 'Lost Managers or Industrial Dinosaurs? A Reappraisal of Front-Line Management', *Australian Journal of Management*, 16(1): 35–48.

Dawson, P. (1994) *Organizational Change: A Processual Approach*. London: Paul Chapman Publishing.

Dawson, P. (1994a) 'Total Quality Management' in Storey, J. (ed.) *New Wave Manufacturing Strategies*. London: Paul Chapman Publishing.

Dawson, P. (1994b) 'Quality Management in the Multi-Cultural Workplace' in H. Willmott and A. Wilkinson (eds) *Critical Perspectives on Quality*. London: Routledge.

Dawson. P. and Palmer, G. (1993) 'Total Quality Management in Australian and New Zealand Companies: Some Emerging Themes and Issues', *International Journal of Employment Studies*, 1(1): 115–36.

Dawson, P. and Patrickson, M. (1991) 'Total Quality Management in the Australian Banking Industry', *International Journal of Quality and Reliability Management*, 8(5): 66–76.

Dawson, P. and Webb, J. (1989) 'New Production Arrangements: The Toally Flexible Cage?', *Work, Employment & Society*, 3(2): 221–38.

De Cieri, H., Samson, D. and Sohal, A. (1991) 'Implementation of TQM in an Australian Manufacturing Company', *International Journal of Quality and Reliability Management*, 8(5): 55–65.

DeMeyer, A., & Ferdows, K. (1991) 'Quality Up, Technology Down: Manufacturing Improvement Programs in Europe', *International Journal of Technology Management* (Special Publication on the Role of Technology in Corporate Policy): 136- 153.

Deming, W.E. (1981) *Japanese Methods for Productivity and Quality*. Washington: George Washington University.

Deming, W.E. (1982) *Quality, Productivity and Competitive Position*. Cambridge, Mass: MIT Press.

Deming, W. (1986) *Out of Crisis*. Cambridge, Mass: MIT Press.

DiMaggio, P.J. and Powell, W.W. (1983) 'The Iron Cage Revisted: Institutional Isomorphism and Collective Rationality in Organizational Fields', *American Sociology Review*, 48: 147–56.

Dobyns, L. and Crawford-Mason, C. (1991) *Quality or Else: The Revolution in World Business*. Boston: Houghton Mifflin.

Dore, R. (1973) *British Factory, Japanese Factory*. London: Allen & Unwin.

Dunphy, D. and Stace, D. (1990) *Under New Management: Australian Organizations in Transition*. Sydney: McGraw-Hill.

Ealey, L.A. (1988) *Quality By Design: Taguchi Methods and U.S. Industry*. Michigan: ASI Press.

Eisman, R. (1990) 'Government Gridlock: Could A Motivated Work Force Cut Your Taxes?' *Incentive*, January: 24–29.

Feigenbaum, A. (1956) 'Total Quality Control', *Harvard Business Review*, 34(6):93–101.

Feigenbaum, A. (1961) *Total Quality Control*. New York: McGraw-Hill.

Feigenbaum, A. (1991) *Total Quality Control: Fortieth Anniversary Edition.* New York: McGraw-Hill.

Foley, K. (1987) *Report of the Committee of Review of Standards, Accreditation and Quality Control and Assurance.* Canberra: Australian Government Publishing Service.

Forker, L.B. (1991) 'Quality: American, Japanese, and Soviet Perspectives', *The Executive*, 5(4): 63–74.

Foucault, M. (1977) *Discipline and Punish: The Birth of the Prison.* London: Macmillan.

Fox, R. (1991) *Making Quality Happen: Six Steps to Total Quality Management.* Sydney: McGraw-Hill.

Gabor, A. (1990) *The Man Who Discovered Quality: How W. Edwards Deming Brought the Quality Revolution to America—The Stories of Ford, Xerox, and GM.* New York: Times Books.

Gardner, M., Littler, C., Palmer, G., Quinlan, M. (1986), *Management and Industrial Democracy: Structures and Strategies* (Canberra, AGPS) pp. 552.

Gardner, M., Palmer, G. and Quinlan, M. (1988) 'The Industrial Democracy Debate' in Palmer, G. (ed.) *Australian Personnel Management:* pp.336–371.

Gardner, M. and Palmer, G. (1992) *Employment Relations: Industrial Relations and Human Resource Management in Australia.* Melbourne: Macmillan.

Garvin, D. (1991) 'How the Baldridge Award Really Works', *Harvard Business Review*, Nov–Dec.

Giles, E. and Starkey, K. (1987) 'The Japanisation of Xerox' *New Technology, Work and Employment.* 3(2): 125–33.

Goldsmith, W. and Clutterbuck, D. (1984) *The Winning Streak: Britain's Top Companies Reveal Their Formulae for Success.* Harmondsworth: Penguin Books.

Gospel H. and Palmer, G. (1993) *British Industrial Relations* (2nd edn), London: Routledge.

Gray, J.L. and Starke, F.A. (1988) *Organizational Behavior: Concepts and Applications.* Columbus: Merrill.

Grint, K. (1991) *The Sociology of Work.* Cambridge: Polity Press.

Hames, R. (1991) 'Managing the Process of Cultural Change', *International Journal of Quality & Reliability Management*, 8(5): 14–23.

Hill, S. (1991a) 'How Do You Manage A Flexible Firm? The Total Quality Model', *Work, Employment & Society*, 5(3): 397–415.

Hill, S. (1991b) 'Why Quality Circles Failed but Total Quality Management Might Succeed', *British Journal of Industrial Relations*, 29(4): 541–568.

Hill, S. (1992) 'People and Quality', in K. Bradely (ed.) *People and Profits*. Aldershot: Gower.

Hill, R.C. and Freedman, S.M. (1992) 'Managing the Quality Process: Lessons from a Baldridge Award Winner. A Conversation with CEO John W. Wallace', *The Executive*, 6(1): 76–88.

Hoernschemeyer, D. (1989) 'The Four Cornerstones of Excellence', *Quality Progress*, August: 37–40.

Hofstede, G. (1990) 'The Cultural Relativity of Organizational Practices and Theories', in Wilson, D. and Rosenfeld, R. *Managing Orgnizations: Text, Readings and Case*. London: McGraw-Hill.

Holpp, L. (1992) 'Making Choices: Self-Directed Teams or Total Quality Management?', *Training*, 29(5): 69–76.

Hunt, J. (1990) 'Budgeting for Quality', in Lock, D. and Smith, D. (eds) (1990) *Gower Handbook of Quality Management*. Aldershot: Gower.

Hurd Jr. W.L. (1992) 'Quality in the Asia Pacific Region', *International Journal of Quality & Reliability Management*, 9(3): 14–20.

Imai, M. (1986) *Kaizen: The Key to Japan's Competitive Success*. New York: McGraw-Hill.

Ishikawa, K. (1985) *What is Total Quality Control? The Japanese Way*. Englewood Cliffs, N.J.: Prentice Hall.

Ishikawa, K. (1985) *What Is Total Quality Control? The Japanese Way*. Englewood Cliffs: Prentice Hall.

James, D. (1991) 'Business Lacks Commitment to Total Quality Management', *Business Review Weekly*, July 5: 66–70.

Jennison, K. (1991) 'Total Quality Management—Fad or Paradigmatic Shift?', in Couch, J.B. (ed.) *Health Care Quality Management for the 21st Century*. Forida: American College of Medical Quality.

Juran, J.M. (1988) *Quality Control Handbook*. New York: McGraw-Hill.

Juran, J.M. (1991) *Juran's New Quality Road Map*. New York: Free Press.

Juran, J.M. (1993) 'Made in U.S.A.: A Renaissance in Quality', *Harvard Business Review*, 71(4): 42–50.

Kanter, R.M. (1991) 'Transcending Business Boundaries: 12,000 World Managers View Change', *Harvard Business Review*, May–June: 151–64.

Kanter, R.M. (1983) *The Change Masters: Corporate Entrepreneurs at Work*. London: Unwin.

Kanter, R.M. (1989) *When Giants Learn to Dance: Mastering the Challenges of Strategy, Management and Careers in the 1990s*. London: Unwin.

Kanter, R.M., Stein, B.A., and Jick, T.D. (1992) *The Challenge of Organizational Change: How Companies Experience It and Leaders Guide It*. New York: Free Press.

Kreitner, R. and Kinicki, A. (1992) *Organizational Behaviour*. 2nd edn, Homewood: Irwin.

Kriegler, R., Dawkins, P., Ryan, J. and Wooden, M. (1988) *Achieving Organizational Effectiveness: Case Studies in the Australian Service Sector*. Melbourne: Oxford University Press.

Lansbury, R., Gardener, M., Quinlan, M. and Palmer, G. (1988) 'The Industrial Democracy Debate' in G. Palmer (ed.) *Australian Personnel Management*. Melbourne: Macmillan.

Lawrence, P. and Lorsh, J. (1967) *Organisation and Environment: Managing Differentiation and Integration*. Cambridge: Mass, Harvard University Press.

Lewin, K. (1947) 'Frontiers in Group Dynamics', *Human Relations*, 1: 5–42.

Lewin, K. (1951) *Field Theory in Social Science*. New York: Harper & Row.

Littler, C. (1982) *The Development of the Labour Process in Capitalist Societies*. London: Heinemann.

Littler, C.R. (1985) 'Taylorism, Fordism and Job Design', in D. Knights, H. Willmott, and D. Collinson (eds), *Job Redesign: Critical Perspectives on the Labour Process*. Aldershot: Gower.

Macdonald, J. and Piggott, J. (1990) *Global Quality: The New Management Culture*. London: Mercury.

McConnell, J. (1988) *Safer Than A Known Way: A Quality Approach to Management*. Dee Why: Delaware Books.

Merli, G. (1990) *Total Manufacturing Management: Production Organization for the 1990s*. Massachusetts: Productivity Press.

Mitroff, I. and Mohrman, S. (1987) 'The Slack is Gone: How the United States Lost its Competitive Edge in the World Economy', *Academy of Management Executive*, 1: 65–70.

Morgan, G. (1980) 'Paradigms, Metaphors and Puzzle Solving in Organisation Theory', *Administrative Science Quarterly*, 28: 601–7.

Morgan, G. (1986) *Images of Organisation*. London: Sage.

Morrison S. (1990) 'Managing Quality: A Historical Review', in B. Dale and J. Plunkett (eds) *Managing Quality*. Exeter: Philip Allan.

Newton, D. (1990) 'An Introduction to Statistics for Quality Applications' in D. Locke (ed.) *Gower Handbook of Quality Management*. Aldershot: Gower.

Oakland, J. (1989) *Total Quality Management*. Oxford: Heinemann.

Oliver, N., & Wilkinson, B. (1989) 'Japanese Manufacturing Techniques and Personnel and Industrial Relations Practice in Britain: Evidence and Implications', *British Journal of Industrial Relations*, 27(1): 73–91.

Ouchi, W. (1981) *Theory Z: How American Business Can Meet the Japanese Challenge*. Reading, MA: Addison-Wesley.

Palmer, G. (1983) *British Industrial Relations*. London: Allen & Unwin.

Palmer, G. (1987) 'Human Resource Management and Organisational Analysis', *Human Resource Management Australia*, Vol. 25, No. 2, pp. 5-17; also in Palmer, G. (ed.) *Australian Personnel Management*: pp. 148–163.

Palmer, G.(editor) (1988) *Australian Personnel Management: A Reader*, Sydney: Macmillan Australia, pp. 371.

Palmer, G. (1988) 'Personnel Management in Australia Today', in Palmer, G. (ed.) *Australian Personnel Management* pp. 1–14.

Palmer, G. (1989) 'Corporatism and Australian Arbitration' in S. Macintyre and R. Mitchell (eds) *Foundations of Arbitration*. Melbourne: Oxford University Press.

Palmer, G. and Saunders, I. (1992) 'Total Quality Management and Human Resource Management', *Asia Pacific Journal of Human Resources*.: 67–78

Palmer, G. & Allen, C. (1992) 'Yet Another Panacea? The Quality Management Movement in Australia', in J. Marceau (ed.) *Reworking the World: Organisations, Technologies and Cultures in Comparative Perspective*, Berlin, New York: de Gruyter, pp. 277–294.

Palmer, G (1993a) 'Industrial Relations, Gender and the Management of Culture', paper presented at the British Universities Industrial Relations Association (BUIRA) conference, York University, 2–4 July.

Palmer, G (1993b) 'A Comment on Sex in Management: Gender Stereotypes and their Impact on the Management Process' paper presented at the 11th European Group for Organisational Studies (EGOS) at the Ecole Supérieure de Commerce de Paris, (ESCP) 6–8 July.

Palmer, I. and Dunford, R. (1993) 'Liberating Managerial Knowledge? A Critical Assessment of Reframing' paper presented to the EGOS Colloquium, Paris.

Parker, M. and Slaughter, J. (1988) *Choosing Sides: Unions and the Team Concept*. Boston: South End Press.

Patrickson, M. and Dawson, P. (1994) 'The State Bank of South Australia', in Patrickson, M. and Bamber, G. (eds) *Case Studies in the Strategic Management of Industrial and Organisational Change*. Melbourne: Longman Cheshire.

Peters, T. and Waterman, R. (1982) *In Search of Excellence: Lessons from America's Best-Run Companies*. New York: Harper & Row.

Peters, T. (1987) *Thriving on Chaos*, Basingstoke: MacMillan.

Pugh, D. and Hickson, D. (1976) *Organisational Structure and its Context*. Farnborough: Saxon House.

Read, D. (1993) 'State Bank to Close NZ Office', *The Advertiser*, December 1: 7.

Reed, M. (1989) *The Sociology of Management*. Hemel Hempstead: Harvester Wheatsheaf.

Rieley, J.B. (1992) 'How to Make TQM and CI Programs Work', *Quality Progress*, October: 92–99.

Robbins, S.P. (1991) *Organizational Behaviour: Concepts, Controversies, and Applications*. 5th edn. Englewood Cliffs: Prentice-Hall.

Roberts, P. (1990) 'Still a Long Way to Go', *The Australian Financial Review*, 9 November: 50.

Rose, M. (1988) *Industrial Behaviour*. Harmondsworth: Penguin.

Roth, W.F. (1992) *A Systems Approach to Quality Improvement*. New York: Praeger.

Ryan, T.P. (1989) *Statistical Methods for Quality Improvement*. New York: Wiley.

Sashkin, M. and Kiser, K. (1992) 'What is TQM?', *Executive Excellence*, 9(5): 11.

SBS (1993) 'Organisational Behaviour. Quality Improvement: The Implementation'. *Episode 14*, December 19.

Schonberger, R.J. (1982) *Japanese Manufacturing Techniques: Nine Hidden Lessons in Simplicity*. New York: Free Press.

Schonberger, R.J. (1986) *World Class Manufacture: The Lessons of Simplicity Applied*. New York: Free Press.

Schonberger, R.J. (1992) 'Total Quality Management Cuts a Broad Swath—Though Manufacturing and Beyond', *Organizational Dynamics*, Spring: 16–28.

Sewell, G. (1992) '"Someone to Watch Over Me": A Tale of Shop Floor Surveillance in a Total Quality Organisation', paper presented at the *ISA's Joint Symposium on Comparative Sociology and the Sociology of Organisations*, Tokyo and Kurashiki, Japan, 3–7 July.

Sewell, G. and Wilkinson, B. (1992a) '"Someone to Watch Over Me": Surveillance, Discipline and the Just-in-Time Labour Process', *Sociology*, 26(2): 271–89.

Sewell, G. and Wilkinson, B. (1992b) 'Empowerment or Emasculation: A Tale of Shop Floor Surveillance in a Total Quality Organisation', in P. Blyton and P. Turnbull (eds) *New Perspectives on Human Resource Management*. London: Sage.

Slaugher, J. (1987) 'The Team Concept in the US Auto Industry: Implications for Unions', paper presented at the *ERU Conference on the Japanisation of British Industry*, Cardiff.

Sohal, A. (1991) 'Editorial', *International Journal of Quality and Reliability Management*, 8(5): 7–8.

Sprouster, J. (1984) *Total Quality Control: The Australian Experience*. Cammeray: Horwitz Grahame.

State Bank of South Australia (1984) *Annual Report*. Adelaide: State Bank.

State Bank of South Australia (1989) *Annual Report*. Adelaide: State Bank.

Taguchi, G. (1986) *Introduction to Quality Engineering*. Dearborn, Mich: American Supplier Institute.

Taguchi, G. (1988) *Systems of Experimental Design*. Detroit, Mich: American Supplier Institute.

Taguchi, G. (1986) *Introduction to Quality Engineering*. Dearborn: American Supplier Institute.

Taguchi, G. (1987) *System of Experimental Design*. Dearborn: American Supplier Institute.

Tenner, A. and DeToro, I. (1992) *Total Quality Management: Three Steps to Continuous Improvement*. Massachusetts: Addison-Wesley.

Tillery, K.R. and Rutledge, A.L. (1991) 'Quality-Strategy and Quality-Management Connections', *International Journal of Quality and Reliability Management*, 8(1): 71–7.

Tuckman, A. (1994) 'The Yellow Brick Road: TQM and the Restructuring of Organisational Cultures', paper presented at the 8th International Standing Conference on Organisational Symbolism, University of Copenhagen, revised version to be published in *Organisation Studies*.

Tuckman, A. (1994a) 'Out of the Crisis? Quality, TQM and the Labour Process', in H. Wilmott and A. Wilkinson (eds) *Critical Perspectives on Quality*. London: Routledge.

Twiss, B. and M. Goodridge (1989) *Managing Technolgoy for Competitive Advantage*. London: Pitman.

Vesey, J.T. (1991) 'The New Competitors: They Think in Terms of "Speed-to-Market"', *Academy of Management Executive*, (5)2: 23–33.

Vries, J. de and Water, H. van de (1992) 'Quality Circles, the Production Function and Quality of Working Life: Results of a Study in Seven Large Companies', *International Journal of Quality & Reliability Management*, 9(4): 30–45.

Walton M. (1986) *The Deming Management Method*. New York: Dodd, Mead and Company.

Ward, P. (1989) 'State Banks on Growth', *The Australian*, 11 October: 33.

Waterman, R.H. (1987) *The Renewal Factor: How the Best Get and Keep the Competitive Edge*. New York: Bantam.

Weber, M. (1947) *The Theory of Social and Economic Organisation*. Translated by T. Parsons and A.M. Henderson, New York: Free Press.

Weber, M. (1948) *From Max Weber: Essays in Sociology*. Translated by H.H. Gerth and C.W. Mills, London: Routledge and Kegan Paul.

Weber, M. (1976) *The Protestant Ethic and the Spirit of Capitalism*. Translated by T. Parsons, London: Allen & Unwin.

Weisbord, M.R. (1988) *Productive Workplaces: Organizing and Managing for Dignity, Meaning and Community*. San Francisco: Jossey-Bass.

Whittle, S. (1992) 'Total Quality Management Redundant Approaches to Culture Change', *Quality of Working Life*, 110: 8-13.

Wilkinson, A. (1993) 'Managing Human Resources for Quality' in Dale, B. (ed.) 2nd edn. *Managing Quality.* Prentice-Hall.

Wilkinson, A., Redman, T. and Snape, E. (1993) *Quality and the Manager.* Corby: Institute of Management.

Wilkinson, A., Marchington, M., Goodman, J. and Ackers, P. (1992) 'Total Quality Management and Employee Involvement', in *Human Resource Management Journal.* 2.4: 1–20.

Williams, A., Dobson, P. and Walters, M. (1991) *Changing Culture.* London: Institute of Personnel Management.

Williamson, O. (1975) *Markets and Hierarchies: Analysis and Antitrust Implications.* New York: Free Press.

Zeithaml, V.A., Parasuraman, A., and Berry, L.L. (1990) *Delivering Quality Service: Balancing Customer Perceptions and Expectations.* New York: Free Press.

Zeitz, G. and Mittal, V. (1993) 'Total Quality Management—The Deming Method as New Management Ideology: Institutionalisation Patterns in the United States', paper presented at the EGOS Colloquium, Paris.

Index

Accom Industries Pty Ltd 70–5, 152, 168, 179, 182
Albrecht, Karl 22, 78–9
Alcoa's Kwinana Refinery 107–15, 152, 155, 163, 165, 166, 179, 185
American Society for Quality Control 56
Australian Organisation for Quality Control (AOQC) 20, 21, 36
Australian Quality Authority (AQA) 20
Australian Quality Council 36

Baldridge Awards 18–19, 53, 163
Barnett, N. S. 4
Bell Laboratories 15, 23
bureaucratic element of management 7, 42, 45, 46–8, 58, 151, 152–60, 171–2, 191
bureaucratic personnel policies and TQM 46, 155–7
bureaucratic task controls and TQM 154–5

bureaucratic theories 7, 152, 160
change
  analysing 62, 64–5, 137, 170–3
  data, analysis of 6–7, 62, 64–5
  context of 7, 63, 65–6, 108–9, 178, 182, 183, 188, 190
  Lewin's model of 61, 62–3, 191
  organisational 6–7, 61, 62–5, 137, 141–4, 172–3, 174–8, 190, 191
  politics of 7, 65, 66–8, 178, 182, 188, 190
  substance of 7, 65, 66, 178, 190
computerised information technology 41, 44, 51, 165, 171, 172
continuous improvement in TQM 18, 30–1, 41, 61, 66, 104, 162, 172, 179–80
Contingency Theory 41
Crosby, Phillip 17, 23, 26–8, 36, 186, 201–2
cultural element of management 7, 13,

17–18, 21, 37, 41, 45, 54–7, 58, 137, 151, 167–73, 183, 188, 191
cultural control strategy of TQM 13, 17–18, 37
customer
    expectations 3–4, 18, 19, 27, 77–83
    supplier relations 17, 18, 26, 27, 29, 32–3, 61, 66, 90–1, 102–4, 153–4, 179, 181–2

Dawson, P. 3, 6, 7, 62, 65, 176, 188, 189, 190
Deming Award 56
Deming, W. Edward 3, 4, 12, 15, 19, 23–5, 28, 36, 87–8, 159, 186, 199–200

economic environment, context of change and 41, 57, 65, 158
employee participation in TQM 4, 5, 29, 30, 31–3, 40–4, 48, 49–53, 54–5, 56, 61, 66, 74–5, 98–100, 155–60, 161–7, 172, 179–81, 191
empowerment of employees 48, 49–52, 56, 161–7, 172
Enterprise Australia (EA) 20, 21, 36

Feigenbaum, Armand 3, 15, 22
Forker, L.B. 4–5

government and TQM 20–1, 53–4, 188
group problem-solving techniques and TQM 29, 30, 31–2, 33, 41, 43, 44, 50, 51–2, 54, 56, 61, 66, 161–7, 172, 179–81, 183

Hendersons Automotive (SA) 95–106, 152, 154, 155, 162–3, 170, 181, 186, 188
Human Relations, managerial reform and 7, 40, 41, 43

human resources, management of 3, 4, 13, 37, 45, 56, 65, 91–2
Human Resource Management 55, 156, 157–60, 163

Imai, Masaaki 22, 30
industrial development, quality management and 41, 42
industrial relations and TQM 29, 33–4, 66, 179, 182–3, 189
inter-organisational relations 13, 17, 37
Ishikawa, Kaori 22, 32

Jennison, K. 15
Juran, Joseph M. 3, 4, 12, 15, 19, 23, 25–6, 28, 36, 186, 200–1

Kaizen management strategy 22, 30–1, 97, 104, 162

Laubman and Pank Group 116–24, 153, 155, 182, 187, 189
Lewin, Kurt 61, 62, 191

Malcolm Baldridge National Quality Award 18–19, 53, 163
management
    of attitudes and behaviours 17–18, 177
    bureaucratic perspective to 7, 42, 45, 46–8, 58, 151, 152–60, 171–2, 191
    cultural perspectives to 7, 45, 54–7, 151, 167–70, 172–3, 188, 191
    human resources and 7, 45
    ideas, development of 7, 38, 41–4, 57–8, 152, 170–3
    multiple perspective approach to 7, 38–9, 44–5, 57, 151–2, 190–1
    political perspective to 45, 48, 160–7, 151, 191

political processes in 48–54, 178
processes 38–9, 44–58, 152, 170–1, 177–8
thought, history of 38, 39–44, 54, 57, 61, 170–1
women in 55
managerial reform
Human Relations and 40, 41, 43
quality management ideas and 7
Socio-technical Systems Theory and 40–1, 43, 190
Total Quality Management and 38, 41, 171, 190
managerial responsibilities
for quality management 25–6, 36
managerial theories
development of ideas about 7, 38, 39–44
perspectives of 7
Scientific Management and 39–40, 41, 42, 46, 47, 49, 55, 57, 155, 164, 165, 190
Total Quality Management and 38, 39–41, 57–8, 151–74, 190
manufacturing industries 22
mass production 42
multiple-perspective approach to management 7, 38–9, 44–5, 57, 151–2, 190–1

National Industry Extension Service (NIES) 20, 53

organisational
change, analysis of 6–7, 61, 62–5, 137, 141–4, 172–3, 174–8, 190, 191
context, internal 65–6, 183
excellence, elements of 174–5
flexibility, politics of 166–7

Organisational Development 62, 63, 184

Pareto analysis 32
personnel policies 46, 155–60
Peters, Tom 22
Pirelli Cables Australia Limited 137–147, 163, 168, 170, 180, 181, 182, 185, 186, 188
Plan-Do-Check-Action (PDCA) cycle 24–5, 31, 111
political
element of management 7, 45, (TQM)160–7, 172, 191
environment, influence on context of change 65, 178, 182, 190
influence on managerial ideas 41, 42, 57
processes in management 48–54, 58, 178, 183
processural framework
for analysing change 64–5, 177–8, 179, 189, 190
context of change in a 7, 65–6, 178, 182, 183, 188
defined 62, 67, 178
politics of change in a 7, 65, 66–8, 178, 182, 188
substance of change in a 7, 65, 66, 178

Quality Assurance (QA) 12, 14–15, 18, 71–3
'quality circles' 16–17
quality
control 31, 33
defined 4–5, 15–17, 23, 33, 61
principles of 23
group problem-solving techniques for 29, 31–2, 33, 41, 43, 44, 50,

51–2, 54, 56, 61, 66, 161–7, 172, 179–81, 183
  zero defects and 26–7
quality management
  in Australia 19–21, 34, 36, 53–4, 62, 64, 189–90, 191
  in Britain 16, 19, 42–3, 53, 54, 159, 189
  Cosby's absolutes of 27, 201–2
  development of 22–8, 35–7
  ideas of 7, 17, 41
  industrial development and 41
  in Japan 16, 17, 19, 22, 23, 25, 43, 44, 156, 158, 169
  in New Zealand 62, 64, 157, 189–90, 191
  Juran's managerial processes for 25–6, 200–1
  in United States 16, 17, 19, 24, 28, 34, 35, 42, 43, 53, 55, 56, 159
quality management movement, history of 13, 14, 171
Quality Society of Australasia (QSA) 21, 36

reframing perspective and management theory 44–5, 57–8, 151–2, 190–1

Schonberger, Richard J. 3, 4, 22
Scientific Management 7, 39–40, 41, 42, 46, 47, 49, 55, 57, 155, 164, 165, 190
service industries 22
Shewhart, Walter 23, 25
Shewhart-Demming wheel 24, 31
social
  environment, influence on context of change 65, 66, 172
  ideas, quality management and 7, 42

Socio-technical Systems Theory 7, 40–1, 43, 190
Standardise-Do-Check-Action (SDCA) cycle 24–5
State Bank of South Australia 76–84, 152, 156, 166–7, 168, 170, 183, 184, 187–8
Statistical Process Control (SPC) 100–2, 155, 186
Statistical Quality Control (SQC) 24, 171
Strategic Human Resource Management 157–60

Taguchi, Genichi 22
Taylor, F.W. 42
Taylorism 40, 42, 164
Tecpak 85–94, 152, 153, 155, 156–7, 159, 168, 180, 181, 185, 187, 189
Total Quality Control (TQC) 12, 13, 14, 15–17, 18, 22
Total Quality Management (TQM)
  analysing 7, 38, 41, 44–5, 61, 64–5, 68, 174–7, 183
  bureaucratic process of management and 46–8, 58, (152–60), 171–2, 191
  continuous improvement and 18, 30–1, 41, 61, 66, 104, 162, 172, 179–80
  cultural elements of 13, 17–18, 21, 37, 54–7, 58, 137, 167–70, 172–3, 183, 188, 191
  customer-supplier relations and 17, 18, 26, 27, 29, 32–3, 61, 66, 90–1, 102–4, 153–4, 179, 181–2
  defined 12–13, 14–19, 36–7, 66
  development of strategies for 3–4, 17–19
  elements of 29–37, 179–83, 190–1
  employee participation 4, 5, 29, 30, 31–3, 40–4, 48, 49–53, 54–5,

56, 61, 66, 74–5, 98–100, 155–60, 161–7, 172, 179–81, 187, 191

establishing 58, 64–5, 177–8, 183–91

group problem-solving techniques 29, 31–2, 33, 41, 43, 44, 50, 51–2, 54, 56, 61, 66, 161–7, 172, 179–81, 183

Human Resource Management and 55, 156, 157–60, 163

industrial relations and 29, 33–4, 66, 179, 182–3, 189

management theory and 38, 39–41, 57–8

market-orientation of 153–4

philosophy of change and 17, 18, 29–30, 66, 179, 183–4

political process in management and 48–54, 58, 160–7, 172, 183, 188

principles of 17, 61, 66

quality control techniques and 29, 31, 165, 179, 180

research programme for 5–6, 68

total management approach to 29–30, 188–9

Total Quality Service 22

trade unions 52–3, 189

Vicbank 125–36, 155, 159–60, 168, 182, 184, 187, 189

Weber, Max 42, 155

women in management 55

workteams in TQM 29, 31–2, 33, 41, 43, 44, 50, 51–2, 54, 56, 61, 66, 161–7, 172, 179–81, 183

zero defects 26–7, 36